Dr. BBQ's
Big-Time
Barbecue Cookbook

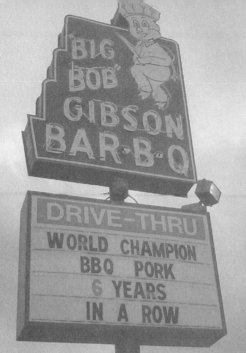

BIG BOB GIBSON BAR-B-Q

DRIVE-THRU
WORLD CHAMPION
BBQ PORK
6 YEARS
IN A ROW

JACK'S BAR·B·QUE

BAR-BQ
BREAKFAST 7·30 A.M.–11·30 A.M.

Dr. BBQ's Big-Time Barbecue Cookbook

**A REAL BARBECUE CHAMPION BRINGS
THE TASTY RECIPES AND JUICY STORIES
OF THE BARBECUE CIRCUIT TO YOUR BACKYARD**

RAY LAMPE

aka Dr. BBQ

Introduction by Dave DeWitt

St. Martin's Griffin ⚞ New York

www.stmartins.com

Book design by rlf design

Library of Congress Cataloging-in-Publication Data

Lampe, Ray.

Dr. BBQ's big-time cookbook : a real barbecue champion brings the tasty recipes and juicy stories of the barbecue circuit to your backyard / Ray Lampe (aka Dr. BBQ). — 1st ed.

p. cm.

ISBN 0-312-33979-8

EAN 978-0312-33979-1

1. Barbecue cookery. I. Title

TX840.B3L36 2005

641.5'784—dc22   2004060162

10 9 8 7 6 5 4 3 2

This book is dedicated to
all the pitmasters who have
helped make true barbecue the
greatest American cuisine.

Contents

Ray's High-Falutin' Barbecue Dishes

Chef Ray Transforms Leftover Barbecued Favorites into Spectacular Main Course Meals

187

Side-Steppin'

Side Dishes and Desserts from Ray's Kitchen

231

Acknowledgments

I'm still not really sure how I got from Chicago truck driver to cookbook author, but I do know there have been many good people who have played a role in the journey. The best part of it all is that we were just having fun. It never crossed my mind that I was writing a book.

To the people below, you have played many different roles in my life, but this book could not exist without each and every one of you. I thank you with all my heart.

My mom and my dad

My grandma Julia

Dean and Denise Zentz

Dan Burdick

Jim Burns

Scott Barrett

John Petitti

John and Sue Beadle

Gary and Carolyn Wells

Bill Myers

Ed Roith

Mike Lake

Brian Andersen

Ray Basso

Nick Nicholas

Steve Benson

Mike Jay

John Ford

Marsha Russell

Bruce Ring

Anne Rehnstrom

Stephanie Wilson

Fast Eddy

Jim Nufer

Judy Stuckey

Mary Baran

Dave DeWitt

Scott Mendel

Michael Flamini

Katherine Tiernan

Amelie Littell

James Sinclair

Cheryl Mamaril

John Karle

Ralph Fowler

Marian Lizzi

Alice Baker

Introduction

I have watched Dr. BBQ cook barbecue. I have eaten his wonderful culinary creations. I have watched him do a cooking demonstration where he displayed his knowledge of butchering. I have carried his entries to the judges at a cookoff. I have cheered when he won Best Brisket. I have edited his writing in "Ask Dr. BBQ" in *Fiery Foods & BBQ* magazine. With all this Dr. BBQ experience, I have an observation to make: Ray Lampe is the real thing. Ray is not some dilettante food writer who studies other people's books and then comes up with a compilation grilling guide. Rather, he is the most hands-on, from-the-heart, experienced barbecue cook that you will ever meet. And the weird thing about it is that's he's a naturally gifted writer.

Ray had no idea that he was a writer until he started to write about barbecue from his own experiences. I admit that I encouraged him and helped him find a publisher, but hey, he bribed me with barbecue, some of which is in my freezer as I write this. This may be his first book—but it won't be his last.

What I like about this book is Ray's utter transparency. He doesn't make picky distinctions about what is "real barbecue." He doesn't preach about which smoker or grill to use. He doesn't take a stand on which meat or sauce is best. He believes, like I do, that it's all a matter of personal preference. And presented here are Ray's own personal preferences, along with his attitude. There aren't many barbecue cookbook authors who are also cookoff circuit champions.

Another thing I like about this book is that Ray gives us a lot of recipes for the excess barbecue (okay, okay, leftovers) that is produced when you, say, smoke a brisket and you have a family of two. He also gives us some great side dishes and desserts in addition to a graduate course in smoking and grilling.

I have learned more about barbecue from working with Ray than from any other sources. I think you will, too. You'll also eat some great 'cue.

—Dave DeWitt

Preface

A Bit of Barbecue Background

I'm often asked how I got started in barbecue, so it seems like the right place to begin my first book. The truth is that I signed up for my first cooking class as a sophomore in high school because it seemed like a good way to slack off and I figured there would be a lot of chicks in the class. Turns out both were true. I think Miss Perkins would be very surprised at how things have turned out for me. I was surprised to find out that I did have an interest in what was going on in the kitchen. I learned to cook a crab quiche and an apple pie that I made many times. Sadly, I don't have either recipe anymore.

After high school I joined the family trucking business and that, combined with the excessive lifestyle of a young man in the 1970s, kept me pretty much out of the kitchen. But in 1982, my friend Bruce Romanek signed us up for the first Annual Mike Royko Ribfest being held in Grant Park in downtown Chicago. Bruce just intended to go for the party, but, as long as we were going, I figured I could probably cook some pretty good ribs. Well, I did cook some mighty fine ribs on a borrowed kettle grill, and we had a great time along with about four hundred other teams. That first Ribfest sparked my interest in barbecue. I bought a kettle grill for home and began cooking ribs on a regular basis. It seemed that I had found my calling in life: barbecue. I realized that it was more than just some smoky ribs. It was a bunch of fun people hanging out in a nice park while cooking and having some beers. And, I fit right in.

The next year I had my friend Scott Barrett build a grill for me out of a metal barrel. Scott worked at the place where I got my trucks fixed, The Berwyn Lubritory. You can't make this stuff up. It was a typical fifty-five-gallon drum. First he cut it open and then we welded legs on that were made out of automobile exhaust pipe. We fixed up a grid for cooking and painted it red. This type of grill is a time-honored tradition and you see them everywhere. I had the pleasure of cooking on a couple of them last year at the Jamaican Barbecue Championship in Montego Bay. You put charcoal in the bottom of a grill like this. For slow cooking the charcoal all goes on one end while the meat stays on the other end.

A couple of years later my barrel grill burned out from all the use, and it was time for an upgrade. My buddy Scott has built me all kinds of crazy things over the years, so as usual I went to him again. He had an old truck-side toolbox in the backyard that was in bad shape. It had stood on end for years and the one end was rusted out. Never fear; Scott can fix anything. He welded and cut and once again went with his favorite legs made out of exhaust pipe. Before I knew it he had made me another beautiful red rib cooker. It was a direct setup, so I had to use aluminum foil as a barrier, but it looked totally cool and I could cook twenty-two slabs of ribs at a time.

Needless to say, my barbecue addiction was in full swing. The Royko Ribfest morphed into the *Chicago Tribune* Ribfest and grew to seven hundred teams. We continued to compete, and while we never won anything, I was getting better and better at cooking barbecue.

In 1991, the *Tribune* announced that there would be no more Ribfest. The organizing had changed hands a few times and it seemed nobody wanted to handle the logistics. But in reality it had grown to be a big event with unattended fires burning everywhere, food being handed out with no regard to the health department, and lots of unauthorized drink-

Dr. BBQ's Top 5 Barbecue Cookoffs

1. **Amazin' Blazin' in Lebanon, Tennessee**

2. **Pigfest in Lakeland, Florida**

3. **Jack Daniel's World Championship Invitational Barbecue in Lynchburg, Tennessee**

4. **Illinois State Championship in Shannon, Illinois**

5. **The American Royal in Kansas City, Missouri**

ing. Sounds like a party to me, but bureaucracy apparently won out. Almost like it was meant to be, I soon found out about the first ever Kansas City Barbecue Society (KCBS) Illinois State Barbecue Championship. The event would be about a half hour from my house and would be hosted by Jim Burns. Jim was an early participant on the barbecue circuit and he decided to host a cookoff at his restaurant. He is surely on a short list of people that I thank for helping me to get started in barbecue. I signed up immediately and was told that there would be four categories to compete in: poultry, ribs, pork loin, and beef brisket. I decided to cook my favorite dish, injected smoked turkey, in the poultry category. I didn't realize I

was supposed to cook in all four categories if I wanted to be the Grand Champion, but it really didn't matter. I won third place with my turkey, and I was as proud as I could be. I convinced a couple of friends to join me in a team the following year. Scott Barrett, John Petitti, and I became the "Bonesmokers," a name coined by John that I still use for fun and business. While the other guys had growing families to attend to, I got more and more involved in barbecue. I started traveling to cookoffs by myself. I bought a new van to carry my barbecue stuff around and applied for a vanity license plate. One of my requests was "Dr. BBQ." Well, that's the one I got and I have been using that name ever since. It didn't seem like that big a deal at the time, but I now have the Florida "Dr. BBQ" plate and my Web site is *www.drbbq.com*.

In 1994, I attended the first ever Michigan State Barbecue Championship and became the Grand Champion. They gave me a check for $1,000 and I was thrilled. There was no trophy at all, though, so I had a copy of the check framed and I am sure glad I did that all these years later. I now have a back room full of trophies, plaques, and ribbons from all over the country, but it would be complete without that first Grand Champion plaque.

After winning that first championship I was honored with an invitation to the American Royal Invitational, where I got a fifth-place ribbon in the sausage category. What a thrill! All of these awards just fed my hunger to do more and more of this. So I got some cash together and bought a real barbecue pit, one that I could tow around on a trailer.

I was still working in the family business, so barbecue just remained a hobby that I was fanatical about until the end of 2000, when my twenty-five-year trucking career came to an end. It had just run its course and it was time to move on. I was thrilled at the chance to pursue my dream job in midlife. I had a wristwatch tattooed on my arm that said 5:01 to signify quitting time, put my house up for sale, and moved to Florida. You see, barbecue isn't real popular in Chicago during the winter.

My successful history as a competition cook opened many doors for me. I've cooked in hundreds of cookoffs and won hundreds of awards. I have never won any award that can be called a World Championship, but I have been in the World Championship top five more times than you can count on one hand and in the top ten more than you can count on both. I'm very honest about my awards, as I think all competitors should be. I'm also not anywhere near done yet. I'm still winning regularly and still have that World Championship goal.

Since my career change, I've operated a roadside barbecue stand, done some catering, sold barbecue at some of the premier vending events around the country, sold barbecue sauce and seasoning, demonstrated grills at stores and trade shows, found some sponsors, taught some barbecue classes, and even written some articles and columns about barbecue.

Writing was just a lark. One day I was talking to Bruce Ring about his new magazine, *The BBQer,* and I offered to write an "Ask Dr. BBQ" column. A couple years later when Bruce left the magazine my friend Mary suggested I contact Dave DeWitt about hosting my column in *Fiery Foods & BBQ.* I did and Dave was interested so I moved over. Since then *The BBQer* has been saved and has now teamed up with *Fiery Foods & BBQ.* This has all served me well in preparing to write this book. I have made many lifelong friends in the barbecue world and it has been a great life's path. I thank them all—those that I have named and those that I have not.

So now it's time to share my knowledge, gained over more than twenty years of cooking barbecue. So, pop a top and let's go cook!

The story of barbecue is the story of America:

Settlers arrive on great unspoiled continent,

discover wondrous riches, set them

on fire, and eat them.

—Vince Staten

Rubbing Me the Right Way

Rubs, Marinades, Mops, and Sauces to Give Your Barbecue That Championship Flavor

Getting Started

I've looked at a lot of barbecue books and almost all of them start out with a boring chapter about equipment, tools, and charcoal. I'm not going to do it that way. I will address the equipment and tools as I go along, relative to the dish and the cooking technique being used. I am, however, going to spend a little time here telling you about my feelings about some taboo barbecue subjects. You see, there is great controversy in the barbecue world about where the progress should stop. Predictably, the different camps are content that it stops wherever they are standing.

For example, some people think that you should only cook a whole hog in a pit made out of concrete blocks. That's *Traditional Barbecue,* they say. Some even argue about whether a piece of corrugated steel should be allowed as a cover. Then there is the camp that says you should only use an offset firebox big ol' hunk of steel cooker. That's *Traditional Barbecue,* they say. Some guys only cook in a hole in the ground. That's *Traditional Barbecue,* they say.

My friends with the Big Green Egg will tell you that theirs is the best cooker out there. That type of equipment has been in use for three thousand years. That's *Traditional Barbecue,* they say. But of course we all know that the real original and absolutely *Traditional Barbecue* was cooked over an open fire as a caveman made antelope kabobs.

There is a whole group that takes great pride in having giant cookers, and another group that takes great pride in cooking great barbecue on the smallest cookers. There's a big debate over meats: pig vs. cow vs. mutton vs. cabrito. And one over woods: mesquite vs. hickory vs. oak vs. apple vs. pecan vs. cherry.

Then there is the multifaceted argument about fuels. Here is a list of the stances:

- Logs only! No charcoal ever in my cooker!

- Natural lump charcoal is the best! Nothing else works!

- Brand X Natural Lump is much better than the others!

- No logs! They must be burned down to coals first! (Isn't that the same fuel as the guys above?)
- Pellets are cheating!
- Pellets are wood, too.
- Charcoal briquettes are okay.
- Charcoal briquettes are not okay.
- Gas is okay.
- Gas is not natural.
- There is a whole fight about using aluminum foil to wrap your food for part of the cooking. Some say it ruins the bark (crust on the meat) and steams the meat instead of barbecuing it. That's not *Traditional Barbecue,* they say.
- Grilling isn't barbecue!
- Sweet barbecue sauce isn't supposed to be served on real barbecue.
- In fact, some insist that barbecue shouldn't be sauced at all, just rubbed.

Dr. BBQ's Favorite Barbecue Tools

1. **Instant-read thermometer**

2. **Sharp knives**

3. **Wood flavor pellets**

4. **Aluminum foil**

5. **Bamboo skewers**

Those of you who don't know me will quickly learn that I am very opinionated and not afraid to speak my mind. Here's what I think. Cook on whatever you have, like, or can afford. It's all good. I have fourteen cookers at this time and I like them all. They are big, small, cheap, expensive, ceramic, steel, grills, smokers, pellet-fueled, briquette-fueled, natural lump–fueled, and even gas-fueled.

Cook whatever meat you have, like, or can afford. (See a trend here?) The old traditions of which meat and which type of wood were very regional and defined by what was available. That's why they cook hogs with hickory in North Carolina and beef over mesquite in Texas. There has always been a big hog-raising industry in North Carolina and there are lots of hickory trees there. In Texas cattle has always been a big business and there is an abundance of mesquite bushes, although I can't believe the first guy who used mesquite for cooking actually tried it a second time.

Now we have access to all the different woods and they are all good and should be tried, with the possible exception of mesquite. To borrow a line from *Maxim* writer Paul Bibeau, mesquite smoke smells like it came "straight from the devil's ass crack." The fuel arguments are fun, but for me the line is pretty simple. All the major cookoff sanctioning bodies allow wood, charcoal, or pellets. None allow gas. That seems like a fair line, although I wouldn't fuss much if they allowed gas. The best food wins and I've seen great food cooked using all those fuels. Pick your favorite. I would pass on burning all that wood down to coals, though. It's really a lot of hassle and a mess. Lump charcoal is the same thing only it's pre-burned.

The aluminum foil argument is futile. Almost every barbecue champion I know these days is using it in some fashion and judges consistently score their food high. So much for that argument.

To most people grilling *is* barbecue. Get over it.

Most people like sweet barbecue sauce on their food. Look at how much is sold in the grocery and specialty stores. (Dr. BBQ's Bonesmokers Honey BBQ Sauce is my favorite—it's also mine. Get it at *www.peppers.com*.)

As you can probably tell, I am all for progress and innovation in cooking barbecue both at home and at cookoffs. I've proposed a cookoff where we all show up in a loincloth and nothing else and see who can make a weapon, hunt a dog, dig a hole, create fire, and get it cooked first. Now *that* would be *Traditional Barbecue*. Okay, the loincloths would be cheating, but if you'd ever been to a cookoff you'd want them to be allowed, too.

By the way, I've also proposed a cookoff where the judging is done by a dog. What could be more fair? You all put your box of food on the ground and then they let the dog go. The first one he tries gets a prize and the first one he finishes gets a prize. If he sniffs yours and doesn't eat any you have to put an extra $20 in the pot. Nobody has taken me up on that one yet, either.

So now we get to an issue related to the competitions themselves, blind vs. on-site cookoff judging. These are two distinctly different schools of thought. "Blind" judging is done in a secluded area where the judges have absolutely no indication of who has cooked the meat. There are even rules to limit the creativity of the presentations so this will be pure. The bad

news is the public isn't usually allowed to watch and most teams don't feel a need to dress up their area or themselves. "On-site" judging is quite different. It is done at the team's cook site and there is absolutely no question of who has done the cooking. Boasting of one's accomplishments is an accepted part of the process. This is very public-friendly and makes for a fun and colorful event. Dressing up the

Dr. BBQ's Top 10 Favorite Cooking Team Names

1. **The Staggering Chef**

2. **Two Hog Nuts**

3. **The Smokin' Elvis**

4. **Dirty Dick's Legless Wonders**

5. **The Beverly Grillbillys**

6. **Buttrub.com**

7. **BBQ Gods of the Universe**

8. **Meat Mitch**

9. **Squeal of Approval**

10. **Mean Dean's Smokin' Machine**

team and the site is always done and enjoyed by all. There are teams that dress as Elvis and teams that dress as Miss Piggy. You'll see fine china and crystal at some sites and denim tablecloths at others.

There is usually also a substantial number of points given via a second set of judges that are using the blind system at these events, but the "on site" is what sets these contests apart.

The primary on-site group is Memphis in May (MIM). MIM is actually a month-long festival that hosts the World Championship Cookoff in Memphis every May and has been doing so for many years. It's the world's largest pork barbecue cookoff. The largest blind judging group is the Kansas City Barbecue Society (KCBS), although there is the International Barbeque Cookers Association (IBCA) and some splinter groups in Texas also use a blind judging system. KCBS was started many yeas ago by a group of friends who had the common interest of barbecue and a bit of a wild hair that inspired them to stay up all night cooking in a parking lot. The American Royal, also a month-long festival, hosts the world's largest cookoff in October every year. It is known as the World Series of Barbecue, and it's held in Kansas City, Missouri. While it really isn't run by KCBS, it is sanctioned and has surely become their signature event. I have cooked almost exclusively in KCBS contests in my time. I am also on their Board of Directors, so that is obviously my preference. It's mainly a product of where I used to live (Chicago) and the fact that I often cooked by myself. If I had been here in Florida when I got started I would have probably become an MIM cook.

I have many good friends who cook mainly MIM and they much prefer it and, of course, I have many friends who cook mainly KCBS and they much prefer that. The food is top-notch on both circuits. Many of us come together in the fall at the Jack Daniel's World Championship Invitational Barbecue in Lynchburg, Tennessee. I'd venture to say that the awards have been pretty equally distributed over the years.

I love barbecue in all its incarnations. I can find enjoyment in any sauce, any style, and just about any barbecue meal I can find. The diversity and uniqueness of each style aren't really that different. Kind of like a Ford and a Chevy—the difference makes for good conversation, but they both seem to be pretty good.

Barbecue is a very important cuisine, but it's so much more than that. It is truly a culture and a phenomenon. I have made many good friends on the barbecue trail. I am lucky enough to count many of the most prolific barbecue cooks and business people in the world as my friends. I have proudly included some of their recipes in this book.

Enough of this, let's get to the food!

Ray's Ruminations

Pork is pork! And beef is beef. The different cuts do have their own characteristic flavors, but what really sets one dish apart from another is the way we season it. Many of the old and legendary barbecue joints and pitmasters use very simple seasonings, even just salt and pepper. This makes great barbecue. Some will use a mop or a baste to add another layer of flavor and some will even toss the meat with a thin sauce before serving. I saw a great TV show once where these guys cooked a whole hog, took all the meat off the bones, tossed it with a sauce and some red pepper, and then served it back in the hog skin. It sure looked like something I would like to eat. Rest assured that this was not a thick, sweet barbecue sauce, though. It was probably more like one of the mops I use or a thin vinegar sauce.

In my experience, the thin vinegar sauces are not very complicated. They consist mainly of white or maybe cider vinegar, cayenne pepper, and very little else. Sometimes mustard seed or Worcestershire sauce is added. This does make a very unique and tasty accompaniment to smoked pig meat, but in truth it's a very limited preference. So is mustard-based sauce, and even more limited is the white barbecue sauce from upstate Alabama.

I've included recipes for all of the above, but by far the most popular barbecue sauce is a

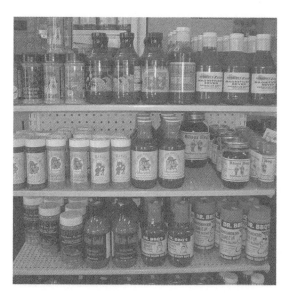

tomato-based sweet sauce. I've included a couple recipes for these, too, but I must also tell you that there are many very good and interesting bottled sauces available these days from specialty stores, on the Internet, and even in most large grocery stores. I like to serve a few choices on the side to my guests. I always prefer to serve the sweet sauces as a condiment because they are so apt to burn if brushed on the food early in the cooking process. Now, I know some folks like that burned sugar taste, so I recommend adding the sauce after the meat is fully cooked and allowing it to sit on the heat for just a few minutes to caramelize the sugar. Otherwise, you'll be ordering pizza, since there is a very fine line between caramelized and burned.

Back to the seasoning. The dry seasonings have progressed to a very complex and important part of barbecue cooking. We have discovered that turbinado sugar doesn't burn as easily as white or brown sugar. Of course, we have also acquired these great barbecue cooking machines that control temperature so beautifully that we can cook at the precise temperature to caramelize while cooking low and slow, avoiding the temperature spikes that would char the rubs.

These blends that we call "rubs" have become an important part of competition barbecue. It would be tough to win using just salt and pepper. My preference is a very basic blend, usually three parts sugar to two parts salt and a little onion, garlic, chili powder, and some herbs. Anything too off-center could distract the judge and result in a lower score. I sometimes mix the rub with a small amount of apple juice to create a "schmear." This helps the spices stick to the meat. Brisket seems to need

this more than the pork cuts. I consider apple juice to be the barbecue cook's equivalent of a chef's chicken stock. Anytime that you need some liquid but don't want to water things down, use apple juice. It blends in without changing the flavor.

Marinades aren't very popular for the big cuts of meat such as pork butt/shoulder or brisket. At a cookoff, you would only have a few hours to do it and it wouldn't be very effective. Encountering this problem created the technique of injection. Many cooks now take big food-grade syringes, available through the Internet as curing pumps, and use them to inject their meat. This helps add moisture and flavor deep inside. The "injections" are typically a blend of vinegar, fruit juices, and spices.

Chicken can certainly benefit from marinating, and I always do it. Sometimes I will inject some of the marinade as well. You will probably need to strain it, though. Many cooks like to brine their chicken and turkey, but for me it creates a texture that I don't care for. I have

seen many cooks do well with brining, though, so I have included a couple of recipes.

Ribs can be approached many different ways. I once had a thought that I would marinate my ribs in root beer. I was afraid the color would be too dark, so I decided to switch to 7UP. I won the Ohio State Championship that day. I really wasn't sure if it had any effect, but I figured I had better try it again. The next time I didn't win anything, so I never tried it again. These days I just dry-rub them and then cook them in foil partway through. I like to add some flavorings to the foil such as honey, brown sugar, and apple juice. You'll have to look at the rib recipes for the rest of that story.

Burgers, steaks, chops, and anything else you can think of to grill directly do very well with these same seasoning methods. Just be aware that these spice blends can only be subjected to the hot fires of grilling for a short period of time.

So here are a bunch of recipes for seasonings and such. Some are used within this book's recipes and some stand alone. There are still others within recipes later in the book. I've even included some salsa recipes. Feel free to mix and match and adjust them to your liking.

If I could teach you one thing with this book it would be to develop your own barbecue style. When I teach people how to barbecue, I always suggest that they keep a log of all the cooking that they do. I've given you places within the book to keep your own log of times, temperatures, and personal preferences. Use the tools I give you along with your own experiences to do it the way you and your guests enjoy most.

Rubs

These are the basis of the flavor of your barbecue creation. They will flavor the meat and help with the color and caramelized flavor that barbecue is built on. Depending on whether you want things spicy, sweet, or seasoned with herbs, you can mix and match these rubs with a variety of different meats.

▼▼▼

Big-Time Barbecue Rub

½ cup salt

½ cup turbinado sugar

¼ cup granulated brown sugar

1 tablespoon granulated* garlic

1 tablespoon granulated* onion

2 tablespoons paprika

2 tablespoon chili powder

2 tablespoons freshly ground black pepper

2 teaspoons cayenne pepper

1 tablespoon dried thyme

1 tablespoon ground cumin

1 teaspoon ground nutmeg

*Granulated garlic and onion are coarser than powder, but the powders can be substituted.

This is a very good basic barbecue rub. It works well on any food for smoking or grilling. • **Yield: 1½ cups**

Combine all ingredients, mix well, and store in an airtight container.

Sweeter Big-Time Barbecue Rub

½ cup salt

½ cup turbinado sugar

½ cup granulated brown sugar

1 tablespoon granulated garlic

1½ tablespoons granulated onion

2 tablespoons paprika

2 tablespoons chili powder

2 tablespoons freshly ground black pepper

2 teaspoons cayenne pepper

1½ tablespoons dried thyme

1 tablespoon ground cumin

1 teaspoon ground nutmeg

1 teaspoon cinnamon

For those who like sweet with their sweat.

• Yield: 1¾ cups

Combine all ingredients in a bowl, mix well, and store in an airtight container.

Spicy Big-Time Barbecue Rub

½ cup salt

½ cup turbinado sugar

¼ cup granulated
brown sugar

1½ tablespoons granulated
garlic

1 tablespoon granulated
onion

2 tablespoons paprika

3 tablespoons chili powder

2 tablespoons freshly
ground black pepper

1½ tablespoons cayenne
pepper

1 tablespoon dried thyme

1 tablespoon ground cumin

1 teaspoon ground nutmeg

For the chiliheads in the crowd, here's my rowdy rub.
• **Yield: 1¾ cups**

Combine all ingredients in a bowl, mix well, and store in an
airtight container.

Big-Time Herb Rub

¼ cup salt

¼ cup turbinado sugar

1 tablespoon chili powder

1 tablespoon dried thyme

1 teaspoon freshly ground
black pepper

1 teaspoon granulated
garlic

1 teaspoon granulated
onion

1 teaspoon dry mustard

1 teaspoon dried oregano
leaves

1 teaspoon ground cumin

1 teaspoon dried tarragon
leaves

½ teaspoon cayenne
pepper

½ teaspoon ground
nutmeg

Here's one that's just a little different. It's also great as a vegetable seasoning. • **Yield: about 1 cup**

Combine all ingredients in a bowl, mix well, and store in an airtight container.

Big-Time Creole Barbecue Rub

2 tablespoons salt

2 tablespoons granulated garlic

2 tablespoons granulated onion

2 tablespoons freshly ground black pepper

2 tablespoons dried thyme

2 tablespoons paprika

2 tablespoons cayenne pepper

No carbs! This also makes a great steak seasoning.
• **Yield: ¾ cup**

Combine all ingredients in a bowl, mix well, and store in an airtight container.

The Barbecue Log

My Favorite Rubs

A barbecue mop is really just a basting liquid named after the process of applying it. The barbecue tradition of cooking large cuts of meat has created the use of many different tools not normally associated with cooking, and a dishwashing mop is one of those items. You'll need to find the wood-handled cotton rag mop.

As a matter of fact, real floor-washing mops are used in some instances for large cuts of meat. These are used to apply the "mop" during the cooking process. Of course we always use a new one. A brush or a spray bottle works well, too.

▼▼

Big-Time Barbecue Mop

1 can beer of choice

½ cup olive oil

½ cup cider vinegar

¼ cup Worcestershire sauce

½ cup prepared yellow mustard

1 onion, finely chopped

2 cloves garlic, crushed

1 jalapeño chile, seeds and stem removed, finely chopped

This is the one you use for big, long-cooking cuts like pork shoulder, beef brisket, and whole hog. Use a metal bowl and keep it warm in the cooker while the meat cooks. • **Yield: about 3 cups**

In a saucepan, combine all the ingredients and bring to a boil. Reduce the heat and simmer for 15 minutes. This can be made the night before, but it must be refrigerated.

Whiskey Spray Mop

1 cup apple juice

2 tablespoons Tennessee whiskey (Old No. 7 for me)

1 tablespoon soy sauce

This is nice and simple and good on everything.

- **Yield: about 1¼ cups**

In a bowl, combine all ingredients, mix well, and apply as needed from a spray bottle.

Spicy Lemon Mop

¼ cup olive oil

3 tablespoons freshly
squeezed lemon juice

½ teaspoon cayenne

2 cloves garlic, minced

2 teaspoons chopped
parsley or rosemary

Freshly ground black
pepper, to taste

This mop is different from the traditional ones. It's really good on fish and chicken, but you can also use it on grilled vegetables like asparagus or broccoli.

• **Yield: about ½ cup**

Combine all the ingredients in a small bowl and mix well.

To so many people, all barbecue is defined by the sauce. The purists among us prefer to have it on the side so that we can taste the meat by itself, but there is no denying that at home or at a cookoff, people love barbecue sauce slathered all over their meat.

I don't like to classify barbecue sauces by region. When I go to these regions I don't see the people using the exclusive sauces they've been labeled with. Contrary to popular belief, not everyone in South Carolina uses a mustard-based sauce and not everybody in Texas skips the sauce. I see people using all different kinds of sauces in all different places. There are surely different styles, but like so many other things in the food world these days, cooking styles and flavors cross the old boundaries all the time. I like to serve a few different choices on the side at the same meal.

▼▼

Big-Time Barbecue Sauce

1¼ cups commercial chili sauce

3 cups ketchup

1 cup prepared yellow mustard

¼ cup Worcestershire sauce

¼ cup cider vinegar

1 tablespoon garlic powder

1 tablespoon onion powder

1 tablespoon freshly ground black pepper

1 tablespoon salt

½ tablespoon dried thyme

1 teaspoon chili powder

1 teaspoon cayenne pepper

½ teaspoon Liquid Smoke

¼ teaspoon ground nutmeg

¼ teaspoon ground cumin

½ cup honey

1 cup brown sugar

This is a very good all-purpose barbecue sauce that can be used for basting, glazing, and dipping. • **Yield: about 2 quarts**

Combine all the ingredients except the honey and brown sugar in a saucepan and very slowly bring the mixture to a simmer. Remove from the heat and add in the last 2 ingredients. Mix well and mix again occasionally as it cools. Store in a covered glass or plastic container in the refrigerator for up to 1 month.

Red Rose Barbecue Sauce

2 tablespoons vegetable oil

1 cup chopped onion

¼ cup chopped green bell pepper

2 cloves crushed garlic

1¼ cups commercial chili sauce

1 ¼ cups ketchup

½ cup cider vinegar

1 teaspoon allspice

½ teaspoon cayenne pepper

1 cup brown sugar

This started out to be my "chunky" barbecue sauce, but when I got done it wasn't that chunky. (That's probably because I don't care for chunky barbecue sauce.) It reminded me of a sauce that I really like from an old barbecue restaurant in Kansas City, so I kind of named it after that restaurant. The restaurant is called Rosedale and it has a cornerstone by the door that says "Founded July 4, 1934." You gotta figure the food is good if they are still around after seventy years. They do have a new building, but the site and tradition are unchanged. On my last trip there the food was as good as usual and there was a sweet young bartender with a full bicep tattoo of Elvis. That is the kind of thing that makes a great barbecue joint for me. • **Yield: about 1 quart**

Heat the oil in a saucepan. Add the onion and bell pepper and sauté for a few minutes, stirring occasionally. Add the garlic and continue to sauté until the vegetables are all soft. Add all the other ingredients except the brown sugar and slowly bring the mixture to a simmer. Then add the brown sugar and blend well. Remove from the heat and cool, stirring occasionally. Store in a covered glass or plastic container in the refrigerator for up to 1 month.

Thick and Sticky Barbecue Sauce

2 cups ketchup

1 cup dark molasses

½ cup white vinegar

1 teaspoon chili powder

1 teaspoon paprika

1 teaspoon onion powder

1 teaspoon garlic powder

½ teaspoon allspice

½ teaspoon cinnamon

½ teaspoon mace

½ teaspoon freshly ground black pepper

¼ teaspoon Liquid Smoke (optional)

This is the type of sauce that is typically associated with Kansas City, but like many local favorites it's not exactly what you'll find in the original joints.

• **Yield: 3½ cups**

Combine all ingredients in a saucepan over low heat. It doesn't need to boil; as soon as the molasses dissolves, it is ready. Store in a covered glass or plastic container in the refrigerator for up to 1 month.

Vinegar-Based Barbecue Sauce

2 cups cider vinegar

¼ cup brown sugar

3 teaspoons salt

½ teaspoon cayenne pepper

1 teaspoon freshly ground black pepper

1 teaspoon white pepper

This is the thin vinegar sauce in the tradition of eastern North Carolina that is becoming popular everywhere as barbecue continues to spread like kudzu. Folks that try this get very attached to it. For a rough idea of the western North Carolina version, add 1 cup ketchup, 1 teaspoon Worcestershire sauce, and ½ teaspoon cinnamon to this recipe. The difference between the sauces stems from the fact that the original settlers of the Piedmont, or eastern portion of North Carolina, believed that tomatoes were poisonous. The western portion of the state was settled after tomatoes became a common ingredient. For a low-carb version just skip the brown sugar. This is best served over smoked pork in any form—chopped or pulled. • **Yield: 2 cups**

Combine all the ingredients in a large bowl, mix well, and let stand for a couple hours to blend the flavors. Store in a covered glass or plastic container in the refrigerator for up to 1 month.

Big Squeeze Yellow Mustard Barbecue Sauce

¾ cup yellow "ballpark" mustard

¾ cup cider vinegar

½ cup sugar

1½ tablespoons margarine

2 teaspoons salt

2 teaspoons Worcestershire sauce

1¼ teaspoons freshly ground black pepper

2 teaspoons Louisiana-style hot sauce, or more to taste

In South Carolina and parts of Georgia, mustard-based barbecue sauce originated and is still very popular. Now mustard fans from all over are catching on to this idea. There seems to be a mustard sauce in every barbecue joint I see. The sauce is primarily used over smoked pork, but you could serve this over grilled pork chops. • **Yield: 1¾ cups**

Combine all the ingredients in a saucepan, stirring to blend, and simmer over low heat for 30 minutes. Let stand at room temperature for 1 hour before using. Store in a covered glass or plastic container in the refrigerator for up to 1 month.

Alabama White Barbecue Sauce

1 cup mayonnaise

¾ cup white vinegar

1 tablespoon lemon juice

1 tablespoon freshly ground black pepper

1 teaspoon sugar

1 teaspoon prepared horseradish

1 teaspoon salt

White barbecue sauce is something that you won't see very far outside of northern Alabama. But when you are there you really should stop and try some. Big Bob Gibson's BBQ in Decatur, Alabama, is where it all began. They still serve it every day. They use it to make their world-famous barbecued chicken the same way they've been making it for almost eighty years. In the back by the old-fashioned wood burning pits, they dunk the chickens immediately in the white sauce as they come off the fire. Great stuff! • **Yield: about 2 cups**

Combine all ingredients in a bowl, mix well, and refrigerate. Store in a covered glass or plastic container in the refrigerator for up to 1 month.

Big-Time Mango Barbecue Sauce

2 ripe mangoes, peeled and sliced

½ cup ketchup

¼ cup brown sugar

3 tablespoons freshly squeezed lemon juice

⅓ cup bourbon

½ teaspoon habanero hot sauce (optional)

1 teaspoon ground ginger

1 teaspoon salt

½ teaspoon soy sauce

½ teaspoon ground cinnamon

¼ teaspoon ground nutmeg

¼ teaspoon ground allspice

I feel obliged to include a barbecue sauce that is a little less than traditional. Many people like to experiment, so this one is for them. It's really good on pork and chicken. • **Yield: 2½ cups**

Place the mango slices in a blender or food processor and puree until smooth.

Combine the puree and all the remaining ingredients in a saucepan and bring to a boil.

Reduce the heat and simmer over medium-low heat for 15 minutes, stirring occasionally, until it thickens. If prepared ahead of time, refrigerate, and reheat before using.

The Barbecue Log

My Favorite Mops and Sauces

Marinades

Marinades are a very popular tool for grilling. They help keep things nice and juicy and flavor the meat completely as long as the cut isn't too big. Fruit juices and vinegars will help tender-ize, too. Here are some interesting examples but, as always, feel free to experiment. Just about anything goes here.

▼▼

Italian Dressing Marinade

⅓ cup olive oil

⅓ cup balsamic vinegar

⅓ cup apple juice

1 tablespoon honey

1 tablespoon salt

1 tablespoon black pepper

1 tablespoon dried basil

1 tablespoon dried oregano

1 teaspoon dry mustard

2 cloves garlic, crushed

Many championship barbecue cooks use Italian dress-ing straight out of the bottle as a chicken marinade. Here's my homemade version. • **Yield: about 1 cup**

Combine all ingredients in a blender and puree. Store in a covered glass or plastic container in the refrigerator for up to 2 weeks.

Bear Game Teriyaki Marinade

1 cup soy sauce

¼ cup pineapple juice

⅓ cup brown sugar

1 teaspoon sesame oil

1 tablespoon minced garlic

1½ tablespoons chopped ginger root

This recipe comes from my friends in Chicago. We used it for many tailgating parties at Soldier Field when Da Bears were tearing up the league in the 1980s. It works best with chicken or pork. • **Yield: about 1½ cups**

Combine all ingredients in a nonreactive bowl and mix well and marinate. Store in a covered glass or plastic container in the refrigerator for up to 2 weeks. Marinate meats in it at least 6 hours.

Spicy Margarita Marinade

⅔ cup tequila

⅓ cup Triple Sec

2 tablespoons vegetable oil

1 tablespoon chopped cilantro

1 tablespoon finely chopped onion

2 serrano or jalapeño chiles, seeds and stems removed, finely chopped

1 teaspoon chipotle chile powder

Here's a perfect spicy Southwestern marinade for shrimp, chicken, or fish that's headed for the grill. • **Yield: about 1 cup**

Combine all the ingredients in a nonreactive bowl and allow to sit for 30 minutes. Store in a covered glass or plastic container in the refrigerator for up to 2 weeks.

Asian-Style Marinade

¾ cup olive oil

¼ cup sesame oil

⅓ cup rice vinegar

2 tablespoons soy sauce

2 tablespoons honey

2 cloves garlic, minced

1 tablespoon Chinese
five-spice powder

2 teaspoons freshly ground
white pepper

Chicken and pork both do well soaked in this marinade. • **Yield: 1½ cups**

Combine all ingredients in a nonreactive bowl and mix well. Store in a covered glass or plastic container in the refrigerator for up to 2 weeks.

Ray's Florida Marinade

1 cup freshly squeezed
orange juice

½ cup freshly squeezed
lime juice

1 tablespoon soy sauce

1 tablespoon balsamic
vinegar

1 jalapeño chile, seeds and
stems removed, chopped
fine

½ cup finely chopped red
onion

2 cloves garlic, crushed

2 tablespoons sugar

1 tablespoon salt

I moved to Florida in 2001 and have learned to love cooking with fresh citrus. This is great with chicken or flank steak. • **Yield: about 2 cups**

Combine all the ingredients in a nonreactive bowl, mix well, and refrigerate before using. Store in a covered glass or plastic container in the refrigerator for up to 1 week.

Citrus Marinade for Poultry

½ cup vegetable oil

2 dried red New Mexico chiles, seeds and stems removed, crumbled

¼ cup chopped onion

2 cloves garlic, minced

1 teaspoon cumin seeds

1 cup freshly squeezed orange juice

1 tablespoon freshly squeezed lime juice

2 teaspoons achiote paste (available in Hispanic markets)

1 teaspoon dried oregano, Mexican preferred

Pinch of ground cloves

Salt and freshly ground black pepper

Here's one of my favorite marinades for grilled poultry. It's particularly good with the dark meat of chicken and turkey. • **Yield: about 2 cups**

Heat ¼ cup of the vegetable oil in a pan and sauté the chiles and onion until softened. Add the garlic and cumin and continue to sauté for an additional minute. Remove from the heat. Combine the chile mixture along with the remaining vegetable oil, orange juice, lime juice, achiote paste, oregano, cloves, and salt and pepper in a food processor or blender and puree until the mixture becomes smooth. Store in a covered glass or plastic container in the refrigerator for up to 2 weeks.

There was a trend toward barbecue sauce–type salsas in the 1990s, but it never really panned out—probably because there are so many different types of salsas that go well with grilled food. They're really just chunky sauces any-way. Now they have moved from the bowl next to the tortilla chips to the top of the meat. This is a nice eclectic sampling, but the possibilities are endless. Mix and match them with all your barbecue.

▼▼

The Salsa with Six Names

6 serrano or jalapeño chiles, stems and seeds removed, chopped very fine

1 large onion, finely chopped

2 medium tomatoes, finely chopped

2 cloves garlic, minced

¼ cup finely chopped cilantro

2 tablespoons vegetable oil

2 tablespoons (or less, to taste) red wine vinegar or freshly squeezed lime juice

This blend of hot chiles and fresh garden vegetables is known both north and south of the border as *salsa fria, pico de gallo, salsa cruda, salsa fresca, salsa Mexicana,* and *salsa picante.* No matter what it's called, or what part of the Southwest it's from, the Salsa with Six Names will always triumph over bottled salsas for the dipping of *tostadas,* as a taco sauce, or a relish for roasted or grilled meats. The key to proper preparation is to *never use a food processor or blender.* A marvelous consistency will be achieved by taking the time to chop or mince every ingredient by hand. • **Yield: 2 cups**

Mix all the ingredients together in a nonreactive bowl. Let stand at room temperature for at least 1 hour before serving. Serve with tortilla chips as a dip. This salsa is also good with tacos, burritos, and fajitas.

Tomatillo-Mango Salsa

6 red serrano chiles, stems and seeds removed, minced

1 clove garlic, minced

2 tablespoons chopped green onions, including the greens

1 mango, pitted and coarsely chopped

6 tomatillos, husks removed, chopped

½ cup chopped cilantro

Juice of 1 lime

2 tablespoons olive oil

Not all Southwest salsas are tomato-based; this one utilizes tomatillos, the small "husk tomatoes" that are grown mostly in Mexico but are available fresh or canned in many U.S. supermarkets. The natural sweetness of the mango blends perfectly with the tartness of the tomatillos. • **Yield: 2 cups**

Note: This recipe requires advance preparation.

Combine all ingredients in a nonreactive bowl and allow to sit for at least 3 hours or, preferably, overnight to blend the flavors.

Pineapple-Habanero Salsa

2 cups chopped fresh
pineapple

3 fresh tomatillos, finely
chopped

1 tablespoon freshly
squeezed lime juice

1 tablespoon rice wine
vinegar

1 tablespoon vegetable oil

2 teaspoons grated fresh
ginger

1 teaspoon ground fresh
habanero chile

2 teaspoons chopped
fresh mint

This recipe combines hot habanero chiles with sweet pineapple to make a condiment that goes well with almost any type of meat or poultry. Habaneros are really hot, so wear plastic gloves when you cut them. The colors of this salsa make a nice garnish to any plate. • **Yield: 2½ cups**

Note: This recipe requires advance preparation.

Combine all the ingredients in a nonreactive bowl and allow to sit for 2 to 3 hours before serving.

Fiery Avocado Corn Salsa with Four Chiles

2 yellow wax chiles, stems and seeds removed, minced

2 red serrano chiles, stems and seeds removed, minced

1 green New Mexican chile, stem and seeds removed, minced

1 orange habanero chile, stems and seeds removed, minced

1 cup cooked corn

1 cup diced avocado

1 small tomato, diced

1 teaspoon chopped cilantro

1 teaspoon chopped green onion

1 teaspoon chopped red bell pepper

1 teaspoon chopped purple bell pepper

1 teaspoon chopped yellow bell pepper

2 tablespoons freshly squeezed lime juice

3 tablespoons olive oil

Here is a colorful, hearty salsa that can be served either as an accompaniment to grilled meats or atop greens as an interesting and colorful salad.

- **Yield: about 3 cups**

Combine all ingredients in a nonreactive bowl and mix gently. Serve immediately.

Grilled Southwestern Salsa

6 green New Mexican
chiles

4 jalapeño chiles

2 large tomatoes

4 tomatillos

2 medium onions

3 cloves garlic

¼ cup chopped cilantro

Here's a salsa that's partially cooked. This is an all-purpose salsa that can be served with tortilla chips, enchiladas, tacos, as an accompaniment to grilled entrées, as well as an ingredient in recipes. • **Yield: 1½ to 2 cups, depending on the size of the vegetables**

Make a wood or charcoal fire and let it burn down to coals. Place the first 6 ingredients on a grill only a few inches above the coals. Grill the vegetables until the skins burn and pop, turning occasionally.

Peel the vegetables, removing the stems and seeds from the chiles, and chop coarsely. Add the cilantro, mix well, and serve.

The Barbecue Log

My Favorite Marinades and Salsas

▼▼▼

Anything But

At a barbecue cookoff, "Anything but" is the term that is commonly used for the extra categories, as in "Anything but the regular categories." Sometimes the rules are very structured and sometimes they are very limited. I once turned in Fried Peanut Butter and Banana Sandwiches—Elvis's favorite, you know. I'm going to use Anything But as the catch-all section in all the chapters of this book.

▼▼▼

First Trophy Sherry Butter

1 cup melted butter

1 cup sherry

This is the simple injection mixture I used to win my first ever barbecue award. Avoid anything called cooking sherry, as it'll be too salty. Head for the liquor section and find a reasonable bottle. It's wonderful in turkey and chicken. Some great additions would be granulated garlic and onion and some spicy hot sauce. Just don't use anything chunky or it will clog the injector. • **Yield: 2 cups**

Mix the ingredients together in a bowl and inject in chicken or turkey a few hours before cooking.

Scottie's Creole Butter

1 pound butter

1 can beer of choice

1 tablespoon Big-Time Barbecue Rub (see recipe, p. 9)

1 tablespoon paprika

1 tablespoon freshly ground white pepper

1 tablespoon sea salt

1 tablespoon garlic powder

1 tablespoon onion powder

1 tablespoon dry mustard

1 tablespoon freshly and finely ground black pepper

1 teaspoon cayenne pepper

This recipe was inspired by my friend Scottie Johnson from Chicago. We first met via The BBQ Forum on the Internet and realized we were almost neighbors. I wish you could see his adorable little girls. This recipe was first created for deep-fried turkeys but works just great when barbecuing poultry and it makes a great fish marinade, too. • **Yield: about 2½ cups**

Melt the butter in saucepan and add the beer and spices. Mix well. Let cool, then inject.

Big Pig Pork Injection

1 cup pineapple juice

1 cup apple juice

½ cup brown sugar

¼ cup salt

2 tablespoons
Worcestershire sauce

2 tablespoons soy sauce

2 tablespoons hot sauce of
choice

1 tablespoon dry mustard

Here's my version of a competition injection blend. This goes well in a slow-cooked pork shoulder. • **Yield: about 3 cups**

Combine all the ingredients in a saucepan. Heat until they are well blended. Refrigerate before using.

Big Cow Beef Injection

2 cups beef broth

¼ cup Worcestershire
sauce

1 teaspoon onion powder

1 teaspoon garlic powder

½ teaspoon cayenne
pepper

Injecting brisket is a new thing in the cookoff world, but it's catching on fast. This works well with any cut of beef. • **Yield: 2¼ cups**

Combine all ingredients in a bowl, mix well, and refrigerate before injecting.

Barbecue Schmear

1 cup Big-Time Barbecue Rub (see recipe, p. 9)

Apple juice to make a paste, about 2 to 3 tablespoons

I primarily use this on brisket to help the rub stick to the cold meat, but it would work fine on other meats as well. • **Yield: 1 cup**

In a bowl, combine the ingredients, mix well, and apply directly to the meat.

Traditional Jerk Paste

4 to 6 Scotch bonnet peppers (habaneros will work), seeds and stems removed

1 cup chopped scallions

1 cup chopped onion

2 teaspoons salt

2 teaspoons allspice

2 teaspoons dried thyme

1 teaspoon ground nutmeg

½ teaspoon ground cinnamon

2 tablespoons olive oil

T his is a spicy paste that is used on fish, pork, and chicken. When you visit Jamaica you quickly realize that jerk is not a gimmick for the tourists. It's eaten and served everywhere and it's very spicy. You may want to use fewer peppers if you don't want as much heat. Jerk paste is best when applied one hour before cooking.
• **Yield: about 2½ cups**

Combine all the ingredients in a blender and puree.

Sweet and Sticky Barbecue Glaze

2 cups Thick and Sticky Barbecue Sauce (see recipe, p. 21)

½ cup honey

1 tablespoon hot sauce of choice

This is what I always use to finish my ribs and chicken at barbecue cookoffs around the country. • **Yield: 2½ cups**

Combine all ingredients in a saucepan, stir well, and simmer for 15 minutes to reduce and thicken.

Honey Mustard Pineapple Glaze

¾ cup honey

½ cup Dijon mustard

1 cup pineapple juice

2 tablespoons cornstarch combined with ¼ cup cold water

Here's a glaze with a tropical flavor that makes a great finishing sauce for teriyaki chicken. • **Yield: 2 cups**

In a saucepan, heat the first 3 ingredients to a boil. Add the cornstarch-water mixture and stir to thicken. Cook about 3 minutes, stirring constantly.

Brines

Brining meat is a very old technique that was originally used for preservation. While it still often is, I also use it as a tool for flavoring and helping the meat to retain its juiciness. It's not something I personally do very often because I don't much care for the texture that is created. I must tell you, though, that many great barbecue cooks and many great chefs disagree with me on this one. Here is a very basic brine and another one that's kind of uptown. They both work the same. One or two days' soaking is good for a chicken or a piece of pork loin, and two to four days is good for an eighteen-pound turkey. The longer you brine, the more effect it will have on the flavor and texture. Be sure to rinse the meat well and don't use a very salty rub.

▼▼

Real Simple Brine

1 cup kosher salt

1 cup white sugar

1 gallon water

½ cup white vinegar

1 tablespoon whole black peppercorns

1 teaspoon garlic powder

1 teaspoon dried tarragon

• Yield: about 1 gallon

Dissolve the salt and sugar in half the water in a large pot. Bring to a boil and let cool. Add the rest of the water, the vinegar, and the spices. Mix well. Chill before using.

Big-Time Chef's Brine

1 cup kosher salt

1 cup honey

1 gallon water

½ cup cider vinegar

4 cloves garlic, chopped

1 large onion, chopped

4 carrots, chopped

1 teaspoon dried thyme

1 teaspoon dried tarragon

2 tablespoons whole black peppercorns

• Yield: about 1 gallon

Dissolve the salt and honey in half the water in a large pot. Bring to a boil and let cool. Add the rest of the water, the vinegar, the vegetables, and the spices. Mix well. Chill before using.

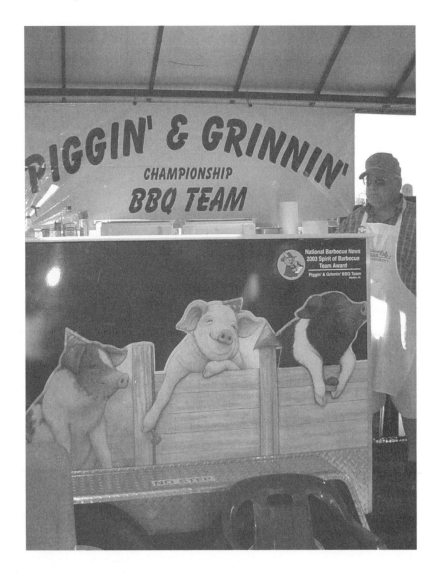

Smoke 'Em If You Got 'Em

Ray's Award-Winning Ribs, Brisket, Pork Butt, Chicken, and Other Smoky Favorites

ROSEDALE BARBEQUE FOUNDED JULY 4, 1934

BIG HOUSE BAR-B-QUE TEAM

Ray's Pit: Smoking Concepts, Techniques, and Equipment

Real barbecue is created by taking a lesser cut of meat and cooking it slowly over some form of wood fuel for a long period of time, thus tenderizing the meat and creating a smoky, caramelized outer surface known as the "bark."

That's the bottom line, but I thought I'd put it at the top to start this chapter. It is my belief that this style of cooking was perfected by the slaves and peasants of old who only had access to the lesser cuts of meat, probably discarded by the folks lucky enough to be eating the more desirable parts. This cooking method has sure changed things. Now the bones cut from the loin of a hog (baby back ribs) cost twice as much as the boneless meat that was attached to them. That is a bizarre tribute to the real pioneers of barbecue.

The term "smoking" is often interchangeably used with "barbecue," but that can be misleading. Cold smoking is done at very low temperatures and is more of a flavoring and preserving technique than what I'm talking about here.

I call it barbecuing. When pressed I will accept the term "hot smoking." The cooking temperature should be between 210° and 275°F. There should be some smoke involved. If using a log wood fire there is a distinct possibility of oversmoking the food. You will need to practice to keep the temperature right without restricting the exhaust. This is what is referred to as a clean fire. My preference to avoid oversmoking is to use charcoal with some wood for flavoring or a pellet cooker.

The original barbecue fuel is wood, of course. Split logs and whole logs are used in many barbecue cookers. Some will have a burn barrel where you can burn the wood down a bit before putting it in the cooker.

There are two main types of charcoal, briquettes and natural lump. Briquettes are processed and formed and usually contain fillers and binders. I don't mind them, but I do try to buy good quality. The cheaper stuff seems to leave considerably more weird-looking ash than the better stuff. That can't be a good thing. Natural lump charcoal is just that, partially burned wood with no additives. Some brands will occasionally include an old beer can, a rock, or what seems to be a melted plastic bottle, but I'm pretty sure that is an accident. There are brands that are primarily oak, maple, or mesquite. The flavors won't be very different because it's all partially burned. There is an amazing Web site devoted to the different brands of lump: *www.lumpcharcoal.com*. This guy clearly has too much time on his hands to devote so much attention to this subject.

Wood pellets are a manufactured fuel product. One variety is made for heating your home and another is made for cooking. You know which ones to buy. There are specific cookers designed to use them, which I will tell you about a little later. It's a very unique and interesting concept. The pellets are wood sawdust that has been extruded, resulting in a product that looks eerily similar to rabbit chow. If the manufacturing process is done at the right temperature with the right moisture content and

pressure, the pellets can be made without any foreign binders. The typical cooking pellets are from 10 to 33 percent of the named flavor with the balance being a consistent wood base. The base wood is usually something common to the region. Many pellets are made in Missouri, where oak is abundant, so they use oak. The pellets made in the Northwest are based with alder, which is abundant there. There are two main reasons for the use of a common base. The first goes right to the origin of pellets, lots of sawdust as a by-product of logging. This explains the heavy use of the locally abundant wood. The second reason is consistency among different flavors. The cherry pellets need to have the same degree of hardness and the same amount of BTUs as the apple, hickory, pecan, and so on. Blending these flavor woods with the right amount of the base wood allows for the uniformity of hardness and BTUs that is necessary to create good consistent pellets of all flavors. These cooking pellets are typically available in twenty- or forty-pound bags.

There are also pellets that are intended mainly for flavor, as opposed to fuel. They are composed of 100 percent of a specific wood. These are more expensive and typically sold in smaller quantities. My friend Candy Weaver and her company BBQr's Delight are the leaders in this field. She has developed beautiful packaging and a wide variety of flavors. Have you ever tried mulberry, orange, or sassafras? BBQr's Delight has them. She even has a savory herb variety (see p. 177 for her lamb recipe in which these are used). Flavor pellets are the perfect way to sample the many different types of wood flavors that used to be only available regionally. I also think pellets are great for blending flavors. A combination of a fruitwood and a heavier smoke wood such as hickory or oak is a good thing. I always keep a few varieties around. A one-pound bag of flavor pellets provides ten uses. These are used much like chips and chunks, mainly for flavoring when grilling or barbecuing. Candy recommends a foil packet or a little cast-iron pot to keep the pellets smoking rather than just burning up, but sometimes I will drop a handful right through the grate and quickly shut the lid for a quick dose of smoke while grilling.

My personal preference for choice of wood flavor has always been a combination of two-thirds cherry to one-third hickory. I like the color and flavor that cherry imparts, but it just seems to need a little kick. Hickory is the classic barbecue flavor to me, but it can easily overpower most foods. If I'm cooking just chicken I like straight cherry, but since I'm usually cooking different things at the same time the above combination is usually what is in my cooker. I like pecan as a substitute for the combination when I can get it, but it doesn't make the food the nice color that cherry does.

Dr. BBQ's Top 5 Barbecue Tips

1. Don't put any barbecue sauce on until the food is almost done or it will burn.

2. Learn to control the temperature of your grill. They are all different.

3. Don't use too much wood. You can oversmoke the food.

4. Take your time. Cooking barbecue can take a while. Savor the opportunity to relax and enjoy the smell.

5. Learn to use a thermometer and to tell when the food is done. Many meals are ruined by overcooking.

Types of Barbecue Cookers

Charcoal and wood can be used in many different types of cookers. You name it and someone has built a cooker out of it. I prefer to have the heat source under the food. It just makes sense to me since heat rises. The heat can be deflected in many ways. My Big Green Egg has a ceramic deflector option that also holds a drip pan. My Cookshack FEC 100 Pellet cooker has a two-layer deflector plate, with the bottom one directly over the fire to disperse the direct heat and the top one on an angle to carry the grease off to a drain pan. These are both very good setups. There are many nice cookers that use a water pan as a deflector. This works well, too. It does create a messy cleanup and I prefer dry

heat, but there are many great cooks who swear by the water bath cookers. There are flat plates that are close to the fire and will vaporize the grease and still others that just have the food high enough above the direct fire. All of these cookers typically burn charcoal or wood that is pre-burned down to embers, which are then added to the cooker. All of these work very well once you get used to them.

The other popular barbecue cooker is commonly referred to as an offset or Texas style. It's my belief that these originated in and around Texas, where they had scrap oil pipe readily available. These guys wanted to make cookers out of the pipe, but it just wasn't big

enough to get the meat far enough from the fire. So they devised a design where the fire is in one chamber and the food is in another with an opening between them letting heat and smoke in on one end and exhausting out the other end. This actually works but is not very fuel efficient and of course it's much hotter on the end nearest the fire. There are now some very successful designs being built and sold that even the heat out across the cooker. They conserve wood by insulating the firebox and spreading the heat with a steel plate or some other baffle setup. These new high-tech designs work well, but it still makes much more sense to me to have the heat rising to the food. Offset smokers are mostly fueled by split logs or branches. They are usually big and black and really cool-looking, so it is a very macho way to cook. You'll need to learn to keep a clean hot fire though, or your food will be too smoky. I would plan to use charcoal later in the cooking or plan to wrap the food in aluminum foil along the way to prevent this from happening.

Backyard electric cookers are becoming very popular. They are easy to operate and can be left unattended all night with no worries for those long cooks. Just don't use very much wood in these—you won't need it. My friends at Cookshack make a beauty.

Back to wood pellets. There are special cookers built with a system to feed pellets into a fire pot on a regular basis regulated by a timer or a thermostat. This process, along with a draft to stir things up, creates a clean-burning fire. These pellet cookers compete very well with the other types of smokers on the cookoff circuit.

I must tell you that backyard kettle grills and good old gas grills still outsell these true-

blue cookers by a big margin, and the truth is you can cook real barbecue on just about anything. The kettles are easily set up for indirect cooking by putting the coals on one or both sides with a drip pan underneath. The gas grills are a little trickier. They use many different burner configurations, so you'll need to follow the manufacturer's instructions for indirect cooking on yours.

A barbecue cooker is a very personal item. They can cost as little as forty bucks and as much as you could possibly imagine. A price tag of ten to fifteen thousand dollars is common. No matter which one you choose, you'll need to learn the way it cooks. That's one reason for the acceptable temperature range of 210° to 275°F. The cooking times may vary, but there is an old saying around barbecue: "It's done when it's done."

I had an old-timer once suggest that I quit fighting my cooker over a 15° variation and just let it cook where it wanted to. That cooker always settled in at 210°F, which I had thought was too low. I became a much better cook after that advice.

Building a Fire

I'd like to talk here about starting and building a fire for cooking. You sure can't cook without a fire. If you've got a gas grill, an electric or gas smoker, or a pellet cooker, you should have no problem because they are all self-starting. Just follow the manufacturer's instructions.

For a charcoal fire it's pretty simple. There are a few very good ways to start charcoal and they all work for both lump and briquettes. The briquettes will always take a little longer to get going, though. First off is the old standby electric starter. You'll need an outlet nearby and you'll have to stay close by to keep an eye on it, but once purchased it's pretty much free to use. Just be sure to take the charcoal out as soon as the coals are going or the fire will get hot and burn up the starter.

Another very good and popular way to start a charcoal fire is with a charcoal chimney. They are readily available these days and work well. The concept is the charcoal is in a sort of great big metal mug with holes in the bottom. You crumple up some newspaper underneath and light it. The configuration is such that it will light the charcoal and the whole load will be going cleanly and quickly. Then you can dump it into your grill or smoker and add as much more charcoal as you need. As with any fire, once you have a good bed of hot coals going, any new fuel will ignite easily. The chimney is virtually free to use once purchased.

There are also some very good single-use products available to start charcoal and wood fires. The most common are made of paraffin and sawdust. They come in different shapes and sizes but are all essentially the same. This is a good combination, since the sawdust is wood and the paraffin burns off quickly. It's just there to get the sawdust going and then the sawdust acts as kindling.

Last but certainly not least is a blowtorch. These come in sizes from a small MAPP gas torch with a one-pound cylinder up to a very macho weed burner that uses a big propane tank and a hose. These can light a fire in no time at all and are very popular on the barbecue circuit. You want to scare your neighbors? Get one of these. I once bought one for Stephanie in the KCBS office for Christmas and she cried. What a gal. Of course, the big blowtorch is a great option for an all-wood fire. Anything less would just get tiresome. One other good option is to build a charcoal fire as a base and then add the wood. I always prefer a combination of charcoal and wood anyway. Depending on the size and type of your cooker, you'll need more of one or the other, but I always try to use the charcoal for fuel and the wood for taste.

Please stay away from starter fluid because the food will pick up that taste. If you must use it, light only a small amount of coals and let them gray over completely before adding more charcoal and don't add any more starter fluid. This will take a while, but you should end up with a clean fire.

Once you get the fire established and the cooker warmed up, you should have a pretty consistent plan for adding more fuel. Add as often as is necessary to keep an even temperature inside the cooker. For some cookers this means a small amount of fuel every hour, and for others it can mean one big load that will burn evenly all night. Can you guess which one I'd like to have?

The Smoke Ring

That nice reddish color that you see around the outside of a piece of cut barbecue is called the smoke ring. It is something that we barbecue competitors are very aware of. Now pay close attention here, because this is the science class part of the book. The coloring that we refer to as the smoke ring is the result of a chemical reaction between the nitrites in the smoke and the protein in the meat. The chemical reaction that causes the coloring ceases at approximately 130°F. That's why it penetrates the meat a quarter or half inch and then stops. The smoke flavoring of the meat does not cease. Let me repeat that. The smoke flavoring of the meat does not cease, ever, regardless of the temperature. Unless the meat is wrapped in foil or in a covered pan, it will continue to pick up smoke flavor if it's in the cooking chamber.

The penetration of the smoke flavor into the meat may slow down as the crust forms, but the outside is where almost the entire smoke flavor is anyway. Smoke penetration beyond a half inch is a myth. When you eat a piece of barbecue the smoke flavor is in the caramelized, smoked, seasoned bark of the meat. Period. This flavor is akin to a roux. It is developed by the slow cooking process and is a result of the heat, smoke, and drying effect of a barbecue pit. When done properly it is not like anything else you will ever taste.

I must tell you here about a product called Tender Quick. It's a curing salt that is readily available and it contains a high level of nitrites. If it's applied to a piece of meat in a controlled fashion it can simulate a beautiful smoke ring. If it's not used properly it can produce a corned beef taste in a matter of a couple of hours. It is legal and used by quite a few competitors. I've never tried it because the cookers I use have always produced a good smoke ring during normal cooking. Some don't.

Based on what I just told you, I will now tell you that I always put my pork, brisket, and ribs on the cooker directly from the ice chest or refrigerator to encourage the maximum smoke ring. I know some very good cooks who believe it is best to let the meat come to room temperature before putting it in the cooker. One theory is that the meat goes through some sort of convulsion when it is shocked by the great temperature change. I disagree. For one, to allow meat to sit at room temperature is bad food safety practice and besides, it's only going from 40° to 75°F. If that shocking was real, it would happen anyway when the 75°F meat went into the 250°F cooker. Now, chicken is a different story. The beautiful reddish color that we desire in the other meats can scare off judges and guests when it comes to chicken. I always let my chicken sit out for a half hour to discourage the chemical reaction that can make the bones red and the meat pink. I've seen more than a few cookoff disqualifications for raw chicken. I always wonder if it was raw or just looked raw. I've also seen more than a few barbecue restaurants put something on their menu about the chicken looking pink because of the smoking, but some people just can't enjoy it, so I think it's best to try to minimize it. Cooking chicken at higher temperatures helps, too, getting it past that 130°F line quicker.

Cookoffs

The style of cooking we're discussing here is exactly what the barbecue cookoffs that have become so popular are based on. I've been competing in them for years, but at first it was kind of a subculture. They began to get popular locally, and they got real popular in the barbecue hotbeds like Kansas City, Memphis, and all of Texas, but now they have gone uptown in their appeal. In the last couple of years I've seen myself and all my friends on the Food Network, CNN, The Travel Channel, and in many independent productions. Camera crews from all over have become a common site at our events. At this writing I know of at least three different barbecue TV shows that are being proposed, and they are all receiving serious consideration. The best cooks are becoming names that are known around the country. I even know one who has written a book (hint: you're reading it). The equipment we use is getting popular, and sponsors are coming on board with the cooks. Some sponsors are starting up their own teams. Many of the backyard grill companies are teaming up with the high-profile pro barbecue cooks to promote their products at trade shows and throughout the year. There are classes to teach you how to judge being held regularly throughout the country. They won't tell you what you should like to eat, but they will teach you about the procedures and the rules so that you can score the food according to how well you like it. There are seminars and meetings held during the slow season to train contest officials and organizers. There are awards banquets and a year-end ranking of all the teams that have competed. This sport is smokin' hot right now with no indication of slowing down.

Classes

There are even a few of us teaching competition barbecue cooking classes. Now keep in mind that cooking a brisket can be a twenty-four-hour process, so these are not your normal cooking classes. I do quite a few of these classes, and mine last twenty-four hours. I stay near the cooker the whole time. I don't know any other way to cook barbecue. I tell the students up front that they can go home or to a hotel if they want, but they very well might miss something because the class is in session the whole time. I cover everything in agonizing detail. I want the students to leave with all the information I have gathered in twenty-plus years of doing this. I cover meat selection, prep, cooking, cooker maintenance, rubs, sauces, fuels, contest presentation, and the whole mentality of becoming a barbecue champion.

It's no different from any other type of competition. You have to have a winner's mentality and the drive to succeed. There is no magic secret ingredient that only a few know about. It's the motivation to go the extra mile in every respect that makes winners. I know a cook who regularly drives forty-five minutes each way the day before a cookoff so that he can get the best parsley. That is extreme, but I do drive an hour each way to get briskets when I'm in Florida. The all-night hard-core cooking class offers the whole package as a lesson.

I also do some classes that are limited in their scope. There are many people interested in a little entertainment, a little cooking

knowledge, and a good meal, but they're really not interested in staying up all night to learn all the little details. I like to think of these as an orientation to the barbecue cookoff world. These work great in an area where cookoffs are new. I can teach the guests all about what a team puts into the prep, show them a few cooking tricks, and feed them a meal unlike anything they've ever had. These classes help promote the local event, but they also bring new cooks, judges, and contest organizers into the fold. Before you know it, some of these people are traveling to the next state to judge, or showing up with a brand-new trailer cooker to compete. We like to call this kind of thing "promoting barbecue." There are many of us who do it every chance we get.

This rest of this chapter features my tried-and-true contest techniques. I hope you like them.

The Barbecue Log

Reminders About My Smoker and a
Record of Wood and Charcoal I've Used

Beef

The all-time favorite cut of beef for real slow-cooked barbecue is the brisket. It is also the only cut of beef regularly cooked at barbecue cookoffs. The brisket comes from the chest of the steer. It is a very tough muscle with little internal fat. Brisket fits perfectly in the category of lesser cuts that I talked about at the beginning of this chapter. Do not confuse brisket to be smoked with corned beef brisket, which is the same cut that has been corned (processed in a seasoned brine). Incidentally, corned beef is very good when cooked in a barbecue pit, and I have included a recipe, but it's not a typical barbecue brisket.

Fresh brisket is regularly available as the "flat" cut or as the "whole" or "packer" cut. The whole brisket consists of two distinct muscles with two textures and very different fat percentages. The grain in both muscles is very coarse, but it runs in different directions. This makes brisket difficult to properly carve when left whole. Whoever decided to leave these two muscles together in the first place must not have been a cook. This is one of the many challenges to cooking a brisket.

The flat cut is the leaner, more uniform, and just plain prettier muscle of the two. The "point" is fattier and more free form in shape. It is rarely seen sold by itself by the butcher. It

usually becomes hamburger after it is separated from the flat. The flats are popular with restaurants because they cook faster, slice better, and have much less waste.

Unlike chicken and pork, beef is regularly graded for quality by the USDA. I find USDA Choice briskets to be right for me. Whenever possible, I will seek out Certified Angus Beef (CAB). Not to be confused with all the meaningless "Angus" names in supermarkets, CAB is a program that really does select a better quality of beef to put its name on. It's not just about black cows being better. I also like to age the meat in the sealed plastic (Cryovac). It's not traditional dry aging and not everyone agrees that it helps, but if I can I will always do it until it's thirty to fifty days old. You'll need to know the actual packing date as opposed to the sell-by date, and you'll need to keep the meat very cold. A spare refrigerator that doesn't get opened very often is best, and it should be kept under 40°. If the seal breaks on the package you'll need to cook or freeze the meat within a couple of days.

Nothing else is even close to brisket in popularity for real barbecue, but there are some fun options for cooking it. My first Barbecue All Star recipe shows up in this section, too, on pages 63–64. It is a good one.

Dr. BBQ's Big-Time Competition Brisket

1 whole brisket (12 to 15 pounds)

1 recipe Barbecue Schmear (see recipe, p. 41)

Big-Time Barbecue Sauce (see recipe, p. 19)

When I discovered barbecue, nobody was cooking brisket in Chicago, so I had to learn from the ground up. There were no videos and no books about it, so I just looked and listened when I went to cookoffs. It's amazing what guys will tell you if you hang around and act neighborly. I'm not sure any of them even know it, but guys like Mike Scrutchfield, Jim Erickson, Jeff Shivers, John Willingham, Guy Simpson, and the late Bill Myers all helped me out a whole lot along the way. In case you don't know those names, they are all barbecue cookoff legends. It took a few years, but I got my way of doing it worked out and I consider myself a very good brisket cook these days. • **Yield: 12–15 servings**

Note: This recipe requires advance preparation.

Trim most of the fat from the pockets on the sides of the brisket. Then cut along the outside edge where needed to shape the whole brisket and to get rid of anything that doesn't look good. This will help you when it's time to carve the cooked brisket. The fat cap should remain mostly intact, unless there is an extremely thick piece of fat, and that can be trimmed to even things up for cooking.

About 12 hours before cooking, rub the Barbecue Schmear all over the exposed meat areas of the brisket. Wrap in plastic and return to the refrigerator.

Prepare your cooker for indirect cooking at 235°F, using 2 parts cherry and 1 part hickory wood for flavor. Place the brisket fat side down and with the thicker end facing the hotter side if you have one. Now just keep the door closed and let the brisket cook for about 12 hours before

Dr. BBQ's Big-Time Competition Brisket (continued)

you even peek. As long as your temperature gauges are working properly things will be fine. After 12 hours, check the internal temperature of the thickest part of the flat muscle. When it reaches 190°F, it's time to take the brisket off. Lay out a double layer of wide heavy-duty aluminum foil and place the brisket fat side up. Wrap it up tightly and place in a dry, empty ice chest. Cover the brisket with more briskets or crumpled-up newspaper and leave it alone for at least 3 hours and up to 6 hours. It will stay plenty hot.

Remove the brisket from the ice chest and take off the foil. It will be very tender and there will be very hot liquid in the bottom of the foil, so don't ever do this naked. Reserve the juice and skim the fat.

Take a long carving knife and separate the two muscles, being very careful not to cut into either one. Once you have them apart you should trim the fat off the point muscle and chop the point. Place it in a bowl and add the reserved juice and a little bit of barbecue sauce. Next trim all the fat off the flat and slice it across the grain. There will only be bark and a smoke ring on one side, but that's okay. It will be so intense that it will easily flavor the whole slice.

For my cookoff presentation, I make a bed of the chopped point and put the slices on top in a layered fashion. I always brush each slice with barbecue sauce for competition. At home I prefer to serve it on the side.

Dr. BBQ's Shortcut Brisket

1 cup Big Cow Beef
Injection (see recipe,
p. 40)

1 brisket, flat cut (5–6
pounds), fat left on

Big-Time Barbecue Rub
(see recipe, p. 9)

Many of the top competition teams cook brisket flats and many wrap the briskets midway through the cooking process. This hurries things up and helps maintain a nice juicy brisket. Many teams are also now injecting their briskets, so for this recipe I am going to combine all of these techniques. • **Yield: 6–8 servings**

Note: This recipe requires advance preparation.

A couple hours before you plan to start cooking, inject the Big Cow Injection into the brisket, spreading it around as best you can. Season the brisket with the Big-Time Barbecue Rub as heavily as you can.

Prepare the cooker for indirect cooking at 275°F, using pecan wood for flavor. Cook the brisket fat side down for 1 hour, and then flip it to fat side up. Cook to an internal temperature of 160°F. This should take 3 to 4 hours total. Wrap the brisket tightly in a double layer of heavy-duty aluminum foil and return to the cooker. After another hour begin checking the internal temperature. When it reaches 200°F, remove the brisket and let it rest, wrapped, for one-half hour. Slice and serve.

For cookoff presentation I would sauce each slice lightly.

Jalapeño Brisket

1 brisket, flat cut (5–6 pounds), fat left on

Big-Time Barbecue Rub (see recipe, p. 9)

1 large onion, chopped

6 to 8 large jalapeño chiles, seeds and stems removed, chopped

1 cup beef broth

This is similar to the Shortcut Brisket, but we're going to add the great flavor and heat of fresh jalapeño peppers and skip the injection. I would not recommend this for a cookoff. • **Yield: 6–8 servings**

Note: This recipe requires advance preparation.

The night before, rub the brisket with the Big-Time Barbecue Rub, wrap it in plastic, and return to the refrigerator.

Prepare the cooker for indirect cooking at 275°F, using pecan wood for flavor. Cook the brisket fat side down for 1 hour, and then flip it to fat side up. Cook to an internal temperature of 160°F. This should take 3 to 4 hours total. Lay out a double layer of heavy-duty aluminum foil and spread half the onion and jalapeño in the middle. Lay the brisket fat side up on them. Top with the remaining onion and jalapeño. Crimp up the sides and add as much broth as you can before closing up the package. Be careful not to puncture it or you'll have to start over. If you have the right size aluminum foil pan, feel free to substitute that, but be sure to cover it well with aluminum foil. Return to the cooker. After another hour begin checking the internal temperature. When it reaches 195°F, remove the brisket and let it rest, wrapped, for one-half hour. Slice and serve.

Dirty Dick's Cajun Ribeye Roast

A Recipe from Barbecue All Star Dirty Dick Westhaver

Dirty Dick's Cajun Seasoning Mix

- ½ **cup dark brown sugar**
- ¼ **cup kosher salt**
- 6 **tablespoons garlic powder**
- 2 **tablespoons ancho chile powder**
- 2 **tablespoons paprika**
- 2 **tablespoons freshly ground black pepper**
- 2 **tablespoons dried oregano**
- 2 **tablespoons cumin**
- 1 **tablespoon cayenne pepper**
- 1 **tablespoon freshly ground white pepper**
- 1 **tablespoon ground coriander**
- 1 **tablespoon onion powder**

1 boneless ribeye roast (8 pounds), USDA Choice

½ **pound unsalted butter, melted**

Dirty Dick's Curry Horseradish Cream Sauce (recipe follows)

This is the first of the "Barbecue All Stars" recipes that are spread throughout this book. These are recipes with interesting stories from great folks who have played a big role in the world of barbecue. I'm proud to include them just as they came to me. Dirty Dick's Legless Wonders is a very old barbecue team. That name is kind of catchy and I remember seeing it when I first got started in the early 1990s. Dirty Dick, a.k.a. Richard Westhaver, doesn't really look like a guy who should be named Dirty Dick. He looks much more like the Boston indoor landscape designer that he is in real life. He's become a good friend over the years and is a spectacular kitchen cook as well as being a world-class barbecue cook with plenty of championships to his name. I think his recipe speaks for itself. • **Yield: 12 servings**

To make the seasoning mix: Combine all the ingredients in a bowl and mix well.

To make the roast: Let the roast rest on the counter for an hour so it won't be cold to start. In a big pan, roll the roast around in the melted butter to thoroughly coat it. Sprinkle heavily on all sides with the seasoning mix.

Prepare your cooker for indirect cooking at 275°F, using hickory and cherry wood for flavor. Put the roast in the cooker and cook to an internal temperature of 130°F. This should take about 3 hours.

Remove the roast from the cooker, tent loosely with foil, and let rest for one-half hour.

Slice and serve with Dirty Dick's Curry Horseradish Cream Sauce on the side. I'd serve some barbecue sauce, too.

Dirty Dick's Curry Horseradish Cream Sauce

¾ cup sour cream

½ cup heavy cream

2 teaspoons prepared horseradish (freshly grated is best), or more to taste

1 tablespoon chopped cilantro

1 tablespoon Dijon mustard

2 teaspoons sugar

1 teaspoon curry powder

Salt and freshly ground black pepper, to taste

In a bowl, whisk all the ingredients together and check for salt and pepper. Chill until ready to serve.

Meat Loaf for Lisa Marie

We had to get to this sooner or later, so here goes. The Big Green Egg is an all-ceramic barbecue cooker that I happen to use very often. There was a time when I scoffed at it because of the quirky design and the cultlike following it has on the Internet, but then a very wise man named Jim Nufer gave me one to try. I promptly named it Lisa Marie as a jab at the eccentric folks who worship these things. Well, I carried it around all summer and really took a liking to it. I've since cooked many award-winning dishes on my Big Green Eggs and I have a very good relationship with the company. I now carry two large eggs, a small one, and a mini with me all the time. Lisa Marie has taken her place of honor at my house, where she will stay. A longtime egger named "Woo Doggies" even gave me a custom-engraved handle for her. When it came time to test my meat loaf recipe I cooked it on Lisa Marie. Seems only fitting to name the recipe after her. Yes, I am an Elvis fan and I carry a fake EP driver's license with me at all times. • **Yield: 8–10 servings**

3 pounds ground chuck

¾ cup beef consommé (canned is fine)

¼ cup Worcestershire sauce

1 small onion, chopped fine

1 small bell pepper, seeds and stem removed, chopped fine

1 jalapeño chile, seeds and stem removed, chopped fine

2 cloves garlic, crushed

1 cup seasoned breadcrumbs

4 large eggs, lightly beaten

2 teaspoons salt

2 teaspoons freshly ground black pepper

2 teaspoons chili powder

2 medium aluminum foil loaf pans

Barbecue sauce (optional)

In a big bowl, mix all the ingredients well. Punch a few holes in two medium aluminum foil loaf pans and split the mixture between the two, packing it tightly in the corners.

Prepare the cooker for indirect cooking at 275°F, using cherry and hickory wood for flavor. Put the loaves in the cooker for one hour. At that time check them for firmness. They should be ready to be turned out of the loaf pans, and put onto the grate and stay together. Cook for another hour and begin checking the internal temperature. When it reaches 155°F, they are done. Remove to a plate and glaze with barbecue sauce if you wish. Tent with foil and let rest for 10 minutes. Slice and serve.

The leftovers make great meat loaf sandwiches.

Barbecue Pot Roast

1 chuck roast (4 pounds)

Big-Time Herb Rub (see recipe, p. 12)

1 pound carrots, peeled and sliced

6 medium potatoes, peeled and halved

1 medium onion, chopped

2 cloves garlic, crushed

2 cups beef broth mixed with 1 tablespoon cornstarch

Here's a good old-fashioned pot roast but with a smoky twist. • **Yield: about 6 servings**

Prepare the cooker for indirect cooking at 275°F, using hickory and cherry wood for flavor. Coat the chuck roast liberally with the rub and put it in the cooker. Cook for 1 hour. Flip the roast and cook for another one-half hour. Remove the roast to an aluminum foil pan. Cover with the vegetables and pour the broth over the top. Sprinkle some more rub on the vegetables. Cover tightly with foil and return to the cooker. Cook for about another 3 hours, until the roast is tender. If you can, run the heat up to 350°F during this time and check it in 2 hours instead of 3. Remove the roast and vegetables to a platter and serve the gravy on the side.

Smoky Corned Beef

1 piece of corned beef, flat cut (3–4 pounds)

Freshly ground black pepper, to taste

It won't be your average St. Patrick's Day when you serve this with a head of smoked cabbage (see recipe, p. 252). • **Yield: 6–8 servings**

Prepare the cooker for indirect cooking at 275°F, using hickory and cherry wood for flavor. Take the corned beef out of the package and sprinkle it with black pepper. Put it in the cooker and cook for 1½ hours. Wrap in foil with one-quarter cup of water. Cook to an internal temperature of 185°F, about another 2 hours. Remove from the cooker and rest for 20 minutes. Slice thinly and serve with boiled potatoes and smoked cabbage.

The Barbecue Log

Things to Remember About
Barbecuing the Best Beef

▼▼▼

Did you know that Louis Armstrong coined the word "chicks" as a nickname for girls? He's also responsible for "reefer," but my favorite from the jazz great is the use of the word "barbecue" to refer to a sexy woman. That's right; when Satchmo wrote "Struttin' with Some Barbecue" he was not referring to a carry-out from the local pitmaster.

I love that story and I thank Doug Worgul from the *Kansas City Star* for leading me to it. The real lesson from it is that barbecue is something people are very passionate about. I think Mr. Armstrong must have been thinking about a slow-cooked piece of pork shoulder when he felt the urge to compare barbecue to a sexy woman. Nothing fits the bill as a great piece of barbecue quite like slow-cooked pork shoulder. It seems whoever was the Great Creator of the swine constructed it so that the shoulder area would be the perfect cut to use in the slow-smoking, fat-rendering, and meat-tenderizing way we know as barbecue. I know that just about everyone east of the Mississippi River would agree with me. It has the perfect texture and fat content and it tastes so good.

In barbecue cookoff terms, a whole pork shoulder consists of the shoulder blade, the picnic, and a portion of the shank. The shoulder blade when separated is known as the butt or Boston butt because it is the butt end of the shoulder. No butt jokes, please. The upper arm or lower part of the shoulder is known as the picnic or picnic ham. Any or all of these cuts make great pulled pork or chopped pork, but in many places it's just called barbecue. It's not that hard to cook great pork barbecue. My advice to first-timers is to cook it until you think it's done and then cook it for another three hours. It's amazing what that thorough cooking does to the taste—not to mention the texture—of pork. Pork shoulder cooked like this just off the cooker doesn't need much seasoning at all. We cook these cuts slowly to an internal temperature much higher than the 160°F that the USDA suggests as safe. The meat should be judged by temperature and feel, but the guideline for done will be an internal temperature of 190° to 200°F. This is confusing to some educated cooks, but the outcome is the complete breakdown of the meat and rendering of most of the fat, combined with a nice caramelization of the exposed areas. The key is the cooking temperature. This won't work that well cooking at 350°F, but at 235°F it's the greatest. It takes a long time, though. Just plan on it and enjoy the ride. Have a couple of beers.

There are other cuts of pork that can be done in the barbecue pit, but none of them compare to the shoulder, with the obvious exception of ribs, which get their own section in this book. I've also provided a nice loin recipe and another for a double-smoked ham that's a real crowd pleaser.

Dr. BBQ's Big-Time Championship Pork Butt

1 pork butt (7 pounds), bone in

Big-Time Barbecue Rub (see recipe, p. 9)

I always cook pork butts in competition. I really do take the very simple approach and I've always done pretty well. I had the honor of winning the first two "Butt to Butt" invitationals. It's strictly a winner-takes-all pork cooking contest held the day before the Illinois State Championship in Shannon, Illinois, each July. Cash and bragging rights are there for the winner, but the award we all want is the coveted boar's tooth necklace. It's a real boar's tooth harvested (knocked out) by Mike Lake and inscribed in his garage. They are two of my most treasured trophies. • **Yield: 12 servings**

Note: This recipe requires advance preparation.

Unless I find something weird on the outside, like a piece of tough cartilage or a hunk of fat that should have been cut off at the packing house, I really don't trim anything off the butt. I pack the rub on as heavily as I can in the exposed meat areas. No need to season the fat cap. Return it to the refrigerator for at least a half hour but up to 12 hours.

Prepare the cooker for indirect cooking at 235°F, using hickory and cherry wood for flavor. Put the butt in fat side up. Cook for at least 10 hours before even peeking. After that, check it every hour until it reaches an internal temperature of 190°F. If the bone is sticking out and the meat feels soft, it is done. If it's still a little tough, cook it a little longer, but not past 200°F.

Take it out of the cooker and let it rest for one-half hour. Using big neoprene gloves or two forks, slide the fat cap off and discard it. Slide the bone out and discard it. Now just work through the butt, shredding the good meat and discarding any fat. Toss the meat all together with a little more rub and serve.

For cookoff presentation I toss it with a little Big-Time Barbecue Sauce, too, and make sure to have some nice bark pieces on top so the judges can see them.

Injected and Wrapped Pork Butt

2 cups Big Pig Pork Injection (see recipe, p. 40)

1 pork butt (7 pounds), fat cap trimmed off

Big-Time Barbecue Rub (see recipe, p. 9)

This is a common technique among my fellow cookoff competitors. It's a different texture than mine, but there are plenty of awards being won this way, too.

• **Yield: 12 servings**

Note: This recipe requires advance preparation.

Inject 1½ cups of the injection liquid into the pork butt, spreading it as evenly as you can. Rub the meat liberally with the Big-Time Barbecue Rub. Put it in the refrigerator for at least a half hour and up to 12 hours.

Prepare the cooker for indirect cooking at 275°F, using hickory and cherry wood for flavor. Put the butt in the cooker and cook to an internal temperature of 160°F. This should take about 6 hours. Lay out a big double piece of heavy-duty aluminum foil and put the pork butt in the middle. As you begin to close up the package pour the last half cup of injection fluid over the top and then seal the package, taking care not to puncture it. Put it back in the cooker. Now bring the internal temperature up to 195°F. This should take another 2 to 3 hours.

Remove the package from the cooker. Open and let it rest for one-half hour. Use neoprene gloves or two forks to shred the meat. It should just fall apart. Mix some of the juice and a little more rub with the meat.

For a cookoff I would toss it with a little barbecue sauce, and then I would present it in a nice pile with as much bark on the top as possible.

Kansas City–Style Pork Butt

Big-Time Barbecue Rub
(see recipe, p. 9)

1 pork butt (7 pounds),
boned, rolled, and tied (if
you don't know what this
means, have your butcher
do it)

When I cook in different regions I really don't change much at all. I may make a slight adjustment in the pepper, but that's really all I do, with one big exception. I serve sliced pork butt in Kansas City. I know the folks in Tennessee would think this is crazy, but that's the way it is. When I go out to eat or act as a barbecue judge in Kansas City, I regularly see the pork butt served sliced. It's different than serving it pulled or chopped, but it's still very good. Since sliced brisket is so popular in Kansas City, I guess they just figured they should cook their pork the same way. The truth is I usually cook two, one each way, and turn in some of each. Old habits are hard to break. • **Yield: 12–15 servings**

Note: This recipe requires advance preparation.

The cooking process is very simple. Just apply as much rub as you can to the meat. Let it rest for at least a half hour and up to 12 hours.

Prepare the cooker for indirect cooking at 275°F, using hickory and cherry wood for flavor. Put the butt in the cooker and cook to an internal temperature of 175°F. This should take about 7 to 8 hours.

Remove the pork butt and wrap it in heavy-duty aluminum foil. Rest for 1 hour. Slice and serve.

When I present this at a cookoff I brush each slice with barbecue sauce and then lay them neatly on a bed of pulled pork. Sometimes I cut each slice in half to make them fit better.

Double-Smoked Ham

1 fully cooked ham
(boneless and bone in will
work equally well)

½ cup canola oil

Freshly ground black
pepper to taste

1½ cups Big-Time Barbecue
Sauce (see recipe, p. 19)

½ cup brown sugar

This is about as simple a barbecue recipe as you could ever find. It's really good, though, and will probably become your favorite way to cook a ham.

• Yield: 2–3 servings per pound of ham

Cut a series of ½-inch-deep slashes in the ham, making a nice cross-hatch pattern. Rub the ham with the oil and sprinkle with black pepper.

Prepare the cooker for indirect cooking at 275°F, using maple or pecan wood for flavor.

Put the ham in the cooker and cook to an internal temperature of 150°F. Mix the barbecue sauce with the brown sugar and glaze the ham with it. Continue cooking the ham to a temperature of 160°F. Total cooking time should be 2 to 3 hours. Remove from the the cooker and let rest for 15 minutes. Slice and serve.

Cuban Mojo Picnic

Living in Florida, I can't help but be exposed to Cuban food. It's just part of the culture and it's good stuff. There is a very popular marinade called mojo criollo that is based on the juice of the vary rare sour orange. If you're not lucky enough to have access to sour oranges there are two options. If you live in Florida or anywhere near a Cuban neighborhood you'll find lots of commercial mojo criollo on the shelf at the grocery store. All the brands I have tried have been good, and I use them often. The other option is to use 2 parts freshly squeezed orange juice to 1 part freshly squeezed lime juice as a substitute for the sour orange juice.

This recipe calls for a pork picnic. I like the "knuckle meat" that is so prevalent in a picnic with this flavor. I like to serve it in chunks. I would not recommend this for a cookoff. • **Yield: 8 servings**

Note: This recipe requires advance preparation.

Mojo Criollo Marinade

⅔ **cup freshly squeezed orange juice**

⅓ **cup freshly squeezed lime juice**

½ **cup extra virgin olive oil**

8 cloves garlic, crushed

1 medium onion, chopped

½ **teaspoon cumin**

1 teaspoon salt

1 teaspoon freshly ground black pepper

1 fresh pork picnic (6 pounds)

Yellow rice and black beans, for serving

To make the marinade: Put all the ingredients in a blender and puree.

To make the pork: Cut a few slashes in the skin of the picnic and stab it a few times all around so the marinade can penetrate. Put the picnic in a cooking bag and pour the marinade over it. Close the bag, getting out as much air as possible. Marinate for two days, turning and massaging a few times a day.

Prepare the cooker for indirect cooking at 235°F, using pecan wood for flavor. Take the picnic out of the bag and put it directly on the cooker. Cook to an internal temperature of 180°F. This should take about 8 to 10 hours.

Wrap the picnic in heavy-duty aluminum foil and let rest for 1 hour. Take it out of the foil and put it in a pan. Discard the skin and bones. Pull the meat off in chunks and transfer it to a plate. If the juice in the foil isn't too greasy, skim the fat off and pour it over the meat. Serve with yellow rice and black beans.

Kind of Like Hawgeyes
Smoked Pork Loin

1 boneless pork loin roast
(8–10 pounds)

Scottie's Creole Butter
(see recipe, p. 39)

1 cup Big-Time Barbecue
Sauce (see recipe, p. 19)

½ cup spicy Dijon mustard

1 cup Big-Time Barbecue
Rub (see recipe, p. 9)

1 cup brown sugar

1 pound good quality
hickory-smoked bacon

2 cups apple juice to spray
or mop

This recipe is inspired by one from Hawgeyes BBQ in Ankeny, Iowa. Mike and Brett are good friends, great cooks, and they run the absolute best Web site for barbecue sauces, rubs, and tools. The pork loin recipe they used to win the prestigious World Pork Expo's "BarbeQlossal" in 1999 is a good one. Mike was generous enough to guide me to a reasonable facsimile for this book. To try the real version you'll need to visit his barbecue stand in Ankeny. Thanks, Mike. I just can't talk about these guys without telling you about their Web site. There are many great and interesting small-batch barbecue products being produced, and these guys have them all. If they hear good things about a new product, they'll get it right away and add it to the long list they already have. They even carry my products. The great selection along with their wonderful customer service has produced a thriving business with a loyal customer base. They are the best by far. Check them out at *www.hawgeyesbbq.com*. • **Yield: 20 servings**

Note: This recipe requires advance preparation.

The night before you plan to cook, inject the pork loin as heavily as you can with Scottie's Creole Butter. In a bowl, mix together the barbecue sauce and the mustard. Coat the loin heavily with this mixture. In a bowl, mix together the barbecue rub and the brown sugar. Coat the loin heavily with this mixture. Wrap the loin in plastic wrap and refrigerate overnight.

Prepare the cooker for indirect cooking at 225°F, using cherry wood for flavor.

Meanwhile, take the loin out of the refrigerator and let it rest on the counter for one hour. Cover the loin with the slices of bacon and put it in the cooker. Spray every 45 minutes with apple juice. After two hours, you should check the internal temperature. It will probably need to cook another hour or two, but you don't want to overcook it. When it reaches 145°F, remove it from the cooker and wrap it tightly in foil. Let it rest for at least 30 minutes and up to 1 hour.

Maxim Hog in the Ground

A few years ago, I got a call from Fast Eddy, who warned me that I might be getting a call from *Maxim* magazine. They were looking for three hog cooking experts to cook three hogs three different ways. Eddy had told them that he was the expert at cooking a hog in a cooker, that I was an expert at cooking a hog in a hole in the ground, and that our friend Chris Lilly was an expert at cooking a hog on a spit. Well, the actual truth was that we all had limited experience cooking hogs in a cooker, but the rest was all B.S. In Eddy's defense, none of us wanted to miss this opportunity, so nobody was complaining. After all, I had watched some drunks cook a hog in the ground once, so I figured I could give it a go. We went to the home of *Maxim* editor Charles Coxe to cook the three hogs. Charles and his lovely wife, Jennifer, had just moved into a suburban New Jersey neighborhood. Not a typical place for a three-hog roast. When we got there, Charles and the writer, Paul Bibeau, had already dug the hole, had had the wood delivered, and had a couple bottles of whiskey waiting for us. Being *Maxim,* they did things a little differently: There was a photographer there for the prep, kind of a warmup for the next day. The next morning brought a full-tilt photo shoot complete with bikini models to pose with the hogs. I'm sure Charles's new neighbors were thrilled. The hogs were all pretty good. Mine was the worst-looking out of the three, but that's just the nature of a hog in the ground. A couple of busloads of *Maxim* employees came over from Manhattan. Everyone ate until they were full and a good time was had by all, unless you count the hogs. These are the instructions I gave to *Maxim*. I hope you can find someone to dig the pit for you. • **Yield: You should be able to easily feed 100 people with a hog this size and might even be able to stretch it with some other entrées.**

1 whole hog (approximately 125 pounds)

1 gallon Big Pig Pork Injection, or more (see recipe, p. 40)

Big-Time Barbecue Rub (see recipe, p. 9)

2 bottles of whiskey

Lots of wood, rocks, chicken wire, foil, and banana leaves or cornstalks

A canvas tarp

Barbecue sauce of choice and apple juice, if desired

First you need to dig a pit about 5 feet long by 2 feet wide and 2 feet deep.

Build a fire in the pit out of hardwood (hickory is my preference) and feed the fire to create a nice bed of coals. The bed of coals needs to be at least 10 inches deep. This will take a long time and a lot of wood. You'll need to allow 8 hours for this. Resist the urge to drink the whiskey during this step. There is still a lot of work and a long time to stay awake. You also want to get the pit of hot coals covered up before you start drinking too heavily.

After the last logs have been started you can start adding some rocks. Your rocks must not have any water in them, since water will expand to steam and the rocks can explode. Rocks with a lot of moisture have been known to shoot rock fragments ten feet from the fire. *This can cause serious injury.* The best rocks are round, no small corners to break off under heat stress, and very dense. In geological terms: "intrusive but fine-grained rocks." If you're not a geologist you might want to get some firebricks instead of using unknown and possibly dangerous rocks. These should be available at any home improvement store. You will need to add enough rocks or firebricks to cover the entire fire as a bed, plus a few to put in the cavity of the hog. While the rocks are heating it's time to prepare the hog. I like a hog around 125 pounds. You should ask the butcher to cut the ribs so it will lie flat on its back. I inject the hog with at least a gallon of Big Pig Pork Injection. It will help keep the hog moist and give it that great island taste. Then I rub the outside and the cavity with Big-Time Barbecue Rub. This will help it get a nice color and add a little barbecue flavor. A hog in the ground is really just steamed, so it needs a little help. Lay the hog on a piece of chicken wire big enough to wrap all the way around.

Now line the cavity with foil and lay a few hot rocks up near where you will put the shoulders part of the hog, as that will be the hardest part to get cooked. Make some handles at the corners of the chicken wire bed for handling. I use a double run of picture-hanging wire and thread it through the chicken wire all the way from corner to corner to act as reinforcement. I then make loops out of the ends of the wire. I have four nice handled hay hooks to inset in the loops for carrying, but you can get by with some heavy gloves. Be sure to do a good job because the hog will be very tender when it comes out and the chicken wire will be the only chance of handling it.

Now you must name the hog. It's also a good time to begin drinking the whiskey. For me the hog is always named after a former girlfriend. My *Maxim* hog was named after my first girlfriend, Rosie. There happened to be a girl working at *Maxim* named Rosie, too, so we all agreed on the name. The Rosie at *Maxim* was flattered. My Rosie doesn't know. I guess she will now. I don't meant to imply anything here, but Fast Eddy named his hog Billy Ray.

Back to the pit. Cover the hot rocks and embers with banana leaves, corn stalks, or something that will serve the purpose of keeping things very moist and acting as a buffer between the hog and the hot rocks and embers. Lettuce will work in a pinch. Now lay the hog down right on the leaves and then cover it with more leaves. Cover the last layer of leaves with a couple layers of canvas tarp. Finally you can put sand or dirt around the edges of the tarp to keep everything in place.

There are many variables that make it hard to say when the hog will be done, but 10 to 12 hours is a good guideline. The size of your bed of coals and amount of rocks will vary and change the time. I use a remote thermometer in the shoulder of the hog to help me determine when it's done. The meat temperature needs to be at least 140°F to be safe, but most people aren't comfortable eating pork under about 160°F.

When you decide that your hog is done it's time to unwrap it. Start by taking off the tarp and remember throughout the process to try not to let any sand or dirt get on the hog. Use heavy neoprene gloves and rakes and shovels to expose the prize. Now you'll need some hooks or a few guys with gloves to get the hog out of the ground. There will be hot grease and steam and liquid dripping everywhere, so be very careful. The hog should be cooked to a very tender state and you'll need to support it. Have a table close by, covered with foil and/or pans on which to set the hog. Slide the hog off the chicken wire if you can; it will look much nicer. Get the hot rocks and foil out of the cavity of the hog, too.

Decorate the table with some fruit and flowers while the hog rests and cools a little. After a half hour or so you can start the "pig picking." It should just fall apart, but if some parts need chopping or a little more cooking just take them to another station. Put the good meat in pans and discard the fat, bones, and skin. If you like, you can toss the meat with a little barbecue sauce. I like to use a 50/50 mixture of apple juice and barbecue sauce.

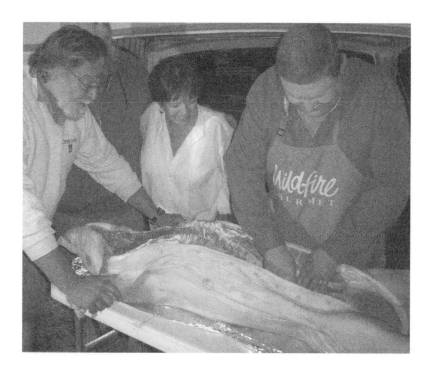

The Barbecue Log

Things to Remember About
Barbecuing the Best Pork

▼▼

Ribs

North and south, east and west, ribs are a barbecue favorite. They seem to transcend all barbecue arguments. Everybody likes ribs. I guess it's the sweet meat near the bone, the convenient built-in handle, and, of course, the holy grail thing because you spend your life seeking out the perfect rib.

I also think there is a mystery for many cooks as to how a pitmaster can get the ribs to that nirvana "falling off the bone" state while still keeping them moist and juicy. In the land of my misspent youth around Chicago there is a horrible theory in place that involves boiling the ribs before taking them out to the grill. I can't imagine boiling ribs and then discarding the broth. If it were a chicken you'd put some noodles in it and call it soup. Enough about that. Don't boil your ribs EVER!!!

First, let's talk about pork ribs. They are by far the most popular and the typical entry at a barbecue cookoff.

The real reason ribs became such a popular barbecue item was that they fit in the lesser cut category and they just happen to finish beautifully when slow-cooked over a smoky fire. Spareribs were just that, spare. When you used up the loins, shoulders, and hams you had the spare parts left. The spareribs come from the side of the hog, where it's just not very meaty. These were the only ribs we knew or cooked for years, and they became very popular as barbecue grew. Then along came the loin back rib, smartly named the baby back rib by some good salesman. You see, these ribs don't really come from a baby hog. They do come from the top of the hog in the middle of the loin. There are two per hog.

There was great demand for boneless loins in Denmark and Canada and there was always a market for the beautiful little tenderloin muscle on the inside. This produced a by-product that was the bones of the loin. Well, if you cut the backbone off you are left with loin back ribs. They began shipping them to the United States, and the baby back rib was born. That's why you still see Danish baby back ribs in the store from time to time. They are still shipped here in huge quantities, but most of them go to the chain restaurants. They are a little smaller and cheaper than domestic ribs, so the restaurants buy them all up. You may notice the long thin bones as opposed to the thicker ones that you see in the grocery store. There's nothing bad about that.

I'm sure that beef ribs made it to the barbecue pit in a similar story. Beef ribs don't really stay together after cooking and the bones are big and almost always end up left on the grill or serving platter. There are also exotic ribs such as lamb and even alligator available in some places. I'm going to leave those for another day. Pork ribs seem to be just right to me, so I'll focus on them.

A whole other subject is country-style pork ribs. True country-style ribs are the last three bones of the loin along with the pork chop meat. These were a popular cut because they were a by-product of the center-cut bone-in pork roast, which was a popular classic cut of pork before the rib revolution. You rarely see a center-cut bone-in pork roast or true country-style ribs anymore. You can't get either of those and baby back ribs from the same hog because they require the same rib bones. The baby back ribs bring a higher price, so they are the chosen cut for most meat processors. Did you catch that? The ribs at this time cost about twice as much as the meat that is cut from them.

Because of the high price and demand for ribs, the marketing folks have come up with interesting names for some other cuts such as "country-style blade ribs," or "shoulder ribs" or "western ribs," or my all-time favorite, "boneless baby back ribs." None of these actually include any rib bones and most come from a completely different part of the hog. But if you can call it a rib, you can mark up the price. It's hard to tell you how to cook these cuts because there are all different things in the package depending on the region and even the store.

Boneless ribs? You gotta be kidding me. They are usually the aforementioned loin meat that is now a by-product of the ribs. (Why don't we ship them to Denmark and Canada?) Butchers butterfly the big muscle, lay it open, and cut slashes in it so it looks kind of like some ribs. It's actually very lean and can't really be cooked like real ribs at all. Buy it if you must, but cook it like a pork chop. It's not a rib.

Back to real ribs. The baby back ribs became so popular that we needed more of them. So some smart meat cutter trimmed the cartilage and breastbone off of a slab of spare ribs and thus created "St. Louis–style ribs." These are my favorite and the best of both worlds. They are nicely shaped like a baby back but have the good taste and fat content of the spares. They

are also priced in the middle if you can find them in the store. They are widely available at wholesale and you've probably eaten them without knowing it, but they just don't show up in the market very often. Not to worry, it's pretty easy to make them yourself.

Starting with a whole slab of spareribs, lay it flat with the bones facing up and pointed at you. Using a sharp knife, cut the flap off from the middle of the ribs. Now feel for the top of the bones where they attach to the cartilage. Cut across the whole slab right above the bones. Be sure to cut the cartilage and you should be fine even if you don't have the greatest knife. As you get to the shorter ribs just go straight across, and you'll have a nicely shaped slab of ribs.

The discarded piece with all the cartilage is known as rib tips. These are very good and can be cooked right along with the ribs. They can also be used for soups or stews or trimmed for sausage meat.

Now it's time to peel the membrane off the back. This goes for all ribs: baby back, spares, St. Louis, and even beef ribs. You have to peel the membrane off. Period. Any vendor, restaurant guy, or backyard cook that tells you he leaves it on because it keeps the moisture in or helps the smoke stay in or anyone who says he just scores it so he can easily burn it off is B.S.ing you. They are skipping this step because it's a bit of a hassle and in a commercial setting it's a big hassle. To make the best ribs they should be doing it and so should you. Using a butter knife or similar tool, you want to get the skin peeling started on one of the wider bones. Then work your finger in there and start to loosen it. It gets slippery so use a paper towel to hang on. I've known guys that use catfish skinners, screwdrivers, skewers, and some tools I couldn't identify. Find the one that works for you. With a little practice it becomes pretty easy.

Most of the ribs we get these days are trimmed very nicely. If there are any big fatty layers, just trim them off. I like to rinse my ribs, too, because there is usually some bone dust from the meat saw left on them. Just swish them around in a pan of fresh water and then pat them dry.

I've offered up some great rib recipes here. Pick one or grab something from each of them and create your own version.

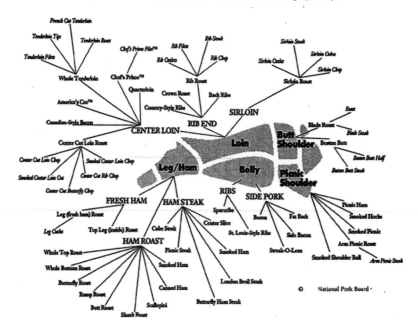

Meat Case Can Be Web of Confusion

Looking for a few simple pork chops? The modern meat case can be a confusing web of choices for consumers in search of a fresh meat cut they recognize and have the confidence to cook.

To help sort it all out, the pork industry is teaching consumers to "shop by shape." No matter what it's called on the label, whether it's thick or thin, with bones or with-out, all fresh pork cuts boil down to six basic "shapes"– chops, cubes, roasts, ribs cut-lets and strips.

For example, a chop is a chop is a chop... it can come from the loin, rib, sirloin or center loin, but it's still a chop. And because of their common shape, all chops cook alike and will work interchangeably in a recipe.

© National Pork Board

Dr. BBQ's Big-Time Championship Ribs

½ cup turbinado sugar

1 cup Big-Time Barbecue Rub (see recipe, p. 9)

3 slabs of St. Louis–style ribs, membrane off and washed

2 cups honey

1½ cups brown sugar

1½ cups apple juice (more may be needed)

2 cups Sweet and Sticky Barbecue Glaze (see recipe, p. 42)

Salt, to taste

This method is really a combination of things I've learned along the way. I started using St. Louis–style ribs when the price of baby backs went sky high a few years back, but I found that I liked them and I was scoring better than I ever had before. Many cooks wrap their ribs in foil for part of the cooking process and many use honey and/or brown sugar during the time the ribs are wrapped. Apple juice isn't very typical during this process, but it's always around most barbecue camps, and the sweetened-up barbecue glaze is something many of us have taken on as well. These ribs are very sweet. Among the many awards these ribs have won is the Amazin' Blazin' Tennessee State Championship two years in a row. • **Yield: 6–8 servings**

Prepare your cooker for indirect grilling at 275°F, using cherry and hickory wood for flavor.

About 30 minutes before the ribs go into the cooker, mix the turbinado sugar and the rub together and rub it on the ribs. Use about ⅔ on the meaty side and ⅓ on the boney side.

Put the ribs in the smoker meaty side up for 2 hours. Flip the ribs and cook another hour.

Remove the ribs to a platter. Tear of 3 long sheets of heavy-duty 18-inch-wide aluminum foil and fold each one over so you have a double-thick piece big enough to wrap each slab of ribs. Lay the foil sheets on the counter and spread about ⅓ cup of honey on each, spreading it where the ribs will lie. Top this with ¼ cup of brown sugar. Place one slab of ribs meat side down on the mixture and then repeat the honey and brown sugar application again on the top of the slab. Now crimp up the edges of the foil and pour ½ cup of apple juice in the bottom. Do this for all three slabs. Close up the packets around the ribs loosely so you don't puncture the foil, and lay them all back in the cooker.

Cook another 90 minutes this way. Take a peek after 1 hour to make sure the apple juice isn't dried up or leaked out. If so, add a little more.

Carefully unwrap the packets and take out the ribs. This is a dangerous time, so be careful. There will be hot steaming juice in there. If your cooker allows, just do it right in the cooker and let the juices flow to your grease catch pan. The ribs will be very tender, so be careful not to break them.

Put the ribs back on the cooker, raising the temperature to 350°F if you can. Brush with the glaze and flip several times for about another 20 minutes.

Place the ribs meaty side down on a board and cut through each rib to serve. Salt to taste.

Friday Night Spareribs

3 racks of whole spareribs

Big-Time Barbecue Rub, to taste (see recipe, p. 9)

Red Rose Barbecue Sauce, to taste (see recipe, p. 20)

These ribs are the simplest of all. That's what makes them so good. We primp and prep everything so much for these contests that sometimes we get away from just plain old meat, smoke, and a little spice. I often cook these on Friday night before the cookoff just so I can have some extra ribs to sort through for my turn-in on Saturday. Miss Trish Trigg, who along with her husband, Johnny, are the only two-time Jack Daniel's World Barbecue Champions, likes these so much that I feel bad if I don't make them when she's around. • **Yield: 6 servings, unless they like the ribs as much as Miss Trish does—then it serves 3**

Trim the flap off the back of the ribs, and peel the membrane off. Trim any loose or thin meat off the meaty edge of the ribs. Season the ribs lightly with the rub.

Prepare the cooker for indirect grilling at 250°F, using hickory and cherry wood for flavor.

Put the ribs in the cooker and cook until tender. Use a rib rack if needed for space. This should take 5 to 6 hours. Check by sticking the ribs with a toothpick. It should slide in easily. I prefer these a little chewier than my contest ribs.

When serving whole spareribs you must always cut them apart individually for your guests. They just won't pull apart like back ribs will. Serve with barbecue sauce on the side.

Backyard Championship Ribs

½ cup turbinado sugar

1 cup Big-Time Barbecue Rub (see recipe, p. 9)

3 slabs of St. Louis–style ribs or baby back ribs, cut in half, membrane off and washed

1 cup honey

1½ cups apple juice

2 cups Sweet and Sticky Barbecue Glaze (see recipe, p. 42)

The original version of these ribs isn't that hard to do, but not every backyarder has a smoker that will run all day at 275°F and have enough room to comfortably spread out three slabs of ribs. So this is a good substitute for a kettle, a smaller smoker, or a gas grill. The only catch is that you'll have to adjust the times and temperatures to your cooker. It may be a little tricky at first, but take notes and you'll have it down perfectly after a few tries. Those first couple batches will be pretty good anyway. • **Yield: 6–8 servings**

Prepare your cooker for indirect grilling at about 325°F, using cherry and hickory wood for flavor.

About 30 minutes before the ribs go into the cooker, mix the turbinado sugar and the rub together and rub it on the ribs. Use about two-thirds on the meaty side and one-third on the bony side.

Put the ribs in the smoker meaty side up. Use a rib rack if you need it for space. The exact cooking instructions will depend on your equipment, but you should cook them slow until they are nicely cara–melized and looking great. About 1 to 1½ hours is a good guideline for this step.

Remove the ribs to a platter or sheet pan and brush them all on both sides with honey.

The next step is a tenderizing process. Put the ribs in an aluminum foil pan with a little apple juice in the bottom, about one inch. Stand them on end in the pan if you need to. Cover with foil and cook at about 325°F until tender. If you have a hard time keeping your grill low, you'll need to check that the apple juice doesn't all cook off. Re-plenish it as needed. This step can even be done in the oven. The time for this step is 1 hour as a guideline; but again, this will vary depending on your equipment. Test the ribs by sticking them with a toothpick to see when they are soft and tender. (At this point you could cool them down, wrap them separately, and reheat later. This is a great way to take ribs to a tailgate party or to prepare ahead for a party at home.)

Transfer the cooked ribs to a medium-hot grill. Brush with the Sweet and Sticky Barbecue Glaze and flip several times for just a few minutes. Cut into pieces and serve.

Fast Eddy's World Championship Ribs

A Recipe from Barbecue All Star Fast Eddy Maurin

That title sure says a lot, doesn't it? This is the second of a handful of recipes from friends that I call the Barbecue All Stars. Fast Eddy sure fits the title. The Food Network says, "He's a legend." Eddy is a world-class barbecue cook, a Kansas City fire fighter, and runs a welding shop on the side. All of these things, as well as a racing background (Fast Eddy, get it?), add up to a guy who really knows how to build barbecue cookers. Eddy pioneered the use of pellet-fueled cookers in the cookoff world. He then began modifying them to make them work better. The next step was to build them himself, and finally he formed a partnership with the legendary smoker manufacturer Cookshack out of Ponca City, Oklahoma. I have a custom-made pellet cooker at home that Eddy helped me with and I usually have one of his FEC-100s with me on the road. They are as good as it gets. Oh yeah, he knows how to cook, too. Fast Eddy Maurin has been one of the top competition cooks in the country for many years. His office is filled with trophies. Not just any trophies. He has all the awards that a competitive barbecue cook covets. Reserve Grand at Jack Daniel's, Grand Champion at The Great Pork BarbeQlossal, and a few Team of the Year awards. These ribs are what he cooked to win the World Barbecue Association Rib Championship in Lebanon, Tennessee, in 2000. You'll notice that they are quite different from mine. There is definitely more than one way to skin a rib. • **Yield: 6 servings**

Note: This recipe requires advance preparation.

Fast Eddy's Rib Rub

½ cup sugar

¼ cup Hungarian paprika

¼ cup Lawry's seasoning salt

2 tablespoons garlic salt

1 tablespoon allspice

1 tablespoon cumin

1 tablespoon onion salt

1 tablespoon freshly and coarsely ground black pepper

1 teaspoon celery seed

Fast Eddy's Rib Glaze

One 18-ounce bottle KC Masterpiece Barbecue Sauce

½ cup honey

1 cup water

3 slabs of baby back ribs

½ cup brown sugar

To make the rub: Combine all the ingredients in a bowl and mix well.

To make the glaze: Combine all ingredients in a bowl and mix well. Put in a foil pan and cook the glaze in the smoker for 3 hours (while you cook the ribs). Remove, cover with foil, and reserve.

To make the ribs: Rub the slabs all over with the brown sugar and refrigerate overnight.

The next morning prepare the cooker for indirect grilling at 275°F, using pecan wood for flavor. Rub the ribs with Fast Eddy's Rib Rub 30 minutes prior to cooking.

Put the ribs in the smoker meaty side up for approximately 3 hours. They are done when the meat starts to separate when you pick up the middle of the rack with tongs.

Brush both sides with Fast Eddy's Rib Glaze 10 minutes before taking them off the smoker.

Chicago-Style Rib Tips

Because of the long history of slaughterhouses and stockyards and the wonderful nickname "Hog Butcher to the World," many people assume that Chicago is a serious barbecue town. Truth is, it isn't. I spent twenty-five years as a Chicago truck driver and I am very well acquainted with the food of the neighborhoods in Chicago. Chicago is a hot dog, pizza, and Italian beef town. There are some barbecue joints, but they are mostly run by emigrants from the South. These joints started in the poorer neighborhoods where the folks couldn't afford ribs, so they began cooking the rib tips. The tips quickly became the staple of Chicago barbecue joints. These are the cheap cutoffs from the spare ribs and the leftovers from a nicely cut slab of St. Louis–style ribs—the part with all the cartilage going in every direction is the rib tip. I once stood in a room with 40,000 pounds of them in a refrigerated warehouse in Chicago. There were big skids of them everywhere. These are not to be confused with riblets, which are a hard-to-find cut also called featherbones. The chains are buying all of those, too. Speaking of the chains, they have all now invaded my beloved Chicago and ruined the overall character of the cuisine. Such is life. Look for the remaining gems if you visit. Want some of my favorites? Mr. Beef on Orleans for Italian beef. Villa Nova in Stickney for the best thin-crust pizza in the world (deep-dish pizzas are for the tourists). Gibson's for giant, expensive steaks. Jimmy's on Grand and Pulaski for hot dogs. They've got a sign with a bottle of ketchup and a red line through it, "No ketchup, don't even ask." (Chicago hot dogs *never* have ketchup on them.) • **Yield: 6–8 servings**

Big-Time Barbecue Rub, to taste (see recipe, p. 9)

Rib tips from 6 slabs of ribs

2 cups Big-Time Barbecue Sauce (see recipe, p. 19)

1 cup apple juice

Prepare your cooker for indirect grilling at 250°F, using hickory and cherry wood for flavor.

Apply a heavy coat of the rub to the tips and put them in the cooker for 4 hours.

Remove them from the cooker and let rest for 10 minutes. Cut across the length of the pieces at 1 to 2-inch intervals. Put all the pieces in an aluminum foil pan. Add the barbecue sauce blended with the apple juice and toss to coat the tips.

Cover with foil and return to the cooker for another hour. They should be very tender. If they aren't, leave them in for another 30 minutes and check again. Serve with white bread.

Beef Ribs Cooked with Beer

2 slabs beef back ribs

Big-Time Barbecue Rub, to taste (see recipe, p. 9)

1 can of beer

Barbecue sauce of choice

The first year they held the Kansas Speedway/ Oklahoma Joe's barbecue cookoff, they added an extra category of beef ribs. At a cookoff a few weeks earlier, I was test cooking some to see what I wanted to do. They were cooking along and looking good, but they just weren't getting tender like I wanted. Well, my typical go-to recipe for anything weird or tough is to put it in a pan with some liquid and cover it with foil, so that's where these were headed. I didn't have any liquid except beer, whiskey, and apple juice, so beer was the choice. I don't generally like cooking with beer, but it just worked out with these. Now I do it this way all the time. • **Yield: 6–8 servings**

Begin by peeling the membrane off the ribs as per the instructions at the beginning of this rib section. Cut the slabs in half. Season the slabs liberally with Big-Time Barbecue Rub on both sides.

Prepare the cooker for indirect grilling at 250°F, using oak and hickory wood for flavor. Place the ribs on a rack in the smoker and cook for 2 hours.

Remove the ribs and place them in a foil pan. Add a can of beer. Cover with foil and return to the cooker for another three hours.

Discard the liquid and serve the ribs with barbecue sauce on the side, or finish them on a hot grill while basting with barbecue sauce for about 20 minutes.

The Barbecue Log

The Greatest Ribs I've Ever Cooked

▼▼▼

_____

_____

_____

_____

_____

_____

_____

_____

_____

_____

_____

_____

_____

_____

_____

_____

_____

_____

_____

_____

_____

Poultry

Some barbecue snobs don't consider poultry to be a legitimate barbecue meat. It doesn't really fit the mold of lesser cuts, but chicken shows up on the menu of just about every barbecue joint in the United States. Turkey is a very popular menu item as well, and probably the item I order most when dining out at a barbecue joint. The turkey at Big Bob Gibson's in Decatur, Alabama, is a meal I often drive a hundred miles out of my way for. I wish I had some right now. I've cooked and eaten a lot of turkey and none even comes close to theirs. They cook only

breasts, and I'm pretty sure there is some of their signature white barbecue sauce involved, but I just can't imagine how they keep the turkey so moist. I guess I could ask, but that would ruin the mystique and might take some of the fun out of visiting Decatur, Alabama. Some things are just best if left alone. I have included my version, but theirs is better.

When I started cooking in KCBS barbecue cookoffs, poultry was a category, and many different kinds were turned in such as duck, Cornish hen, and turkey. I won my first ever culinary award using the Sherry Butter Turkey recipe that appears in the grilling chapter of this book. But as KCBS grew and the rules were being tweaked, the category was changed to chicken. Since then, Cornish hens have been allowed back in because it was determined that the Cornish hens we buy these days are just small chickens.

Many different styles of chicken entries were popular. Many cooks marinated chicken breasts and served them sliced. Many cooked whole chickens and then cut them up and turned in a nice representation of the whole thing, such as two drumsticks, two wings, two thighs, and some cut-up breast meat. I have always liked drumsticks, so I specialized in them and did very well over the years, getting top-five finishes at the American Royal and Jack Daniel's cookoffs.

Then along came Jumpin' Jim. Jim is an interesting guy from Iowa who took up barbecue cooking in a very serious way. I'm pretty sure he has more cookers than anyone else I know, and when he was competing regularly, he practiced more than anyone I have ever known. He became one of the best overall barbecue cooks

in the country and the absolute best chicken cook. He won everywhere he went. He even won the chicken category at the American Royal on both days one year. That means the Invitational on Friday and the Open on Saturday, an amazing accomplishment that will probably never be matched.

Well, one day Jim decided to share his chicken recipe with the world via the Internet.

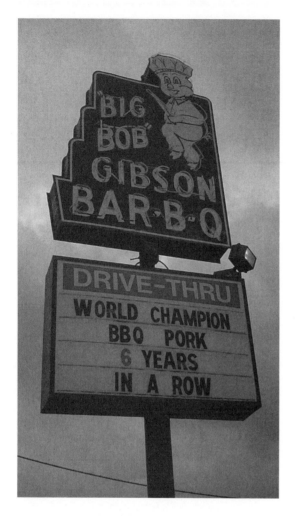

them using Jumpin' Jim's recipe, or at least the basics of it. It became obvious that the recipe Jim shared with us was indeed the recipe he had been spanking us with. So finally I switched to thighs and came up with a modified recipe that used my rubs and sauces, and sure enough I began to do much better. In 2003, I was the seventh-best chicken cook in KCBS. No small accomplishment. Thanks, Jim. Most of the good KCBS cooks are using thighs these days. I'm sure a different trend is right around the corner, but for now thighs rule. Here's Jim's original words on the recipe. Thanks to him for sharing it.

For contests I only cook thighs and I cook 16 of them. I marinate them in Paul Newman's Own (Olive Oil and Vinegar) 4 to 8 at a time in a heavy ziplock bag depending on the size of the thighs. I start them marinating at approximately 4:00 P.M. on Friday.

I have used various rubs but what I really like these days is Head Country (Ponca City, Oklahoma), tweaked for heat, which I get by adding a small amount of cayenne pepper. The thighs come out of the marinade at 7:30 Saturday morning and I lightly and evenly dust them with the rub.

I put them on the smoker and cook them to 180°F internal temperature in exactly 3 hours. If I am using the Ole Hickory I use pecan and if I am cooking on Traeger or a Fast Eddy Smokebox I use hickory pellets.

At the 3-hour mark I test each thigh with a toothpick for tenderness. I put my best 8 in one half-size aluminum pan from Sam's Club with one bottle of Head Country Original Sauce. I put the second best 8 in the other pan.

The recipe was pretty straightforward. He cooked thighs and used a marinade, seasoning, and sauce that were all easily found. There were skeptics who didn't think he was being honest, but there were other cooks who gave this recipe a try. They all started to do very well in chicken. I continued to cook drumsticks for a while, but my scores began to slip and I realized what was happening. *Everybody* was switching to thighs and most were cooking

I loosely tent the pans with foil and let them wallow in the sauce for approximately 1 hour.

One-half hour before turn-in I take 8 to 10 of the best thighs and put them on Weber Kettle or Cajun Grill indirect with a reasonably cool fire so I won't burn the sauce. I taste one of the worst thighs and make an assessment of how it tastes and if I think that taste can do well. If I need to make adjustments, especially with salt, I do it at this time, and then set the seasoning with a light brushing of sauce.

On the next page is my version, which is very similar. I've also included my old chicken drumstick recipe.

Dr. BBQ's Top 5 Barbecue Joints

1. Arthur Bryant's, Kansas City, Missouri

2. Big Bob Gibson's, Decatur, Alabama

3. Jack's Barbecue, Nashville, Tennessee

4. Oklahoma Joe's, Kansas City, Missouri

5. Happy Jack's, Lakeland, Florida

Dr. BBQ's Big-Time Championship Chicken Thighs

12 semi-boneless (one bone only) chicken thighs, trimmed

1 double recipe Italian Dressing Marinade (see recipe, p. 28)

Big-Time Barbecue Rub, to taste (see recipe, p. 9)

Sweet and Sticky Barbecue Glaze, to taste (see recipe, p. 42)

Here's my version of Jumpin' Jim's Chicken Thighs. I've done very well with it. Smoked chicken has a tendency to have rubbery skin. The high heat finish in this recipe will help crisp it up. I trim the thighs all around, including cutting off the oyster. I want two evenly cooked and shaped sides of the thigh. Remember, this is about tasting for competition, not eating dinner. • **Yield: 4–6 servings**

Note: This recipe requires advance preparation.

Marinate the thighs in the marinade in sealable plastic bags for 12 to 18 hours.

Prepare the cooker for indirect cooking at 235°F, using cherry wood for flavor.

About one-half hour before cooking, take the thighs out of the marinade and place them on a tray skin side down. Sprinkle liberally with the barbecue rub. After 15 minutes, turn the thighs to skin side up and sprinkle that side liberally, too. After another 15 minutes, put the chicken thighs in the cooker for about 90 minutes. Transfer the thighs to a grill that is running at about 300°F. Brush the skin side with the barbecue glaze and begin to raise the temperature of the grill. Flip and brush for about a half hour, raising the temperature as you go to a maximum of 400°F. When the chicken has reached an internal temp of at least 180°F, the skin is browned and crispy, and the sauce is sticky and caramelized, the chicken is done.

Big-Time Chicken Drumsticks

12 chicken drumsticks

Big-Time Barbecue Rub, to taste (see recipe, p. 9)

Big-Time Barbecue Sauce, to taste (see recipe, p. 19)

I cooked this in competition for years and won many awards. They are still my favorite and really very simple. • **Yield: 6 servings**

Prepare the cooker for indirect cooking at 275°F, using cherry wood for flavor.

A half hour before cooking, peel the skin back on the drumsticks and season lightly underneath with the rub. Pull the skin back up and season liberally all over. Leave the drumsticks out at room temperature. Put them in the cooker after 30 minutes, being sure to pull the skin up and lay them down neatly. Cook to an internal temperature of 180°F—this should take about 2 hours. Glaze with Big-Time Barbecue Sauce and cook for another 15 minutes.

Remove them from the cooker and let them rest for 10 minutes before serving.

Chef's Choice Brined Chicken

1 frying chicken (4 pounds)

1 recipe Big-Time Chef's Brine (see recipe, p. 44)

6–8 sprigs fresh thyme

Big-Time Herb Rub, to taste (see recipe, p. 12)

1 lemon, quartered

I call this Chef's Choice because I see real chefs using brines at cookoffs more than we parking lot chefs do. I also see those guys wanting to sear the briskets before cooking, too, but that's a whole other story. Brining seems to do well with cookoff chicken, but, as I've said earlier, it's just not my thing. I do like a brined whole chicken cooked with herbs and a lemon in its cavity for dinner. • **Yield: 2–4 servings**

Note: This recipe requires advance preparation.

A day before cooking, submerge the chicken in the brine, add a few sprigs of the fresh thyme, and cover it with a plate to weigh it down.

After 24 hours, remove the chicken from the brine and rinse it thoroughly. Sprinkle lightly with the Big-Time Herb Rub and place the lemon and the rest of the fresh thyme in the cavity. Let this rest in the refrigerator for a couple of hours.

Prepare the cooker for indirect cooking at 235°F, using orange wood or pellets for flavor.

Put the chicken in the cooker breast side up. Cook until the thigh reaches 180°F and the breast reaches 160°F. This should take about 6 hours.

The result will be a smoky, pink, juicy, and delicious chicken. The skin will be a little rubbery and may get dark, but that's just the nature of smoked chicken. If you want it crisper you can run the heat up to 375°F for the last hour.

Smoked Turkey Legs

4 large turkey drumsticks

Big-Time Barbecue Rub, to taste (see recipe, p. 9)

These are something I often cook for a snack along the way to a long-cooked brisket or butt. Many cooks like to brine them—do it if you wish, but for me they do just fine without brining. • **Yield: 4 servings**

Prepare the cooker for indirect cooking at 275°F, using hickory and cherry wood for flavor. If you're already cooking something else at a lower temperature, just look for a hotter spot in the cooker for these and allow a little more time.

Rub the drumsticks with Big-Time Barbecue Rub. Put the legs in and cook until they reach 160°F. This should take about 2 hours. Wrap each leg loosely in heavy-duty aluminum foil and return to the cooker for about another hour, or until they are tender and at an internal temp of at least 180°F.

These may have a rubbery skin—that's just the nature of smoked turkey. You can crisp it up on a hot grill if you like.

Smoked Turkey Breast

1 boneless turkey breast (3–4 pounds), skin on

1 double recipe Alabama White Barbecue Sauce (see recipe, p. 24)

Big-Time Barbecue Rub, to taste (see recipe, p. 9)

This is one of my favorite things from the slow barbecue pit. That might be true because I cook so much pork, but it might also be because it's so good.

• **Yield: 8–10 servings**

Note: This recipe requires advance preparation.

Place the turkey breast in a plastic cooking bag and pour half the white sauce over it. Close the bag up tight and put it in the refrigerator for a whole day. Massage it and flip it over occasionally.

Prepare the cooker for indirect cooking at 275°F, using pecan wood for flavor.

Remove the turkey breast from the bag and sprinkle it liberally with Big-Time Barbecue Rub. Put it in the cooker and cook to an internal temperature of 160°F, no higher. This should take about 2 to 3 hours.

Remove from the heat and wrap it in foil with another cup of the white barbecue sauce poured over it. Let rest 30 minutes.

Slice and serve with the remaining white sauce on the side.

Smoked Duck

1 domestic duck (5–6 pounds), defrosted

Big-Time Herb Rub, to taste (see recipe, p. 12)

I've always wondered why duck isn't more popular as a barbecue item. It has plenty of fat and cooks up beautifully in a low-temperature barbecue cooker. Like most meat these days, it's not as fatty as in the old days, but in the case of duck, that's just fine. • **Yield: 2–4 servings**

Note: This recipe requires advance preparation.

First you'll need to cut all the way down the duck's backbone, splitting it open on that side. Kitchen shears are the best tool for this job. It isn't to be butterflied; just pull the back apart a little bit. This will allow the fat to render and the smoke to get inside the duck. Remove the wing tips or tuck them under the neck. Poke the duck all over with a skewer or an ice pick. This will allow the fat to render out of the skin. Rub the duck generously with the herb rub, inside and out. Let rest in the refrigerator for an hour.

Prepare the cooker for indirect cooking at 275°F, using cherry wood for flavor.

Put the duck in the cooker and cook until the thigh reaches an internal temperature of 180°F. This should take about 3 to 4 hours. If you can, let the cooker temperature rise for the last hour to help crisp the skin. This can also be done on a separate hot grill.

The Barbecue Log

Things to Remember About
Barbecuing Chicken, Turkey, and Duck

▼▼▼

Sausage

Smoked sausage is definitely a part of the barbecue world, and almost all barbecue joints serve some form of sausage. For most of us, slow cooking a sausage stuffed in a casing will produce a rubbery and not very pleasant skin. There are ways to combat this, such as setting up a place where your smoked sausage can be showered with cold water for a few minutes after cooking, soaking the casings in vinegar, or even slicing the sausage thinly before serving. Besides the problem of tough skins, stuffing sausage meat into casings and curing it is a process that requires specialized equipment. To avoid writing a book within a book, I am going to talk about sausage cooked in a loaf rather than in a casing. If you wish to learn how to use the equipment and casings, or buy the equipment, just do a Web search for "sausage making" and you will have 367,000 references. I may not be a casing and curing expert, but I do know how to mix some ground meat and some spices together and then cook it, so that's what we're going to do.

The first part of the recipe will be the same for all the different types of sausage. The ingredients will change and be listed separately. This is a simple and fun project when done this way. Enjoy.

When making sausage, it's very important to keep everything very cold in the name of safety. All these recipes call for some water. Keep it in the refrigerator or even in the freezer during the last five minutes before using it. If grinding your own meat, put it in the freezer before working with it and then again right after grinding. This should all be done in a cool place.

The Basic Technique

Take all the seasonings and spices and mix well with the ice-cold water. Mix the spiced water into the ground meat and stir by hand until well blended. Form 2 or 3 log-shaped loaves. Make them the thickness you'd like your sausage slices to be when they are done. You should allow for a little shrinkage. Wrap each log in plastic wrap and chill again until very cold. Prepare the cooker to run at 200–225°F and no higher, using the recommended wood for the ingredients you've chosen. Put the wrapped logs on the cooker and leave them for 20 minutes. Unwrap them and continue cooking until they reach an internal temperature of 160°F. This should take about 2 hours. You may brush with barbecue sauce after 1 hour if you like. Remove and let rest for at least 10 minutes. You can eat it fresh and hot, or cool the loaves down to be sliced and fried later. Frying is best for the breakfast sausage.

Kielbasa

Recommended wood: cherry

The Meat

2½ pounds coarsely ground pork, approximately 75 percent lean (if grinding your own, an untrimmed pork butt is just about the right amount of fat to lean)

The Seasoning

1 tablespoon salt

1½ teaspoons white sugar

1½ teaspoons freshly ground black pepper

1½ teaspoons marjoram leaves

¼ teaspoon ground allspice

6 cloves garlic, minced

1 cup ice-cold water

Bratwurst

Recommended wood: apple

The Meat

1½ pounds coarsely ground pork, approximately 75 percent lean (if grinding your own, an untrimmed pork butt is just about the right amount of fat to lean)

1 pound ground veal

The Seasoning

1 tablespoon salt

1 teaspoon freshly ground white pepper

1 teaspoon ground nutmeg

1 teaspoon ground mace

½ teaspoon ground allspice

1 cup ice-cold water

Italian Sausage

Recommended wood: cherry

The Meat

2½ pounds coarsely ground pork, approximately 75 percent lean (if grinding your own, an untrimmed pork butt is just about the right amount of fat to lean)

The Seasoning

1 tablespoon salt

1 tablespoon fennel seeds

½ teaspoon dried oregano

½ teaspoon freshly ground black pepper

¼ teaspoon cayenne pepper (optional)

1 cup ice-cold water

Jalapeño Cheddar

Recommended wood: hickory

The Meat

1½ pounds coarsely ground pork, approximately 75 percent lean (if grinding your own, an untrimmed pork butt is just about the right amount of fat to lean)

1 pound 80 percent lean ground chuck

The Seasoning

2 fresh jalapeño chiles, seeded, deveined, and chopped fine

1 tablespoon salt

1 teaspoon white sugar

1 teaspoon freshly ground black pepper

½ cup finely shredded cheddar cheese

1 cup ice-cold water

Breakfast Sage Sausage

Recommended wood: sugar maple

The Meat

2½ pounds coarsely ground pork, approximately 75 percent lean (if grinding your own, an untrimmed pork butt is just about the right amount of fat to lean)

The Seasoning

1 tablespoon salt

2 teaspoons freshly ground black pepper

1 teaspoon ground sage

¼ teaspoon ground nutmeg

2 slices crumbled cooked bacon

½ teaspoon dried parsley

1 cup ice-cold water

Turkey Herb Sausage

Recommended wood: apple or BBQr's Delight Savory Herb Pellets

The Meat

2½ pounds ground turkey

The Seasoning

¼ cup olive oil

1 tablespoon salt

1 teaspoon ground thyme

1 teaspoon dried marjoram leaves

¼ teaspoon ground nutmeg

½ teaspoon cayenne pepper

1 cup ice-cold water

Chorizo (Mexican Sausage)

Recommended wood: pecan

The Meat

2½ pounds coarsely ground pork, approximately 75 percent lean (if grinding your own, an untrimmed pork butt is just about the right amount of fat to lean)

The Seasoning

1 teaspoon salt

½ teaspoon freshly ground black pepper

⅓ cup New Mexican red chile powder

¼ teaspoon ground cloves

¼ teaspoon cinnamon

1 teaspoon dried Mexican oregano

¼ teaspoon cumin

½ cup ice-cold apple cider vinegar

½ cup ice-cold water

▼▼

Smoking the Bologna

1 bologna chub (3 pounds)

3 tablespoons Big-Time Creole Barbecue Rub (see recipe, p. 13)

This is very simple and one of my favorite meals.
• Yield: 10 servings

Prepare the cooker for indirect cooking at 235°F, using pecan wood for flavor.

Unwrap the bologna and cut a few slashes on one side—that will be the top. Sprinkle the rub all over it.

Put the bologna in the cooker for at least 2 hours but up to 5 hours. I like it cooked long, because it gets kind of shrunk down and browns, but since it's already cooked it's fine after only a couple of hours. This is a great dish when you're just not sure when the crowd will want to eat. It's best served on plain white bread.

Cured and Pecan-Smoked King Salmon

The Cure

- 2½ cups kosher salt
- ¾ cup brown sugar
- 1 tablespoon freshly ground black pepper
- 1 teaspoon powdered oregano
- 1 teaspoon crushed dill weed (not seed)

The Salmon

- 2 large fillets of salmon (about 2–3 pounds each), or 5 small but thicker fillets

The key to preparing salmon this way is to make certain that your smoke is rather cool, about 100°F. If it is warmer, decrease the smoking time. I like to serve this on crackers with a hot sauce, a mustard sauce, and a horseradish sauce for topping. Note that this recipe takes a lot of time just to make appetizers, but most of that time is spent waiting (and drinking beer) rather than working. Refrigerate any leftovers, which will keep for weeks.

- **Yield: 10 or more servings**

Note: This recipe requires advance preparation.

Combine the ingredients for the cure in a bowl and mix well. Place a sheet of plastic wrap on an aluminum baking pan and spread a ⅛-inch-thick layer of the cure blend on it. Place the salmon fillets on the cure. Top the fillets with ⅛ inch of cure. Cover the fillets with plastic wrap and cure in the refrigerator for at least 2 hours; a 4-hour cure is preferable.

Remove the fillets from the wrap and rinse the cure off each fillet. Allow the fillets to air-dry for about 2 hours.

Prepare a fire in the smoker's firebox with pecan wood or other fruit or nut hardwood of choice, such as apple, apricot, peach, or walnut. When the fire stabilizes and the smoke is no longer hot, registering about 100°F, place the fillets skin side down on racks or on the aluminum baking pan. Smoke the fillets for 4 to 5 hours, depending on their thickness. Regularly check the fire and fillets to make sure that the fish is smoking, not cooking.

Dr. BBQ's Favorite Lamb Shanks

4 lamb shanks

Big-Time Herb Rub, to
taste (see recipe, p. 12)

8 cloves garlic, chopped

1 yellow onion, chopped

One 28-ounce can diced
tomatoes

1 tablespoon freshly
ground black pepper

I love lamb shanks. They are my absolute favorite cut of
meat to eat. In the barbecue cooker, I give them my common treatment for odd and tough cuts, with a little influence
from my grandma. • **Yield: 4 servings**

Prepare your cooker for indirect cooking at 250°F, using pecan or apple
wood for flavor.

Season the shanks liberally with Big-Time Herb Rub. Cook the shanks
at 250°F for 2 hours.

Put the shanks in a disposable aluminum foil pan. Combine the other
ingredients and pour them over the shanks. Cover with aluminum foil
and return to the cooker for about 3 hours, or until tender. Transfer
the shanks to a plate and spoon the pan sauce over them.

Smoked Leg of Venison

The Marinade

4 cups dry red wine

1 large onion, sliced

5 cloves garlic, crushed

2 bay leaves

1 tablespoon black peppercorns

3 juniper berries

1 leg of venison (6 pounds)

½ pound smoked bacon

The Sauce

⅓ cup maple syrup

⅓ cup port wine

4 tablespoons butter

Salt and freshly ground black pepper, to taste

Here's a nice thing for you hunters to do with your bounty. • **Yield: 8–10 servings**

Note: This recipe requires advance preparation.

Mix together all the marinade ingredients in a bowl. Add the leg and marinate for at least 24 hours and up to 48, turning occasionally. A big cooking bag set in a large bowl works well for this.

Prepare the cooker for indirect cooking at 275°F, using hickory wood for flavor. Drain the meat. Lay the bacon on top of the leg in a single layer, and put it in the cooker. Cook to an internal temperature of 135°F. This should take about 2 to 3 hours. While the venison is cooking, strain the marinade and cook it in a saucepan until reduced by half. Add the sauce ingredients. Cook 5 minutes until well blended. Serve with the venison.

Into the Fire

Heating Up the Grill for
Meat, Fish, and Vegetables

Ray's Grill: Grilling Concepts, Techniques, and Equipment

Grilling has got to be the genesis of all cooking techniques. What could have possibly come first? I guess a chicken could have been caught in some hot lava or a sun-dried tomato could have occurred first, but neither of those has caught on nearly as well as grilling. For a few centuries the popularity waned, but with the boom of suburbia in the 1950s and '60s came backyards and outdoor grills. My earliest recollection of barbecue is my mom cooking ribs for all her friends at an annual party in the '60s. I'm pretty sure the ribs were parboiled and then grilled on a round grill with a three-sided windshield that could also hold the rotisserie option. She made a sauce out of crushed pineapple, molasses, and a local store-bought barbecue sauce. I don't remember wanting any, so I've never tried to re-create it.

The next grill in my family was called a chuck wagon. It was square, fully enclosed with the lid down, and had a little window and a thermometer on the front. The whole thing was a very cool cart with wheels. My dad bought one of these when he was trying to impress some folks who were coming over for a party. It was pretty nice and I think it was high-end for the time. Then came the kettle grill and gas grill revolution. The charcoal kettle grills, made mainly by Weber, are amazing products. They are basically the same as when they were introduced forty-plus years ago. I've used Weber kettles in all shapes and sizes for years and there is just no reason to change them. They work well and can easily adapt to cook low and slow, very hot, or any temperature in between.

I recently had the pleasure of meeting Pete Arnold from PGS Grills, who told me that his dad had invented the gas grill for home use as a means to help sell more gas for his boss. This was a very important invention. Gas grills have become the most popular grills on the decks of America mainly because of the convenience. I have one and I use it, but for me, it just can't reproduce the flavor of a charcoal fire. Gas grills have also become very nice-looking pieces of equipment. The manufacturers have turned them into components of beautiful outdoor kitchens. They have also turned them into very good multi-taskers. Many now include a rotisserie and a smoker option, and some even have a mix of different-type burners for different jobs, such as two typical gas grill burners for slow or medium cooking and a third burner that is a hot infrared type for searing and hot grilling. Some of these new-generation gas grills are downright extravagant, with price tags to match.

I would be remiss not to mention the Big Green Egg because it's one of my favorites. It is an ancient design that Ed Fisher began importing from Japan and selling around Atlanta in the 1950s. The originals were made of clay, but they have been updated to Space Age ceramic. It is a unique grill that doubles very well as a smoker.

Sadly, the crumpled newspaper–fueled grill that was endorsed by Dick Butkus never caught on. I'm a lifelong Chicago Bears fan who could easily fit in one of those *Saturday Night Live* skits (they are pretty much right on the money), but good old number 51 was clearly a better linebacker than a grill inventor.

During the late 1990s and early 2000s the grill evolution has gone wild. The industry has seen the growing interest and has given us an amazing array of options. I enjoy cooking on all the different variations and find that with a little creativity you can do anything on any grill.

There are two distinct ways to grill, direct and indirect.

The direct method is just that and should be used for foods that can be cooked fairly quickly.

You should be able to control your direct flame from low to high, but it's still direct heat and the food should be close to the fire. I like to have a combination of high and low fire so that I can move the food around as needed. Direct grilling can be done with or without a cover; however, the grill manufacturer's instructions should always be followed.

Indirect grilling is a lot more complicated. It's a cross between hot-smoking and direct grilling. The main difference is the cooking temperature. Hot-smoking is done at temperatures from 220 to 275°F, while indirect grilling is done at temperatures above 300°F and up to 400°F. It's much like oven roasting, but with that great smoky grill flavor.

Indirect grilling can be achieved in many ways. Here are a few examples.

- Set the coals off to one side and put the food on the other side.

- Bank the coals on both sides with the food in the middle, not over the coals.

- Use a barrier to deflect the heat. This can be a pan placed on a rack below the food with or without liquid in it, a steel plate, a pizza stone, or just a piece of aluminum foil under the food. All will work to different degrees. A hot trend right now is using a plank of cedar, maple, alder, et cetera. Planks also work great as a barrier from the fire.

- Get the food far enough away from the fire. I'm not talking about a couple of inches. I'm talking a foot or more. This isn't practical with most home grills, but if you are a do-it-yourselfer it's a pretty good setup. This will create the "fat in the fire" flavor that many cooks like.

- In the case of a gas grill, you can turn on one or two burners and put the meat over the unlit burner. You'll need to adjust the burner(s) to get the desired temperature.

- Cooking on a rotisserie. The constant turning takes the meat surface away from the heat part of the time.

Indirect grilling should always be done using a covered grill. The temperature of a covered charcoal grill can be regulated by how much oxygen the fire is allowed to have, as well as how much charcoal is used. I prefer to have plenty of fuel loaded and to use the vents to control the oxygen. You'll have to get used to keeping the lid closed, though, because the fire will grow when it's open. Try using one of the remote thermometers with the wire and outside readout to monitor the temperature inside. Just stick the probe through a potato or a ball of aluminum foil to hold it near the cooking grate. The same thing holds for the internal temperature of the meat. You can be very sure of how things are progressing without peeking if you use one of these remote thermometers. They even make a dual probe wireless version that is the high-tech griller's dream. Yes, I have one.

Thermometers that check the internal temperature of the meat are very important for some of the dishes cooked on the grill. Chicken and pork loin are two meats that just don't have much of a window between being done and being overdone and dried out. When I'm not using the fancy remote thermometers, I use the instant-read digital variety, but a simple bimetal dial thermometer works just fine, too. These are readily available in the kitchen department at many stores.

Some doneness temperatures for grilled food are as follows:

Steak rare: 125°F

Steak medium: 145°F

Ground beef: 155°F

Pork done safely: 137°F

Pork done just a little pink: 145–150°F

Pork done per the USDA: 160°F

Pork done the way your grandma
  did it: 180°F

Poultry, white meat: 160°F

Poultry, dark meat: 180°F

Many chefs use a "feel" method for steaks and chops. The only way to learn this method is to try it. Push down on the meat with the thickest part with your finger when it's raw. It should feel mushy. This is your reference point. As the steak cools it will get firmer. Push on it again every minute or so while it's cooking. The first few times you might want to cut into the steak or chop to make sure it's how you want it, but after a couple of tries you'll know exactly the feel you want for the desired degree of doneness.

White-fleshed fish is done just before it flakes. The best advice for fish is *not* to overcook it. It won't take long at all and is best judged by appearance and feel. With a little practice, you can tell when it's about to get flaky.

Shrimp and scallops cook quickly, and their doneness can be judged by their appearance and feel. When they turn opaque and feel firm they are done. Get them off the heat immediately.

The seafood exception for me is tuna. I love it, but it has to be served rare. Just a sear on the outside and it's done.

Know your grill; be one with it. All of this information can be customized to fit your grill, your choice of fuel, and even your perception of low, medium, and high. You should be able to adapt any of these recipes and techniques to your style with a little practice. Soon you'll be the Grand Champion of your backyard.

Indirect Grilling: Beef

Beef roasts are the chosen cut for indirect grilling. Beef roasts just aren't as popular as they once were. I guess it has to do with the decline of the family dinner, but I think it also has to do with some misleading practices in the grocery stores. The USDA grades beef for quality. The grading is based largely on the amount of fat marbled throughout the meat. This marbling makes for a tasty and tender piece of beef. The most desirable grade is USDA Prime. This stuff is wonderful if you can find and afford it. It's not realistic for most of us, though. Second best is USDA Choice. Not to be confused with Mr. Choice, Managers Choice, or any other misleading names assigned to lesser grades. USDA Choice was the norm in all grocery stores a few years ago. The next grade down is USDA Select. This grade is less tender and less tasty. It is acceptable for the tough cuts that will be cooked with tenderizing in mind and, of course, ground beef, but it just doesn't make for a very good steak or roast beef. Unfortunately, many grocery stores now offer USDA Select as their standard beef. It is marked that way, but there is no fanfare about this. It was just kind of slid into the meat cases behind our backs and many consumers don't even know it. There is often an upgrade option in the grocery store that is USDA Choice. If you're buying a steak or roast, this is money well spent. I prefer to shop where USDA Choice is the only option. Another problem that comes with this new policy is with the "inbetweener" cuts. For example, a bottom round roast from a good USDA Choice carcass could be cooked to medium rare and served as a delicious beef roast. It would be a little chewy but acceptable if sliced thinly. The USDA Select version of the same roast cooked the same way would be pretty much inedible. You wouldn't be very inclined to serve roast beef again anytime soon after one of those.

The following recipes reflect my favorites for roast beef. These are all for the grill, but they would all convert very easily for the kitchen.

▼▼▼

Sirloin Tip Roast

1 USDA Choice sirloin tip roast (4–5 pounds)

3 cloves garlic, peeled and cut into slivers

Big-Time Barbecue Rub, to taste (see recipe, p. 9)

1 cup good quality beef broth

1 cup Red Rose Barbecue Sauce (see recipe, p. 20)

The sirloin is my favorite cut of beef. It has a great beefy flavor and has a firm texture to it. I don't particularly like roast beef to melt in my mouth. • **Yield: 8 servings**

Prepare the grill for indirect cooking at 350°F, using oak wood for flavor, if desired.

With a sharp, pointy knife, stab the roast on all sides and insert a sliver of garlic into each stab hole. Be sure to push the garlic all the way in. Season the roast liberally with the rub. Put it on the grill away from the heat source and cook to an internal temperature of 135°F for medium rare. This should take about 1½ to 2 hours.

While the roast is cooking, whisk together the broth and the barbecue sauce and reserve it to be used as a serving sauce.

Remove the roast to a platter and tent loosely with foil. Let rest for 15 minutes. Slice thinly and serve with the sauce on the side.

Beef Tenderloin on the Grill

1 whole beef tenderloin
(6–7 pounds), membrane
peeled off

¼ cup olive oil

Big-Time Creole Barbecue
Rub, to taste (see recipe,
p. 13)

Béarnaise Sauce (recipe
follows)

The tenderloin is the most expensive and tender cut of beef. When cut into steaks, it is called filet mignon, the most popular cut on the menu in any steak house. Just don't overcook it and it will melt in your mouth. In this recipe I call for whole beef tenderloin, peeled. Any portion will do just fine if you don't want to cook a whole one. "Peeled" refers to a gristly silver membrane that is found on the outside. It is usually removed by the butcher long before you ever see it. The béarnaise sauce is very traditional with this cut of beef. • **Yield: 8–12 servings**

Prepare the grill for indirect cooking at 375°F, using cherry wood for flavor, if desired.

Fold the tail of the roast back up on itself and tie it with string. This will help it cook evenly. Rub the roast with the olive oil. Season it liberally with the Big-Time Creole Barbecue Rub. Put the roast on the grate away from the heat source. Cook to an internal temperature of 135°F for medium rare. This should take about an hour. Remove the tenderloin to a platter and tent it with foil. Let rest 15 minutes. Slice it thick or thin depending on your preference. Serve with the Béarnaise Sauce spooned over it or on the side.

Béarnaise Sauce

• Yield: about 1¼ cups

2 sticks butter

¼ cup white wine vinegar

⅓ cup dry white wine

5 shallots, finely chopped

1 tablespoon dried tarragon

½ teaspoon dried chervil

½ teaspoon white pepper

4 large egg yolks

¼ teaspoon salt

Melt the butter in a medium saucepan over low heat. In a small saucepan combine the vinegar, wine, shallots, tarragon, chervil, and pepper. Bring to a boil and cook until reduced by half. Strain into the top of a double boiler. Whisk in the egg yolks. Place the top over the bottom of a double boiler containing simmering water. Do not let the hot water touch the top section of the double boiler. Whisk constantly. As soon as the yolk mixture begins to thicken, remove the top of the double boiler from above the hot water and continue whisking. Whisk in the melted butter, a little at a time, very slowly. With constant whisking, blend in the salt. When all the butter is incorporated, taste and add more salt or white pepper as needed.

Big-Time Boneless Ribeye Roast

1 USDA Choice boneless
ribeye roast (5–6 pounds)

½ cup Worcestershire
sauce

½ cup Big-Time Herb Rub
(see recipe, p. 12)

1 tablespoon freshly
ground black pepper

This is what we often refer to as prime rib or standing rib roast. Prime isn't very common and definitely not worth the money for a tender and naturally well-marbled cut like this—go with Choice. "Standing rib roast" implies that the rib bones are left intact, and you can go that route if you wish. I much prefer the boneless ribeye roast for even cooking and ease of carving. It's the same meat without the bones. The recipe is very simple. • **Yield: 8–12 servings**

Note: This recipe requires advance preparation.

The night before you plan to cook, place the roast in a big plastic bag. Pour the Worcestershire sauce over it and massage it into the meat. Seal the bag and refrigerate overnight, rubbing and flipping occasionally to spread the sauce around.

When you're ready to cook, combine the herb rub and black pepper. Remove the roast from the bag and season liberally with the herb rub and black pepper mixture.

Prepare the grill for indirect cooking at 350°F, using cherry wood for flavor, if desired.

Place the roast on the rack away from the heat source and cook to an internal temperature of 135°F for medium rare. This should take about 2 hours.

Remove the roast to a platter and tent loosely with foil. Let the roast rest for 20 minutes. I slice it in thick slabs for a small group when I'm sure I have enough, and thin slices if I think I need to stretch it for a larger crowd. It's delicious either way.

Barbecued Tri-Tip

1 tri-tip roast (3 pounds)

Big-Time Barbecue Rub, to taste (see recipe, p. 9)

Whiskey Spray Mop (see recipe, p. 17)

Tri-tip is one of those things that is in every store in some areas and can't be found in others. In California they are everywhere and in Florida I can't find one. It is a muscle of the sirloin and really tasty, so seek it out if you can—it's worth a try. The texture is kind of chewy, but like so many things on the grill, it will be tender as long as you don't overcook it. I like mine medium rare. The traditional flavors of the tri-tips that are celebrated at the festivals in Santa Maria, California, are different from mine. They use a lot of garlic and a vinaigrette to mop. I prefer the traditional barbecue flavors. • **Yield: 4–6 servings**

Note: This recipe requires advance preparation.

The morning you plan to cook, season the tri-tip liberally with the rub. Cover and refrigerate until it's time to cook.

Prepare the grill for indirect cooking at 375°F, using oak wood for flavor, if desired.

Place the tri-tip on the grate away from the heat source. Baste with the Whiskey Spray Mop every 15 minutes, using a brush or a spray bottle. Flip after 30 minutes and continue basting until the roast reaches an internal temperature of 135°F.

Remove the roast to a platter. Tent loosely with foil and let rest 15 minutes. Slice thinly across the grain and serve.

Indirect Grilling: Pork

Just as with beef, indirect grilling pork lends itself to roasts, specifically pork loin roasts. This is not to be confused with pork tenderloin, which is the smaller muscle from underneath the ribs and is much better suited to direct grilling. The boneless pork loin comes from the top of the hog's back. It's a fairly tender muscle that has fallen victim to the "leaning" of American pork. American hog growers saw the need for leaner pork in the meat case and they reacted. The result is a great product for us and them, but the loin muscle was kind of lean to begin with, so now it's very lean. This doesn't mean it has to be dry, though. The trick is to cook it to the proper degree of doneness. When this is done the pork loin is a fabulous cut of meat. This cut is what inspired the term "Pork, the Other White Meat." So what is the proper degree of doneness? Well, it depends whom you ask. Americans have always worried about getting trichinosis from eating undercooked pork. That is very rare in our modern world and even rarer when caused by eating undercooked pork. My grandma always told me you would get worms from eating undercooked pork. When's the last time you heard of somebody who could afford a pork roast getting worms? The USDA suggests we cook our pork to an internal temperature of 160°F. I don't know where they get that number. If the meat is properly handled by keeping it cool and wrapped, 160°F seems like overkill to me. The parasite that causes trichinosis is killed at 137°F. To me that is safely cooked pork. Now I might feel differently if the American Pork Industry wasn't doing such a good job of raising high-quality hogs, but since they are, I'm comfortable with it. The truth is, though, not many people will eat pork at 137°F. Most will start considering it at an internal temperature of about 145°F. Under no circumstances will I cook pork loin or tenderloin past 155°F. However, shoulder and ham cuts wouldn't be desirable at these medium temperatures because they would be tough and these cuts need to have some of their fat rendered at a higher temperature. Most chefs agree with this. I've given you the USDA rule and my personal preferences. Keep those in mind when you make your own choice about how to cook pork that suits you and your guests. This applies to the cuts we will direct-grill as well.

The USDA doesn't grade pork like they do beef; they do inspect it and approve it. It is my experience that the hogs we cook these days are all very similar. This is another great accomplishment of the American Pork Producers.

"Pork, the Other White Meat," is a mild-tasting and attractive meat. Treat it like a blank canvas that can be transformed into many different flavorful dishes. Have some fun twisting these recipes around as you like.

My Mom's Rotisserie Pork Roast

1 boneless pork loin roast (5 pounds), rolled and tied

Freshly ground black pepper

1½ cups ketchup

1½ cups soy sauce

This was a family favorite that we only got about once a year. As it was for many families, grilling was a special event at my house when I was growing up. Happily, that has changed for most of us. • **Yield: 8–12 servings**

Prepare your rotisserie to cook at medium-high heat, using hickory wood for flavor, if desired.

Season the roast liberally with the black pepper. Place the roast on the rotisserie per the manufacturer's instructions.

Whisk together the ketchup and soy sauce. While the roast is cooking, brush with the ketchup and soy sauce mixture every ten minutes. Do it gently so as not to brush off the buildup of caramelization. Continue applying the sauce until the roast reaches an internal temperature of 145°F. This should take 1 to 2 hours, but the time could vary a lot, depending on your equipment.

Carefully remove the roast from the spit and transfer it to a platter. Let it rest 15 minutes, tented loosely with aluminum foil. Slice and serve.

Texas Pork Roast

1 teaspoon salt

½ teaspoon freshly ground black pepper

⅛ teaspoon ground allspice

2 teaspoons New Mexican red chile powder

1 boneless pork shoulder roast (3 pounds)

1½ cups commercial enchilada sauce

2 tablespoons freshly squeezed lemon juice

1 teaspoon hot sauce of choice

1 tablespoon Worcestershire sauce

This is one of my favorite pork recipes. I used to roast it in the oven until I discovered that nearly everything can be cooked on the grill. It is one of those "loose" recipes in which substitutions of ingredients can easily be made. • **Yield: 6 servings**

Combine the salt, pepper, allspice, and New Mexican red chile powder in a bowl. Mix well and rub the mixture on the roast.

Prepare the grill for indirect cooking at 350°F, using oak wood for flavor, if desired. Place the roast directly on the grill for 30 minutes.

Combine the remaining ingredients in a bowl and mix well. Baste the roast with the mixture every 20 minutes. Cook to an internal temperature of 160°F. This should take about 1½ hours.

Remove the roast to a platter and tent loosely with foil. Let rest for 15 minutes. Slice and serve.

Dr. BBQ's Sweet 'n' Spicy Pork Loin

1 boneless pork loin roast
(3 pounds)

½ cup hot pepper sauce

Sweeter Big-Time
Barbecue Rub, to taste
(see recipe, p. 10)

As I said earlier, pork loin is like a blank canvas. One day I was looking for something different and bold and this happened. I still make this often. I usually use common hot sauce like Frank's or Tabasco, but if I'm in an especially spicy mood I'll reach for one of the more exotic and hotter sauces such as She Got Your Balls or Dave's Insanity. These are real products from the really wacky fiery foods industry. If you're not familiar with it, look around on the Internet. If you're using a super-hot sauce, use only a teaspoon diluted in ½ cup tomato sauce. • **Yield: 6 servings**

Note: This recipe requires advance preparation.

The night before you plan to cook, cut a few ½-inch-deep slashes all around the pork roast. Put the pork loin in a sealable plastic bag and pour the hot sauce over it. Toss it around to coat it evenly and put it in the refrigerator.

Prepare the grill for indirect cooking at 350°F, using cherry wood for flavor, if desired.

Remove the pork from the bag and season it liberally with the rub. Place the pork on the grate away from the heat source and cook to an internal temperature of 145°F. This should take about an hour.

Remove the pork to a platter and tent loosely with foil. Let rest 15 minutes. Slice and serve.

Hide the Sausage

1 boneless pork loin roast (2–3 pounds)

1 long link of smoked sausage, fully cooked

Big-Time Barbecue Rub, to taste (see recipe, p. 9)

This is an idea I remember seeing a long time ago. As a cook, sometimes you put things on the back burner for a long time before you get around to them. I like to stuff things for the grill, but I always want it to be something that is fully cooked ahead of time so that when the meat is done, the stuffing will be, too. Using a raw sausage for this recipe would create a situation where the pork would get overcooked while waiting for the sausage to get done. That seems like a really bad idea to me. • **Yield: 4–6 servings**

The goal is to cut a slot all the way through the pork so that we can slide the sausage in to act as a stuffing. With a long, thin, and pointy knife, stab the end of the pork roast and cut into it, reaching for the other end. Cut a slot big enough to fit the sausage. If your knife isn't long enough, do the same procedure from the other end. *Do not* put your finger in the first end to feel for the knife tip. Better to cut both ends and then feel with fingers from both ends to see where you are. When the cut is complete and all the way through, hide the sausage in there. Cut the sausage ends a little shorter than the roast to allow for shrinkage. Season the roast with the barbecue rub.

Prepare the grill for indirect cooking at 350°F, using apple wood for flavor, if desired.

Place the roast on the grate away from the heat source and cook to an internal temperature of 145°F. This should take about 1 to 1½ hours.

Remove the roast to a platter and tent loosely with foil. Let rest for 15 minutes. Slice and serve.

Indirect grilling is best suited for big cuts of poultry cooked whole. The temperature of indirect grilling creates a better texture and a crispier skin than low and slow barbecue cooking, so I much prefer to cook whole birds in this manner.

▼▼

Sherry Butter Turkey

This is the recipe I used to win my first-ever cooking trophy. I've won a bunch since then, but that one is still important to me. There is a running joke on the cookoff circuit that winning your first trophy will cost you thousands of dollars. It's often true, because that first one just gives you a thrill that you want to have again. So you buy a new cooker and some new knives and before you know it you're buying a new truck and spending all your vacation time and money hanging around the circuit. I know—it happened that way for me. I think that a plain old Weber Kettle and the similar oval-shaped Patio Classic are the ultimate turkey cooking machines. If you set it up with the coals banked on the sides and a drip pan in the middle, the radiant heat from the coals will directly heat the thigh joint areas of the turkey. We all know that the thigh joints are usually the last thing to get cooked, so I think this is a great thing. I think it's why people cook such juicy turkeys this way. It's no magical marvel of the grill; it's just that the thighs get cooked before the breast gets overdone. • **Yield: 12–16 servings**

Note: This recipe requires advance preparation.

Sherry Butter Turkey (continued)

2 cups sherry (no need to buy top shelf, but buy something you could also have a glass of—don't buy cooking sherry)

2 cups melted butter

1 turkey (18 pounds)

Salt and freshly ground black pepper

1 red apple, chopped (skin left on)

1 medium onion, chopped

The night before you plan to cook, mix 1 cup of the sherry with 1 cup of the melted butter. Inject this with a syringe evenly all throughout the turkey. Put the turkey in a covered container in the refrigerator.

One-half hour before you plan to begin cooking, take the turkey out of the refrigerator.

Prepare the grill for indirect cooking at 325°F, using apple wood for flavor, if desired.

Sprinkle the turkey liberally with salt and pepper both inside and out. Put the chopped apple and onion in the turkey's cavity. Tuck the wings underneath and tie the legs together with string.

Place the turkey on the grate away from the heat source and cook for 1 hour.

Remove the turkey to a platter. Inject the turkey again with the rest of the sherry mixed with the rest of the melted butter. Return the turkey to the grill and continue cooking until the thighs reach an internal temperature of 180°F and the breast reaches an internal temperature of 160°F. This should taken an additional 1½ to 2 hours.

Remove the turkey to a platter and tent loosely with foil. Let it rest for 20 minutes. Carve and serve.

Roasted Turkey Basted
with Cascabel Oil

1 cup vegetable oil

6 cascabel chiles, stems and seeds removed, crushed

4 cloves garlic, chopped

2 teaspoons dried oregano

Salt and freshly ground black pepper

1 turkey (10 pounds)

This simple dish yields a complex taste. Serve the turkey hot with the chile oil and a salsa on the side, or cold on a crusty roll. Cascabel chiles are the round chiles that rattle when shaken. They are available from mail-order sources, but if you can't find them, substitute dried red new Mexican chiles or anchos. • **Yield: 8–10 servings**

Note: This recipe requires advance preparation.

The night before you plan to cook, heat the oil and sauté the chiles and garlic until softened. Remove from the heat and add the oregano, salt, and pepper. Place the mixture in a blender and puree. Set aside to cool.

Split the turkey in half by cutting in through the breast and backbone with a sharp knife or kitchen shears. Brush the chile oil over the turkey and marinate in the refrigerator overnight (do not discard any leftover oil).

Prepare the grill for indirect cooking at 350°F, using hickory wood for flavor, if desired.

Remove the turkey from the refrigerator, reserving any chile oil that is left. Place the turkey halves, breast side up, on the grate away from the heat source. Baste the turkey with the chile oil every half hour until the turkey sections reach an internal temperature of 160°F in the breast and 180°F in the thigh. This should take about 2 hours.

Remove the turkey halves to a platter and tent loosely with foil. Let it rest for 15 minutes. Carve the turkey and serve.

Beer Can Chicken
{Without the Beer Can}

Beer can chicken under many names has become very popular over the last few years. I can see the appeal. The presentation is great. Standing the chickens up increases the grill capacity and many guys just can't resist the urge to cook with beer. I have a couple of problems with the actual cooking technique and the theory about what happens during the cooking, though. The basic recipe is this. You drink half the beer, you add some seasonings to the beer, you sit the chicken on the beer can and put it on the grill. The theory goes that the beer steams and swirls inside the chicken, thus creating the juiciest chicken known to man. Bull. First off, anytime I've done this, when I take it apart, the beer can is still half full. Not much steaming could have occurred. Of course, the beer wouldn't ever reach a temperature capable of steaming on a slow grill anyway, so there was never any chance of it happening. Here's the other problem. When you stick the beer in the chicken the whole cavity is full. Even if some steaming and swirling did occur, it would be happening inside the beer can, not inside the chicken. I do believe that the beer can inside the chicken helps it cook without drying out because of the can's conductivity, and I know that cooking the chicken standing up seems to keep it from getting dry, but the swirling and steaming concept is a fantasy. So here's my theory on how to get some steaming and swirling to happen. I like to use those wire racks that go up inside the chicken's cavity. They have some that are cone-shaped and others that are made to hold a can. Both work fine, just skip using the can. Place the rack in a round cake pan and then sit the chicken on the rack. You can buy disposable cake pans if you like, or just get a couple that you use exclusively on the grill. Now pour most of a beer in the pan; add some chopped onion, garlic, herbs, and spices. Cook at a temperature hot enough to simmer the liquid and you are now infusing your chicken with the steaming, swirling beer. • **Yield: 8 servings**

2 frying chickens (3–4 pounds each)

Big-Time Barbecue Rub, to taste (see recipe, p. 9)

2 beers

1 medium onion, finely chopped

4 cloves garlic, crushed

1 teaspoon dried thyme

1 teaspoon dried marjoram

You will need 2 upright chicken racks and 2 round cake pans.

Prepare the grill for indirect cooking at 350°F, using cherry wood for flavor, if desired.

Rub the chickens liberally with the barbecue rub.

Place the chickens on their racks. Pour beer in each of the cake pans to about halfway up. Reserve the remaining beer for refilling the pans, if needed, as the chickens cook. Now add half the onion, garlic, and herbs to each cake pan. Place the pans on the grill and place the chickens on their racks in the pans. Cook until the thighs reach an internal temperature of 180°F and the breast reaches an internal temperature of 160°F. This should take about 1½ hours.

Remove the chickens and the racks to a cookie sheet, leaving the pans on the grill. Remove them later and discard the juices. Tent the chickens loosely with foil. Let them rest for 15 minutes. Remove from the racks, carve, and serve.

Fifty-Clove Chicken

1 roasting chicken (6–7 pounds)

Big-Time Herb Rub, to taste (see recipe, p. 12)

50 cloves garlic, separated but unpeeled

With sincere thanks to James Beard for his forty-clove chicken, I give you my fifty-clove chicken. This is not the classic, but it's a fun presentation and makes a good chicken. You'll be surprised at how mellow the garlic is; however, this is not a good choice for a first date dinner. • **Yield: 4–6 servings**

Prepare the grill for indirect cooking at 325°F, using BBQr's Delight Savory Herb Flavor Pellets, if desired.

Season the chicken liberally inside and out with the herb rub, even under the skin where possible. Be careful not to tear the skin. Put the 50 cloves of garlic in the cavity of the chicken. If they won't all fit, just put in what fits comfortably. Tuck the wings underneath and tie the legs together.

Place the chicken, breast side up, on the grate away from the heat source. Cook until the thighs reach an internal temperature of 180°F and the breast reaches an internal temperature of 160°F. This should take about 2½ to 3 hours.

Remove the chicken to a platter and tent loosely with foil. Let it rest for 15 minutes. While the chicken rests, spoon out the garlic. You can serve it in the skin for guests to squeeze out onto crusty bread, or you can squeeze it all into a bowl and serve it that way. Carve the chicken and serve.

Jam-Glazed Cornish Hens Stuffed with Cornbread and Pecans

2 tablespoons butter

1 small onion, chopped

2 medium green bell peppers, seeded and chopped

½ cup chopped celery

3 cups cornbread, coarsely crumbled

½ cup chopped pecans

1 teaspoon each fresh thyme and sage, chopped

½ cup chicken broth

4 Cornish hens

1 cup apricot jam

You can use any jam in this dish, but I like to use apricot. This recipe also works just fine with a chicken or a turkey. You'll just need to adjust the cooking time.

• Yield: 4 servings

Melt the butter in a saucepan and sauté the onion, green peppers, and celery until soft. Combine the onion, peppers, celery, cornbread, pecans, and spices and mix thoroughly. Add enough broth to moisten, but not saturate, the mixture and mix well.

Stuff the hens loosely with the mixture and tie the legs together. Spread the jam over the hens.

Prepare the grill for indirect cooking at 350°F degrees, using orange-flavored wood pellets, if desired.

Place the hens on the grate away from the heat source and cook for about 1 hour, or until the breast meat reaches an internal temperature of 160°F. Remove the hens to a platter and tent them loosely with foil. Let them rest for 10 minutes. Serve whole with additional jam served warm on the side.

▼▼▼

Grill-Roasted Rabbit with
Classic Aioli Sauce

1 rabbit, cut in half lengthwise

Real Simple Brine (see recipe, p. 43)

4 cloves garlic, minced

2 egg yolks

⅛ teaspoon salt

1 slice white bread, crust removed, soaked in milk and wrung out

1 cup olive oil

½ teaspoon cold water

1 teaspoon freshly squeezed lemon juice

Here is a combination of a Spanish technique and a French sauce. Commercially raised rabbit is available at specialty meat shops or through various Web shops. Serve this with garlic mashed potatoes and herbed vegetables. • **Yield: 2–4 servings**

Note: This recipe requires advance preparation.

The night before you plan to cook, submerge the rabbit in the brine in a large roasting pan.

Combine the garlic, egg yolks, salt, and bread in a bowl and beat lightly with an electric mixer. Increase the speed of the mixer and slowly add the olive oil. Then add the water and lemon juice as the sauce thickens.

Prepare the grill for indirect cooking at 325°F, using apple wood for flavor, if desired.

Remove the rabbit from the brine and wipe dry. Brush the rabbit with the sauce and place on the grate away from the heat source. Cook, while basting with the sauce and turning twice, until the internal temperature reaches 160°F.

Remove the rabbit to a platter and tent it loosely with foil. Let rest for 10 minutes. Carve the rabbit and serve.

Direct Grilling

Direct grilling is just that. You cook things that can take the heat and that cook pretty quickly. This is what so many Americans think of as barbecue. Who am I to argue with them? If you learn to control the temperature of your grill you will find that not everything gets seared right away. I say control the temperature, but I really mean to control the fire. Cooking temperatures aren't a good guideline for direct grilling. A hot fire can burn a piece of food before the thermometer ever has a chance to get warmed up. I use "low-medium-high" as the terms for heat levels in direct grilling. Every grill will have a different setting to achieve these levels. Direct grilling can be used to get a nice crispy outside while still getting the inside done. Just don't try to cook anything too big, and remember that fat burns pretty easily. Have a safety (cooler) zone on your grill for food that is cooking too fast, and *never* leave the grill unattended when direct cooking.

I've added appetizers to this section of the book because there were a few recipes that just fit the description. Besides, I couldn't think of anywhere else to put the Spam au Poivre.

▼▼

Mixed Satays with Sambal Marinade

The Marinade

- ½ **cup unsweetened coconut milk**
- **2 green onions, minced**
- **2 tablespoons** *sambal oelek*
- **1 tablespoon freshly squeezed lime juice**
- **1 tablespoon sugar**
- **1 tablespoon chopped fresh cilantro**
- **2 teaspoons fish sauce (*nam pla*)**

½ **pound boneless pork, cut into ¾-inch cubes**

½ **pound chicken meat, cut into ¾-inch cubes**

½ **pound beef steak, cut into ¾-inch cubes**

Bamboo skewers, soaked in water for 1 hour

Alabama White Barbecue Sauce (see recipe, p. 24), for serving

These are a perfect starter for any party. I often like to serve a few different meats cooked the same way to see how they react with the same marinade. This recipe calls for fish sauce, which is an acquired taste, so add more or less, depending on how much you like it. *Sambal oelek* is a condiment commonly used in Indonesia and Malaysia. *Sambal,* which means "hot sauce" in English, is a staple in the Indonesian kitchen and is available in Asian markets. It's very spicy, and can be used as a garnish or accompaniment. Here it used as an ingredient in the marinade. • **Yield: 4 servings**

Note: This recipe requires advance preparation.

The morning you plan to cook, put the coconut milk, green onions, *sambal oelek,* lime juice, sugar, cilantro, and fish sauce in a bowl and mix well. Put the meats in three individual sealable plastic bags and pour ⅓ of the marinade in each one. Seal the bags and toss to coat.

Prepare the grill for direct cooking at high heat. Thread the meat onto the skewers and grill until desired doneness. You will need to cut open a sample piece to be sure. They should be browned and crisp.

Remove the meat to a platter and serve immediately with the Alabama White Barbecue Sauce for dipping.

Grilled Brie Quesadillas

8 ounces brie, rind removed, cut in wide strips, or 8 ounces goat cheese, crumbled

Four 8-inch flour tortillas

Tomatillo-Mango Salsa (see recipe, p. 33)

2 tablespoons olive oil

A quesadilla is simply a grilled cheese sandwich using tortillas instead of bread. These can be made with either corn or flour tortillas, but if using corn, be sure to soften them by frying them in corn oil for 3 seconds per side and then drain them on paper towels. • **Yield: 4 servings**

Prepare the grill for direct cooking at high heat.

Place one-quarter of the cheese on one-half of each tortilla. Top with a little salsa mixture and fold each tortilla in half.

Brush the top of the quesadillas with olive oil and place them on the grill, oiled side down. Cook for a minute, brush the top with oil, and turn and cook for an additional minute.

Cut each quesadilla in thirds, arrange on a plate, and serve with Tomatillo-Mango Salsa.

Grilled Cheese-Stuffed Pepper Pods

10 fresh Italian peperoncinos, or substitute yellow hots

10 thick strips pepper jack cheese

This simple appetizer is amazingly good and seems really exotic. You can vary the type of peppers used as well as the cheese. These can be an appetizer or a side dish. Leave the stems on the pods for a finger-food handle. • **Yield: 5–10 servings**

Prepare the grill for direct cooking at high heat.

Grill the peppers, turning frequently, until the skins blister, blacken, and separate from the pods. Remove from the grill and place in a bowl lined with water-soaked paper towels. Cover with plastic wrap. Allow to cool for at least 10 minutes. Using a dull knife, scrape all the skins off the pods. Make a slit in the side of each pod and use a small spoon to remove the seeds.

Place a strip of cheese into each pod and return them to the grill for an additional 3 minutes, or until the cheese has melted.

Spam au Poivre

Coarsely ground black pepper

1 can of Spam Original, cut in 4 slices (slice it on the flat end so the slices keep the Spam can shape)

Big Squeeze Yellow Mustard Barbecue Sauce, to taste (see recipe, p. 23)

This is another recipe that came about because of my grilling demonstrations. I get bored cooking the same old things and am always looking for something different to cook. This one gets everyone's attention. They all have stories about their moms cooking Spam. Mine's a little different. I figured it was already pretty salty, but that a lot of black pepper and a crusty exterior might make it interesting. It is interesting, if nothing else.

- Yield: 2 sandwiches or 24 bite-size appetizers

Prepare the grill for direct cooking at very high heat.

Apply a heavy coat of black pepper to both sides of the Spam slices. Press it down so that it stays on. Grill the slices over the hot fire for just a few minutes on each side. The exact time will vary, depending on how hot your grill is. When the slices are golden brown and crusty looking they are done.

Remove them to a plate and serve. I often cut the slices into bite-size pieces and serve them with toothpicks stuck in them. Use the Big Squeeze Yellow Mustard Barbecue Sauce for dipping. The slices would also make a great sandwich if you are a true fan of Spam.

I live in Florida, where I'm pretty sure they eat more chicken wings than anywhere else in the world. I think it might be because Hooters was started here, and we all know that everybody loves Hooters. Hooters fries their wings, but I like to grill mine. I cut my chicken wings a little differently than most cooks. I don't like those wimpy single-joint wing pieces, but I also don't like cooking whole wings with the tips on. Those tips are all going in the wrong direction, so they are either sticking up or sticking down in between the grates. Here's what I do. I buy whole wings. First I cut the tips off. We won't be cooking them here, but they should definitely be saved for chicken stock. Then I make a slash with my knife on the inside of the joint, not through the bone, just to cut the skin so the seasonings can get in there and the joint will get cooked. For serving they can be easily cut apart if you need to stretch them for a crowd, or they can be easily pulled apart by a guest if you serve them whole. I've included three wing recipes. The cooking process is the same, but the seasonings and sauces are different.

Apricot Soy Sauce Wings

12 whole chicken wings, cut as described above

1½ cups Gerber Apricots with Mixed Fruit

¼ cup soy sauce

1 tablespoon brown sugar

1 teaspoon salt

1 teaspoon freshly ground black pepper

My mom used to make some wings like this in the oven. They are great on the grill. The baby food gives a fruity flavor without all the sugar of a jam or marmalade. • **Yield: 4 servings**

Note: This recipe requires advance preparation.

The night before you plan to cook, cut the wings and put them in a sealable plastic bag. In a bowl, whisk together all the ingredients and pour the mixture over the wings. Seal the bag and toss to coat.

Prepare the grill for direct cooking at medium heat.

Place the wings directly on the grill, reserving the marinade in a bowl. Grill the wings, flipping occasionally and brushing with the marinade. Continue the flipping until the marinade is gone and the wings are browned and crispy. This should take about 30 minutes. The marinade should not be applied during the last 5 minutes of cooking, and if any is left it should be discarded. Remove the wings to a platter and serve.

Dr. BBQ's Signature Wings

12 whole chicken wings, cut as described on p. 150

Dr. BBQ's Bonesmokers Crank It Up! Pepper Blend, to taste

Dr. BBQ's Bonesmokers Honey BBQ Sauce, to taste

All of the recipes in this book are originals using off-the-shelf ingredients. All except this one. This is the one self-serving recipe that uses my own commercially available products. They may be at a store near you, but if not, you can get them through my Web site at *www.drbbq.com*. The main reason I'm using them for this recipe is because they make such great wings. • **Yield: 4 servings**

Prepare the grill for direct cooking at medium heat.

Season the wings liberally with Dr. BBQ's Crank-It-Up Pepper Blend. Put the wings directly on the grill. Cook the wings, flipping them occasionally, until they start to brown and are close to being done. Begin brushing with the Dr. BBQ's Bonesmokers Honey BBQ Sauce. Continue flipping and brushing until the wings are cooked and nicely browned. This should take about 30 minutes. Remove to a platter and serve.

Grilled Buffalo Wings

12 whole chicken wings, cut as described on p. 150

Big-Time Barbecue Rub, to taste (see recipe, p. 9)

½ cup Frank's Red Hot Sauce

½ cup melted butter

This is a grilled version of the original Anchor Bar recipe, but I really like them and serve them often. The Frank's Red Hot is pretty mild, though, so if you like them hot you might want to try a different hot sauce.

• **Yield: 4 servings**

Prepare the grill for direct cooking at medium heat.

Season the wings liberally with the Big-Time Barbecue Rub. Put the wings directly on the grill. Cook the wings, flipping occasionally, until they are brown and crispy and fully cooked. This should take about 30 minutes.

Remove to a big bowl. Combine the hot sauce with the melted butter in a bowl and pour over the wings. Toss the wings with the sauce mixture to coat well. Remove to a platter and serve.

▼▼▼

Fajita Feast (Part One)

The Marinade

- ½ **cup chopped serrano chiles, stems removed**
- ⅓ **cup freshly squeezed lime juice**
- ⅓ **cup soy sauce**
- ⅓ **cup red wine**
- 2 **tablespoons vegetable oil**
- 2 **cloves garlic, minced**

2 **pounds skirt or flank steak**

Flour tortillas, chopped onions, grated cheese, sour cream, diced avocados, and salsa, for serving

This is the beef version of the fajita feast. There is also a chicken version on page 174. I like to cook both for the same meal so that everyone can have some of each. Typically Texan, these recipes make a great outdoor barbecue party. They are easy to prepare; simply marinate them the night before and grill them when the guests arrive. • **Yield: 8 servings**

Note: This recipe requires advance preparation.

The day before you plan to cook, prepare the marinade by putting all the ingredients in a nonreactive bowl and mixing them together. Put the meat in a sealable plastic bag and pour the marinade over it. Seal the bag and toss the meat to coat.

Prepare the grill for direct cooking at high heat, using mesquite charcoal or chips, if desired. I usually don't like the taste of mesquite, but for a very short cooking time like this it works and imparts that Texan taste.

Grill the steak to an internal temperature of 135°F for medium rare.

Remove the steak to a platter. Carve the steak diagonally against the grain in thin strips as for London broil. Serve with warmed flour tortillas, chopped onions, grated cheese, sour cream, diced avocados, and salsa. Each guest will custom-make their own fajita sandwiches.

Jack and Coke Steak

Ever heard the story about the T-bone steak soaked in Coke overnight and in the morning the steak is gone? I was talking about that one day with some friends and it sounded like nonsense to me, but I couldn't help but get sucked into the idea that there might be something to it that would create a tender steak, so I decided to try it. I like steak and I like Coke, so I figured it would probably taste good. Well, a funny thing happened on my way to the marinade. It was a Saturday afternoon and I was imbibing a Coke with a little bit of Jack Daniel's whiskey in it. So as I was preparing the bowl of Coke for the steak it seemed like an obvious move to add a little of the Jack Daniel's to my marinade. I used a ribeye instead of a T-bone, but it didn't matter. The steak was all still there in the morning. The truth is that the Coke didn't seem to do anything to the texture at all, but the Jack and Coke did impart a great flavor.

This is a good time to discuss how to judge when a steak is done. This works for my Jack and Coke steak, but also for any other type of steak. Now we're talking about good steaks here such as ribeye, porterhouse, T-bone, New York strip, top sirloin, or filet. You should always buy a steak that is graded USDA Choice or Prime. USDA Select grade is just not a very good steak. Steaks should be cooked from rare to medium. Anything beyond that and you are on your own. Always use a hot direct grill. Place the steak on a 45-degree angle to the grate. After a couple of minutes rotate (not flip) the steak 90 degrees. This will give you that nice crosshatch grill-mark pattern. Peek under the steak, and when it looks good and brown flip it over. Push down on the thickest part of the meat with your finger. It should feel mushy. This is your reference point. As the steak cooks it will get firmer. Push on it again every minute or so. The only true way to learn this method is to try it. The first few times you might want to cut into the steak to make sure, but after a couple of tries you'll know exactly the feel you want for the desired degree of doneness. A short rest right after cooking is a good thing. In the case of a steak, 2 to 3 minutes will be fine. • **Yield: 2 servings**

Note: This recipe requires advance preparation.

2 ounces Jack Daniel's Tennessee Whiskey

2 cups Coca-Cola

2 boneless ribeye steaks, 1½ inches thick

Salt and freshly ground black pepper, to taste

The night before you plan to cook, combine the Jack and Coke in a nonreactive dish. Lay the steaks in the dish and refrigerate, covered. Flip them occasionally throughout the marinating time.

Prepare the grill for direct cooking at high heat. Right before the steaks go on you can add some BBQr's Delight Jack Daniel's Flavored Wood Pellets, if you desire.

Remove the steaks from the marinade and pat dry. Season liberally with salt and pepper. Grill to desired doneness.

Remove to a platter. Let the steaks rest 2 to 3 minutes before serving.

Stuffed Flank Steak

The Stuffing

2 tablespoons olive oil

½ cup onion, chopped fine

3 cloves garlic, crushed

4 sun-dried tomato halves (I like the soft dry ones)

2 medium poblano chiles, roasted, peeled, and chopped

1 tablespoon balsamic vinegar

1 tablespoon Worcestershire sauce

½ teaspoon salt

½ teaspoon freshly ground black pepper

2–3 tablespoons breadcrumbs

1 USDA Choice flank steak (about 2 pounds), with a pocket cut in the side

1 bamboo skewer, soaked in water for 1 hour

I like to stuff things for the grill, but I always want the stuffing to start out fully cooked and I never want it too thick. I like the flavor and presentation that stuffing gives, but I never want to have to overcook a piece of meat to accommodate it. I use a finely chopped cooked vegetable dressing for the inside of this flank steak. I add just enough breadcrumbs to soak up the liquids. Getting this steak done just right is a little tricky, and overcooking it is a big no-no. Flank steak gets tough and chewy shortly past medium rare. The proper temperature will be 135°F, but it will be hard to get a reading. The feel method will be a little misleading, too, because the stuffing will be soft. I'd try both and time it, too. On my hot Big Green Egg it's five minutes per side. • **Yield: 4 servings**

Put the olive oil, onion, garlic, sun-dried tomatoes, and chiles in a sauté pan over medium heat. Cook until the onion is soft. Add the vinegar, Worcestershire sauce, salt, and pepper and blend well. Remove from the heat and stir in 2 tablespoons of the breadcrumbs. If it's still too watery add the rest of the breadcrumbs. Cover loosely and let cool.

Try to get the butcher to cut a pocket in the flank steak for you. If not, you should be able to do it yourself. Lay the steak flat and with a sharp knife cut into the side, keeping your knife blade level with the cutting board. Take your time and make a few passes, going deeper each time. Try not to cut through the other side or the ends, but make the pocket as wide as you can.

Spoon the stuffing into the pocket of the flank steak. Spread it out in a thin layer all across the inside of the flank steak. Close the side entry and seal it by weaving a bamboo skewer through the edges, top to bottom to top again.

Prepare the grill for direct cooking at high heat.

Lay the steak directly on the grill at a 45-degree angle to the grate. After about 3 minutes spin (not flip) the steak to 90 degrees. This will give you those nice crosshatch grill marks. After a total of five minutes peek under the steak. If it's nicely browned, flip it over. Cook another five minutes and check for doneness.

When it reaches the desired degree of doneness, remove the steak to a platter. Remember, cooking flank steak past medium rare will make it tough! Tent loosely with foil and let it rest for 10 minutes. Slice and serve, trying to keep the stuffing intact. A very sharp knife will help.

Grande Time Chipotle Steaks

2 thick ribeye steaks

Olive oil

Big-Time Barbecue Rub
(see recipe, p. 9)

1 onion, chopped

3 cloves garlic, minced

2 tablespoons vegetable oil

3 chipotle in adobo chiles,
chopped

1 medium tomato, peeled
and seeds removed,
chopped

½ teaspoon oregano

½ teaspoon sugar

½ teaspoon freshly ground
black pepper

2 cups beef broth

1 cup dry red wine

These are my Mexican-style steaks, mildly spicy and really tasty. I love the smokiness of the chipotle chiles. I use the ones in cans with adobo sauce that are found in the Mexican food section of the supermarket.

• Yield: 2–4 servings

Brush the steaks with olive oil and sprinkle lightly with the rub. Let sit while preparing the sauce.

Sauté the onion and garlic in the vegetable oil until browned. Add the chipotles, tomato, oregano, sugar, and pepper. Sauté for an additional couple of minutes. Stir in the broth and wine and simmer for 20 to 30 minutes, or until reduced by half.

Remove from the heat and puree in a blender until smooth and then strain. Return to the pan and keep warm until ready for serving.

Prepare the grill for direct grilling at high heat, using hickory wood for flavor. Grill the steaks to the desired doneness.

To serve, place some of the sauce on a plate, place the steak on the sauce, and top with additional sauce.

Dr. BBQ's Favorite Burger

I like my burgers to be made of ground beef. That's it. No eggs and breadcrumbs; those are the ingredients for meatballs. No peppers and onions in there, they never get cooked, and definitely no sprouts or cheese or anything like that. If you don't like ground beef, then have something else to eat. I do like ground turkey and you can substitute that. I also like cheese and bacon on the top of my burger, not inside it. I also don't like my burgers to look like meatballs. Ground beef shrinks when you cook it and if you start out with a burger that is plump in the middle, you'll end up with a burger as fat as a meatball. Just make your burger real flat and push down in the middle to make it thinner there. When it shrinks during cooking it will all even out and be a nice flat burger. How is it that my grandma never figured this out? She was a great cook, but her burgers looked like meatballs. This shape will also help the burger cook evenly throughout. Let's talk about cooking your burgers properly. Unfortunately, it's not safe to eat rare hamburgers anymore. *E. coli* bacteria contamination is a very real danger with ground beef and it can't be ignored. All burgers must be cooked to an internal temperature of 155°F. Grinding the meat yourself doesn't change this. The problem is that *E. coli,* if present, is found on the outside of a hunk of beef. It's nothing you can see or smell. If you cook that hunk of beef or a steak to a very rare temperature of 125°F, the outside will easily reach the 155°F required to kill *E. coli*. When you grind a piece of meat, you inevitably fold in some of the outside surface, so now the whole product has to be cooked to the safe temperature of 155°F. Sorry, but that's the deal. No more rare burgers.

- **Yield: 6 servings**

2 pounds 80 percent lean ground chuck

Big-Time Barbecue Rub, to taste (see recipe, p. 9)

6 thick slices Swiss cheese

6 kaiser rolls, split and toasted

6 thin slices tomato

12 slices of cooked bacon

Prepare the grill for direct cooking at high heat.

Split the ground beef into six portions. Form six patties and push down with your finger in the middle to make them very thin there. Season lightly on both sides with the barbecue rub.

Place the burgers directly on the grill. Cook for about four minutes and then peek at the bottoms. If they're nicely browned, flip the burgers. Place the cheese on top. Continue cooking until the cheese is melted and the internal temperature of the burgers is 155°F.

Remove the burgers directly to the buns. Top each one with a slice of tomato and two slices of bacon in an X pattern.

Stacked-Up Blue Cheese Burgers

8 ounces white
mushrooms, sliced

3 tablespoons olive oil

2 teaspoons melted butter

Garlic salt, to taste

4 sesame seed buns

2 pounds 80 percent lean
ground chuck, formed into
4 thick patties

4 slices American cheese

8 strips of cooked bacon

4 lettuce leaves

8 thin slices tomato

4 slices red onion

½ cup blue cheese dressing

Here's a dressed-up burger with a twist, thanks to blue cheese salad dressing that you can buy in any supermarket. • **Yield: 4 servings**

At least a half hour before you plan to grill, sauté the mushrooms in the olive oil, tossing occasionally until soft. This should take about 10 minutes. Set aside to cool.

In a bowl, mix the melted butter with the garlic salt and brush the butter on the inside of the sliced buns.

Prepare the grill for direct cooking at medium-high heat, using pecan wood for flavor. Grill the burgers to desired doneness and, at the last minute, top each with one-fourth of the mushrooms, 1 slice of cheese, and 2 slices of bacon. While the cheese is melting, toast the buns on the grill.

Place the burgers on the buns and top with lettuce, tomato slices, onion slices, and a spoonful of blue cheese dressing.

▼▼▼

Pork Chops Rancheros

6 green New Mexican
chiles, roasted, peeled,
stems and seeds removed,
chopped

½ cup freshly squeezed
lime juice

2 tablespoons vegetable oil

¼ cup chopped onions

2 cloves garlic, minced

1 teaspoon ground cumin

1 teaspoon dried oregano

½ teaspoon ground
coriander

½ teaspoon salt

4 thick-cut pork chops

The addition of cumin and chiles gives these pork chops a wonderful Southwestern flavor that works great on the grill. • **Yield: 4 servings**

Note: This recipe requires advance preparation.

The night before you plan to cook, combine all the ingredients, except the pork, in a blender and puree. Place the pork chops in a glass dish and pour the marinade over them. Cover and refrigerate.

Prepare the grill for direct cooking at medium heat.

Remove the chops from the marinade and place them directly on the grill. Cook until chops reach an internal temperature of 145°F. This should take about 10 minutes per side.

Remove the chops to a platter and tent loosely with foil. Let them rest 5 minutes. The remaining marinade can be boiled until thick and served over the chops.

Peachy Stuffed Pork Chops

6 boneless pork loin chops, 1½ inches thick, with a pocket cut in the side

2 tablespoons butter

¾ cup chopped dried peaches

½ cup crushed pecans

1 or 2 jalapeño chiles, chopped fine

¼ teaspoon salt

¼ teaspoon freshly ground black pepper

½ cup water

Big-Time Barbecue Rub, to taste (see recipe, p. 9)

This is a simple stuffing of dried peaches and pecans with a little excitement mixed in. When you cut up the jalapeño, leave the seeds and veins in if you want some heat, or trim them out if you want it mild. • **Yield: 6 servings**

Have the butcher cut the pockets in the sides of the chops or do it your-self. Lay the chop on the cutting board and cut in on the side with the fat cap, keeping the knife level to the cutting board. Take a few passes to get the pocket as deep as you can without going all the way through.

Melt the butter over low heat in a small sauté pan with a cover. Add the peaches, pecans, and jalapeño and cook for a couple of minutes, stirring occasionally. Add the salt, pepper, and water and put the lid on. Stir occasionally and cook about 5 minutes, until the water is gone. Remove to a bowl and let cool.

Prepare the grill for direct cooking at medium heat.

Stuff each chop with 2 tablespoons of the filling. Push the chops down to flatten and spread the stuffing evenly. Season liberally with the bar-becue rub. Grill over medium heat, turning gently only once, until the pork reaches an internal temperature of 145°F.

Remove to a platter and tent loosely with foil. Let rest for 5 minutes and serve.

Grilled Asian Pork Tenderloin

2 pork tenderloins, about 1 pound each

Asian-Style Marinade (see recipe, p. 30)

Pork tenderloin, the little brother of pork loin, is also a great neutral cut of meat that does well with a flavorful marinade. The tenderloins are usually packed 2 to a pack and weigh around a pound apiece. They have a great texture, really unlike any other cut, and are wonderful served while still pink. For this recipe I'm using my Asian marinade, but feel free to try any others. This cut goes well with almost everything. • **Yield: 4 servings**

Note: This recipe requires advance preparation.

The night before you plan to cook, place the tenderloins in a sealable plastic bag. Pour the marinade over the meat. Seal the bag and toss to coat. Return to the refrigerator.

Prepare the grill for direct cooking at high heat.

Remove the tenderloins from the marinade and place them directly on the grill. Cook, turning occasionally, until they reach an internal temperature of 145°F.

Remove the tenderloins to a platter and loosely tent with foil. Let them rest for 10 minutes. Slice and serve.

Savory Grilled
Country-Style Pork Ribs

A Recipe from Barbecue All Star Chef Ray Tang

A couple of years ago I was attending World Pork Expo to cook in The Great Pork BarbeQlossal. World Pork Expo is a convention and trade show for everyone involved in the pork industry from all over the world. I attend a lot of interesting events, but this one is definitely at the top of the list. As you walk around the Iowa State Fairgrounds, you see live hogs, racing hogs, pictures of hogs, earrings with hogs on them, and just about anything else you can imagine related to the hog business and the love of hogs. These people are really into it. I love the shoelaces with the little hogs on them that I got there and a bumper sticker that says "The World Is My Pork Chop." The cooking and eating side of the pork industry is well represented, too. I was there to cook in one of the most well-respected barbecue cookoffs in the country. They host close to one hundred teams every year, and my dear friend Anne Rehnstrom does an amazing job of keeping it all together. Anne also helps out with other parts of World Pork Expo, and this particular year she needed someone to do a rib-cooking demonstration on the stage that is there for the Celebrated Chefs. This is an impressive group of chefs from around the country who are honored by the National Pork Board annually for their cooking skills and ability to promote pork. I fed them and they fed me and we decided that maybe we should try to do something together someday. Well, these things don't usually pan out, but when I got home I realized that I had the perfect project on my desk. It was the World Barbecue Association Championship, to be held later that year in Jamaica. A big part of the World Barbecue Association's judging criteria is side dishes and plating, so the combination of a seasoned barbecue cookoff man and a real chef looked like a great idea. I called Chef Ray Tang, one of the Celebrated Chefs and winner of the prestigious Taste of Elegance award, and asked him if he was interested. He was. So with great support from the National Pork Board as well as Napoleon Grills and Ken Davis Barbecue Sauce, we were off to Jamaica. It was a terrific trip and a pleasure to work with Chef Ray Tang. We finished ahead of all the other American teams and well up the list of European teams, but the topper was a third-place finish in ribs. The rib presentation was truly our combined effort, and we are both very proud of this accomplishment. I hope we can do it again someday.

Chef Ray and his lovely wife, Shawn, are the owners of The Presidio Social Club in San Francisco. It's in a historic building in the Presidio just inside the Lombard Gate at 563 Ruger Street. They serve "Modest American Cuisine in the San Franciscan Style." I'm not sure what that means, but I do know it tastes good. • **Yield: 4–6 servings**

Note: This recipe requires advance preparation.

The Marinade

2 tablespoons Dijon mustard

2 tablespoons olive oil

¼ teaspoon red pepper flakes

1 tablespoon coarsely chopped fresh rosemary or ½ tablespoon dried rosemary

1 tablespoon chopped garlic

Grated zest of 1 lemon

8–12 pieces boneless pork country-style ribs (2–3 pounds—you can substitute pork chops cut at least ¾ inch thick; cooking time may vary)

½ tablespoon kosher salt

½ tablespoon freshly cracked black pepper

At least one hour before you plan to cook and up to 8 hours before, combine all marinade ingredients in a medium-sized bowl. Put the meat in a sealable plastic bag. Pour the marinade over it. Seal the bag and toss the meat to coat.

Prepare the grill for direct cooking at medium heat.

Remove the meat from the refrigerator 15 minutes before grilling. Remove it from the marinade and season liberally with salt and pepper.

Grill the pork pieces over medium to high heat to form a crust, turning as needed. Continue cooking at medium heat until they reach the desired degree of doneness. Total cooking time is approximately 8 to 10 minutes.

Place the pork on a platter and serve.

▼▼▼

Butterflied Margarita Chicken

1 whole frying chicken (3–4 pounds), butterflied

Spicy Margarita Marinade (see recipe, p. 29)

Butterflying is a great way to cook a chicken. It looks great, cuts apart easily when done, and you only have to turn one piece. It's two chicken halves connected by some skin. Be sure to grab it by the legs to move it around or it will fall apart. • **Yield: 2–4 servings**

Note: This recipe requires advance preparation.

The night before you plan to cook, split the chicken down the backbone. You can do this with a sharp knife or a pair of kitchen shears. After you make the cut, spread the chicken apart and push it down flat on the cutting board. Flip it over and pull out the red keel bone right in the middle of the breast and the white cartilage right underneath it. Tuck the wings underneath themselves and it's ready to go. Put the chicken in a large glass or plastic bowl and pour the marinade over it. Now spread the marinade all over the chicken with your hands, even pushing it up under the skin. The skin will pull away from the meat easily. Try not to tear it. Cover and refrigerate overnight.

Prepare the grill for direct cooking at medium heat.

Put the chicken on the grill flat, skin side up. Cook for about 30 minutes. Grab the chicken by the legs and flip it over. This will probably result in a stirring up of the fire when the juices hit it. Close the lid or spray with water to calm things down. Cook about 10 minutes and flip back over. Now cook until the thighs reach an internal temperature of

180°F and the breast reaches an internal temperature of 160°F. That should take about another 15 minutes. When it's done, flip it over for one final browning of the skin. This will probably only take a couple more minutes.

Remove the chicken to a platter. Tent loosely with foil and rest for 10 minutes. Cut into serving pieces and serve.

El Pollo al Carbon

2 tablespoons vegetable oil

1 small onion, chopped

2 cloves garlic, minced

2 tomatillos, husks removed, chopped

½ cup freshly squeezed orange juice

2 tablespoons freshly squeezed lime juice

1 tablespoon freshly squeezed lemon juice

¼ teaspoon cinnamon

¼ teaspoon ground cloves

¼ teaspoon ground habanero chile

2 small chickens (2–3 pounds), cut in half lengthwise

The concept of marinating chicken in a spicy fruit juice and then char-broiling it originated in Mexico and is becoming quite popular throughout the U.S. The chicken is served with warm corn tortillas, fresh salsa, and a side of pinto beans. Diners remove the chicken from the bones, place the meat in the tortilla, top with salsa, and chow down. • **Yield: 4 servings**

Note: This recipe requires advance preparation.

The night before you plan to cook, heat the oil in a saucepan and sauté the onion, garlic, and tomatillos until soft. Add the remaining ingredients, except the chicken, and simmer for 10 minutes. Place in a blender and puree to make a sauce. Set aside to cool. Place the chicken in a glass dish and pour the sauce over it. Cover and refrigerate.

Prepare the grill for direct cooking at medium heat. Remove the chicken from the sauce and put it on the grill. Grill the chicken, basting frequently with the sauce and turning occasionally, until the dark meat reaches an internal temperature of 180°F and the white meat reaches an internal temperature of 160°F. This should take about 45 minutes.

Remove the chicken to a platter and tent loosely with foil. Let rest for 10 minutes.

Flattened Salsa-Grilled Chicken Breasts

2 large whole chicken breasts, boneless and skinless

1 cup Grilled Southwestern Salsa (see recipe, p. 36)

3 tablespoons dark brown sugar

4 teaspoons Dijon-style mustard

This unusual flavor combination really works. These will cook quickly, so get the basting done early. • **Yield: 2–4 servings**

Prepare the grill for direct cooking at medium heat, using cherry wood for flavor.

Pound the breasts to a one-half-inch thickness.

In a bowl, combine the salsa, sugar, and mustard and mix well.

Grill the breasts for about 4 minutes a side, basting a couple of times with the salsa mixture. Take care that the breasts don't bun.

Teriyaki Chicken Breasts

6 boneless chicken breast halves

Bear Game Teriyaki Marinade (see recipe, p. 29)

Honey Mustard Pineapple Glaze (see recipe, p. 42)

These are really simple and oh so good. They make great sandwiches at a tailgate party. • **Yield: 6 servings**

Note: This recipe requires advance preparation.

The night before you plan to cook, put the chicken breasts in a sealable plastic bag and pour the marinade over them. Seal the bag and toss to coat. Return to the refrigerator.

Prepare the grill for direct cooking at medium heat.

Remove the chicken from the marinade and put it directly on the grill. Cook about 3 minutes on each side and then begin basting with the Honey Mustard Pineapple Glaze. Baste and flip every couple of minutes until the chicken is nicely browned and has reached an internal temperature of 160°F.

Remove the breasts to a plate and tent loosely with foil. Let rest 5 minutes and serve.

Yojerk Chicken

1 whole frying chicken
(3–4 pounds), cut up

1 recipe Traditional Jerk
Paste (see recipe, p. 39)

1 quart container of plain
yogurt

This dish started out with my interest in tandoori chicken and the effect of yogurt in a marinade. I combined the yogurt with a spicy barbecue sauce and it was very good. I was going to make it one day for a cooking class at Poolside near Minneapolis, but Rob Anderson up there is always looking to spice things up, so he suggested mixing the yogurt with a jerk paste. I did and it worked out great. Thanks, Rob. The yogurt seems to have a nice tenderizing influence on the chicken and it mellows the intense flavors of the jerk. • **Yield: 2–4 servings**

Note: This recipe requires advance preparation.

The night before you plan to cook, cut random slashes in the chicken pieces about ½ inch deep. This will help the marinade get to the meat. In a nonreactive bowl, combine the jerk paste with the yogurt. Put the chicken in a sealable plastic bag. Spoon the marinade over it. Seal the bag and toss to coat.

Prepare the grill for direct cooking at medium heat.

Remove the chicken from the marinade and place it directly on the grill. Cook the chicken, turning as needed, until the dark meat reaches an internal temperature of 180°F and the white meat reaches an internal temperature of 160°F. This should take about 40 minutes.

Remove the chicken to a platter and serve.

Fajita Feast (Part Two)

The Marinade

- ½ cup canned jalapeño chiles, chopped fine
- ½ cup chicken broth
- ⅓ cup freshly squeezed lemon juice
- ⅓ cup vegetable oil
- 1 teaspoon ground cumin
- 1 teaspoon dried oregano
- ¼ teaspoon garlic powder
- ½ can beer

3 boneless chicken breasts

Flour tortillas, chopped onions, grated cheese, sour cream, diced avocados, and salsa, for serving

This is the chicken version of the fajita feast. There is also a beef version on page 151. I like to cook both for the same meal so that everyone can have some of each. Typically Texan, these recipes make a great outdoor barbecue party. They are easy to prepare; simply marinate the meat the night before and grill them when the guests arrive. Purists will say that there is no such thing as chicken fajitas, but please, give it up. • **Yield: 8 servings**

Note: This recipe requires advance preparation.

The day before you plan to cook, prepare the marinade by combining all the ingredients in a nonreactive bowl. Put the breasts in a sealable plastic bag and pour the marinade over them. Seal the bag and toss the meat to coat. Refrigerate.

Prepare the grill for direct cooking at high heat, using mesquite charcoal or chips, if desired. I usually don't like the taste of mesquite, but for a very short cook like this it works and imparts that Texas taste.

Grill the chicken to an internal temperature of 160°F.

Remove to a platter. Cut the chicken breasts into thin strips. Serve with warmed flour tortillas, chopped onions, grated cheese, sour cream, diced avocados, and salsa. Each guest will custom-make their own fajita sandwiches.

▼▼

Qsis's Rack of Lamb

A Recipe from Barbecue All Star Lee Fraser

Lee's Lamb Marinade (recipe follows)

2 racks of lamb, bones frenched

Big-Time Herb Rub, to taste (see recipe, p. 12)

Lee Fraser is my first-ever and best-ever friend made via the Internet. Her Internet name is Qsis. We are two people with common interests and similar views of life who would never have met if it hadn't been for the Internet. Lee cooks with my Bonesmokers team when she can, but she also cooks as Back 40 BBQ with her brother Rob. Back 40 refers to their postage-stamp backyard in suburban Boston. Once when we were cooking together at a cookoff in New Holland, Pennsylvania, Lee made a great rack of lamb for the "Anything But" category. She scored a perfect score of 180, for which she won a commemorative pin, but, unfortunately, there were two other perfect scores that day, so we came in third. It was still a great day and it's a great recipe. • **Yield: 4 servings**

Note: This recipe requires advance preparation.

The morning before you plan to cook, prepare the marinade. Put the lamb in a sealable plastic bag and pour the marinade over it. Seal and toss to coat the meat. Refrigerate.

Prepare the grill for direct cooking at medium heat.

Remove the lamb from the marinade and pat dry. Season lightly with the herb rub. Grill on all sides, turning as needed, until the lamb reaches an internal temperature of 125°F to 135°F for rare. This should take about 15 to 20 minutes.

Remove the racks to a platter and tent it loosely with foil. Let them rest for 10 minutes. Slice at the table for presentation.

We've served these on a bed of garlic mashed potatoes with a garnish of tiny diced red and orange peppers and sprigs of fresh rosemary from Lee's garden.

Lee's Lamb Marinade

1½ cups vegetable oil

¾ cup soy sauce

½ cup red wine vinegar

⅓ cup lemon juice

¼ cup Worcestershire sauce

4 cloves garlic, chopped

2 tablespoons dry mustard

1 tablespoon coarsely ground black pepper

2½ teaspoons salt

2 teaspoons chopped Italian parsley

Combine all ingredients in a bowl and mix well.

Spicy Grilled Lamb Chops

A Recipe from Barbecue All Star Candy Weaver

The Marinade

1 cup olive oil

¼ cup wine vinegar

½ teaspoon salt

Dash cayenne pepper

¼ teaspoon freshly ground white pepper

1 tablespoon chopped fresh oregano

1 tablespoon chopped Italian parsley

¼ teaspoon chopped fresh thyme

1 clove crushed garlic

6 lamb chops, cut 1½ inches thick

Salt, to taste

The Herb Blend

2 tablespoons dried oregano

½ tablespoon dried rosemary

1 teaspoon dried thyme

½ cup pepper jelly (hot or mild)

This recipe comes from Candy Weaver. She is the Queen of Pellets. Her company, BBQr's Delight from Pine Bluff, Arkansas, makes those great flavor pellets I talked about earlier. They also make cooking pellets, but it's the variety of the flavor pellets that I think is so great. I currently have open bags of Cherry, Pecan, Jack Daniel's Charcoal, and Orange Pellets at my house. Candy is also a great cook. When I asked her for a recipe, I requested one that used her Savory Herb Pellets. They are not like anything else on the market. They flavor the meat with a combination of wood and herb smoke. Why didn't I think of that? • **Yield: 3–6 servings**

Note: This recipe requires advance preparation.

The night before you plan to cook, combine the marinade ingredients. Put the lamb chops in a sealable plastic bag. Pour the marinade over the chops. Seal the bag and refrigerate.

Prepare the grill for direct cooking at medium heat. Right before putting the chops on, place a foil packet of BBQr's Delight Savory Herb Flavor Pellets in the fire.

Remove chops from the marinade (discard the juice!). Sprinkle chops lightly with salt, then the herb blend. Cover chops and allow to rest 5 minutes before grilling. Grill the chops, turning occasionally, for approximately 8 to 12 minutes for rare and 12 to 16 minutes for medium doneness. Rare lamb is 125° to 135°F internal and medium is 140° to 150°F. Measure the temperature in several places.

Remove the chops to a platter and tent loosely with foil. Warm the jelly in the microwave on high for 30 seconds. Spoon the liquid jelly over the grilled lamb chops and serve.

Wisconsin Bratwurst Cooked the Right Way

This is a subject I have researched for many years. Like much of my research, it involves me, a grill, a lawn chair, and a cooler of beer. My all-time favorite beer is Old Style, formerly made in Lacrosse, Wisconsin. Sadly, they were bought out, and the label is now on a big corporate generic-tasting beer not made in Lacrosse. When you live in Chicago you often go to Wisconsin to escape the city. There are many great little towns on lovely little lakes there, and I've seen many of them. The folks in Wisconsin love to eat sausages of all kinds. I guess it's a natural accompaniment to the great cheese they produce. Their absolute favorite sausage is the "brat" or bratwurst. Bratwurst in its original form is a sausage made with pork, veal, and a distinctive blend of spices. The brats that we see in most stores now are all pork. They are a staple at summertime events in Wisconsin. You will find an assortment of different sausage makers and flavored brats all in the same grocery store. I've actually seen a guy selling Taco Brats. I passed on those.

Cooking the brats properly is a big deal. The typical accompaniments are beer, onions, butter, and sometimes mustard and sauerkraut. Many cooks like to boil or simmer the brats in the beer, butter, and onions and then grill them. The thinking is that the brat will be cooked and all the fat will be gone. Yeah, but so will all the flavor. My method incorporates the required brat ingredients and conserves all their great flavors. • **Yield: 6–8 servings**

1 aluminum foil pan

1 stick of butter

10 links Wisconsin bratwurst

1 large onion, sliced thinly

1 can of beer

Sausage rolls

Mustard, if desired

Prepare the grill for direct cooking at medium heat.

Place the aluminum foil pan on one side of the grill and add the stick of butter. Put the brats on the other side of the grill, directly on the grate. When the butter melts, add the sliced onion to the pan. Toss the onion occasionally. Flip the brats as needed. When the onion gets soft, add the can of beer. As the brats get nicely browned, add them to the pan. Don't worry about them being done all the way because they are going to continue to cook in the pan. You can add more beer if it's needed, but remember that we want to reduce it down by the end, so don't add too much.

When everything is in the pan, cover it with foil and cook for 15 minutes. Remove the foil cover and let the mixture reduce until it's just soft onion and brats. Remove from the heat. Serve the brats on sausage rolls with the onion and some mustard, if desired.

Grilled Scallops Fettuccine

¼ cup freshly squeezed lime juice

1 teaspoon freshly ground black pepper

¼ cup chardonnay wine

2 tablespoons white vinegar

¼ cup finely minced shallots

8 sprigs cilantro, finely minced

1½ pounds large sea scallops

2 sticks (8 ounces) unsalted butter, diced

1 cup chopped mild green chiles

¼ teaspoon turmeric

3 tablespoons Big-Time Herb Rub (see recipe, p. 12)

1 pound fettuccine, cooked al dente

Here's a delicious way to serve grilled scallops. This recipe almost belongs in the chapter Ray's High-Falutin' Barbecue Dishes, but since we are grilling the scallops freshly for this dish it belongs here. Consider it a bonus recipe with the great sauce and the pasta. Use the mild canned green chiles so that the sauce doesn't overwhelm the scallops. This sauce is my chile version of the classic French sauce *beurre blanc*. • **Yield: 4 servings**

Combine the lime juice, black pepper, wine, vinegar, shallots, and cilantro in a nonreactive bowl, add the scallops, and marinate for 15 minutes.

Drain the scallops and transfer the liquid to a saucepan. Bring the liquid to a boil and reduce the volume to one-third of the original amount. Reduce the heat to a simmer, whisk in the butter, and add the green chiles and turmeric. Keep this sauce warm.

Prepare the grill for direct cooking at medium heat. In a bowl, toss the scallops with the Big-Time Herb Rub. Grill the scallops for 2 minutes per side. Remove from the grill.

Place the pasta in the middle of each of 4 plates, add some of the sauce, and top with the grilled scallops.

Grilled Scallops Wrapped in Bacon

12 large sea scallops

12 slices of bacon

Jalapeño hot sauce, if desired

Just about anything wrapped in bacon and grilled is pretty good, but for some reason scallops are just perfect. I do them pretty traditionally except for the way I wrap them. The natural thought is to wrap them around the sides like a filet and secure with a toothpick on the side. This does make for a great-looking presentation, but if you cook it with the scallop down and the bacon around the sides the bacon doesn't get cooked properly and the exposed part of the scallop can get burned. I like to wrap them under the bottom and over the top with the toothpick in the front. That way, the bacon is on the direct heat so it gets cooked while it's protecting the tender flesh of the scallop. When the bacon is done, the scallop will be, too. • **Yield: 2 servings**

Prepare the fire for direct cooking at medium heat.

Wrap the scallops as described above. Place directly on the grill. Cook until the bacon is browned and cooked on the bottom. Flip and cook until the other side of the bacon is browned and done. The total cooking time should be about 12 minutes. Remove the scallops to a plate. Tent loosely with foil and let rest for about 3 minutes. Drizzle with the jalapeño hot sauce, if desired.

Hot Tuna Steaks

2 tuna steaks, 1½ inches thick

Big-Time Creole Barbecue Rub, to taste (see recipe, p. 13)

Grilled Southwestern Salsa (see recipe, p. 36)

I love tuna steaks. They have the taste of great seafood with a texture closer to meat. They don't need to be cooked very long—they should still be raw in the center or they are overcooked. • **Yield: 2 servings**

Prepare the grill for direct cooking at high heat.

Season the tuna steaks with the rub. Put the steaks directly on the hot grill. Cook about two minutes and check the bottom. If it's browned nicely flip the tuna steaks over. Grill another two minutes and check again. Once the outside is browned the steaks are done. It's that quick and they should be very rare inside.

Remove the tuna to a platter and serve immediately with the Grilled Southwestern Salsa spooned over the top or served on the side.

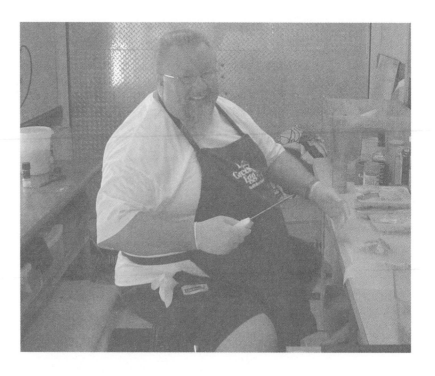

Grilled Citrus-Marinated Whole Red Snapper

1 large whole red snapper, 2–3 pounds, cleaned and scaled

Ray's Florida Marinade (see recipe, p. 30)

Tomatillo-Mango Salsa (see recipe, p. 33)

There is nothing quite as dramatic as a whole grilled fish. I love snapper and it's just the right size for a nice dinner for two. Check for doneness by pushing on the flesh. It should be just starting to flake. • **Yield: 2 servings**

Note: This recipe requires advance preparation.

The morning of the day you plan to cook, cut 3 to 4 slashes in each side of the fish about ½ inch deep. Put the fish in a big sealable plastic bag and pour the marinade over it. Toss to coat the fish. Seal the bag and put it in the refrigerator.

Prepare the grill for direct cooking at medium heat.

Remove the fish from the marinade and place directly on the grill. Cook for 8 to 10 minutes per side, turning occasionally, until the fish is lightly charred on the outside and fully cooked and tender.

Remove the fish to a platter and tent loosely with foil. Let rest 5 minutes. Serve with the salsa spooned over the top or on the side.

Big-Time Grilled Swordfish

½ cup rice wine vinegar

2 tablespoons soy sauce

2 tablespoons oyster sauce

2 tablespoons honey

2 teaspoons curry powder

2 teaspoons ground ginger

2 teaspoons granulated garlic

1 teaspoon wasabi powder

1 teaspoon ground cinnamon

4 swordfish steaks, about 10 ounces each

Big-Time Mango Barbecue Sauce (see recipe, p. 25)

This recipe is for my agent, Scott. He loves swordfish and so do I. • **Yield: 4 servings**

At least 1 hour before grilling, and up to 4 hours ahead, prepare the marinade by whisking together the vinegar, soy sauce, oyster sauce, honey, curry powder, ginger, garlic, wasabi, and cinnamon. Put the swordfish steaks in a glass baking dish and pour the marinade over them. Turn to coat and refrigerate. Turn occasionally while marinating.

Prepare the grill for direct cooking at high heat. When grilling fish, I always make sure to brush the grill well, and then brush it with oil, using a paper towel.

Take the swordfish steaks directly from the marinade to the grill. Grill for 2 minutes, then rotate the steaks 90 degrees. Grill another 2 minutes. Flip and repeat the process. The steaks should be done. Check for firmness.

Transfer to a platter and serve with my mango barbecue sauce on the side.

Grilled Tofu

1 block of firm tofu (1 pound)

¼ cup olive oil

Big-Time Herb Rub, to taste (see recipe, p. 12)

Fiery Avocado Corn Salsa with Four Chiles (see recipe, p. 35)

Here is proof that we can grill anything.
• **Yield: 2 servings**

Cut the tofu lengthwise into 4 slabs. Rub the slabs all over with olive oil. Season liberally with the herb rub.

Prepare the grill for direct cooking at medium heat. Be sure to preheat the grill and brush the grate clean so that the tofu won't stick. Lightly oil the grate just before putting the tofu on.

Put the slabs directly on the grate and cook 5 minutes. Flip and cook for 5 minutes more.

Remove the tofu to a platter and top with the salsa.

The Barbecue Log

Reminders About Great Grilling

▼▼

Ray's High-Falutin' Barbecue Dishes

Chef Ray Transforms Leftover Barbecued Favorites into Spectacular Main Course Meals

Beef

Smoked and grilled meats have always had a dual purpose in the kitchen. Of course, they're great straight off the fire, but the unique smokiness also lends itself beautifully to spicing up other dishes. We all know that smoked sausage, ham hocks, and bacon are used in almost all cuisines as a flavoring agent. This coupled with the leftovers from the large cuts we often cook inspired this chapter. I know many cooks who will always throw on an extra chicken or turkey breast with the sole purpose of using it later to make another dish. For many it's the highlight of the barbecue. A good home cook can use leftovers to create family favorites. My mom called leftovers "Musgo," as in everything in the refrigerator "must go." But what we didn't realize is that she always made an extra piece of corned beef because we like the "Musgo Hash" better than the first meal.

Grilled and smoked meat freezes well, too, so you can have a nice stash in the freezer and enjoy these dishes even if the grill doesn't get fired up. Some of them are very traditional barbecue dishes and others are very exotic. Barbecue is as good as or better than any other cuisine in the world, so I'm proud to serve it anywhere in any fashion.

K.C. Burnt Ends

Burnt ends are a great Kansas City story. The story I have heard about their origin is that when Mr. Bryant at the legendary Arthur Bryant's Barbeque restaurant was slicing the brisket, the "burnt ends" or crumbly edges

would fall off and accumulate next to the slicing machine right near the cafeteria-style line. If you wanted some, you just reached in and grabbed a handful to put on your plate.

These became very popular and now appear on every barbecue menu in Kansas City, as well as many others across the country. Needless to say, the crumbles next to the slicer are no longer enough to meet the demand, so burnt ends have seen a transformation. They are now typically the point cut of the brisket. Most good barbecue joints remove the point muscle before slicing the flat. This actually works out very well because the two muscles are very different. The flat is nicely shaped and great for slicing. The point has much more internal fat and does very well with some extra cooking, eventually becoming burnt ends. Here's my version.

▼▼▼

Bonesmokers Burnt Ends

3 large beef brisket points, pre-cooked as part of whole briskets

Barbecue rub of choice, to taste

2¼ cups barbecue sauce mixed with ¾ cup beef broth

1 aluminum foil pan

The points can be recooked immediately after they are separated from the flats, or they can be frozen for a burnt end cooking session at a later date. If you're lucky enough to have a good meat purveyor in Kansas City, you can get "points" all by themselves, but outside of K.C. I wouldn't even bother looking. For most of us, they are the by-product of cooking a whole brisket, and that is why the recipe is in this chapter. • **Yield 6–8 servings**

Trim as much fat as possible off the points. Apply the barbecue rub to all the exposed areas.

Smoke at 250°F for 2 hours. Remove and let rest for 15 minutes. Cube the meat and put it in an aluminum foil pan. Toss with enough of the barbecue sauce/broth mixture to cover. Return to the cooker for another thirty minutes.

Serve over white bread.

Game Day Smoky Chili

2–3 teaspoons vegetable oil

1 large green pepper, seeded and chopped

1 large onion, chopped

4 cloves garlic, crushed

1 28-ounce can diced tomatoes

4 chipotles in adobo sauce, chopped

2 cups water

One 12-ounce can beef consommé

¼ cup plus 1 tablespoon chili powder

1 tablespoon ground cumin

½ teaspoon salt

3 cups fully cooked barbecued beef brisket, cubed

One 15-ounce can pinto beans, drained (optional)

This combination of the smoked beef and the smoked chipotles makes a bold pot of chili. You can add a couple more of the chipotles if you like it fiery. I call for cubed brisket because that's what I like, but any beef will work, chopped, shredded, or even ground. • **Yield: 6–8 servings**

Warm the oil in a Dutch oven over medium heat. Add the green pepper and onion and cook until soft. Add the garlic and cook a few more minutes. Add the tomatoes, chipotles, water, consommé, chili powder, cumin, and salt. Mix well and bring to a simmer. Add the beef and return to a simmer. Cook for 1 hour. Add the beans and more water only if needed. Cook another 30 minutes.

Smoked Meat Loaf "Chorizo"

1 clove garlic

¼ cup hot red chile powder

½ teaspoon freshly ground black pepper

¼ teaspoon ground cloves

¼ teaspoon cinnamon

¼ teaspoon dried oregano

¼ teaspoon cumin

½ teaspoon salt

½ cup white vinegar

2 tablespoons olive oil

2 pounds (4 cups) Meat Loaf for Lisa Marie (see recipe, p. 65)

This Mexican sausage is often served with *huevos rancheros* for breakfast. Of course, I've untraditionalized it by using smoked meat loaf instead of pork, but hey, we're using up leftovers here. • **Yield: 8 servings**

Note: This recipe requires advance preparation.

Combine all the ingredients, except the meat loaf, and puree in a blender. In a bowl, knead this mixture into the meat loaf until it is thoroughly mixed together. Cover and refrigerate overnight. At this point the chorizo may be frozen.

To cook, crumble the meat loaf mixture into a skillet and fry it. Drain before serving.

Salpicón, Smokin' Style

2 pounds (about 4 cups) smoked brisket, shredded

1 cup diced white cheddar cheese

½ cup chopped cilantro

½ cup diced, seeded tomatoes

½ cup vegetable oil

½ cup wine vinegar

4 chipotle chiles in adobo, minced

Lettuce leaves

Diced avocado for garnish

Flour tortillas, for serving

This is a shredded beef salad popular in El Paso, Texas, but it obviously has Mexican roots. The cooks down there use brisket, but they boil it! Heavens forbid—let's use the smoked brisket. • **Yield: 8 servings**

Note: This recipe requires advance preparation.

In a bowl, toss the shredded brisket with the remaining ingredients, except the lettuce leaves, avocado, and tortillas. Cover and chill the mixture and allow it to marinate for a couple of hours or, preferably, overnight.

Line a platter with lettuce leaves, place the *salpicón* on the leaves, and garnish with the avocado. Serve with hot, buttered flour tortillas.

Thai Brisket Salad

1 head romaine lettuce, torn into pieces in a bowl

1 cucumber, peeled, seeded, and sliced crosswise

1 cup shredded carrots

¾ cup canned baby corn

¼ cup chopped mint leaves

3 serrano chiles, seeded and minced

2 cloves garlic, minced

¼ cup freshly squeezed lime juice

¼ cup soy sauce

¼ cup vegetable oil

2 tablespoons Asian fish sauce

2 teaspoons sugar

1 pound (2 cups) thinly sliced smoked brisket

I love the sharp and spicy taste of a Thai salad and the smokiness of brisket, so why not combine them? I've heard that Thai cooks don't use much lettuce, but they're not making this salad; I am! • **Yield: 4 servings**

In a bowl, combine the romaine, cucumber, carrots, baby corn, and mint.

In a nonreactive bowl, combine the chiles, garlic, lime juice, soy sauce, vegetable oil, fish sauce, and sugar and stir until the sugar is dissolved.

Place the brisket in the dressing and then remove it. Add the dressing to the bowl of romaine and mix well. Transfer the romaine to salad plates and arrange the brisket strips on top.

Brisket Burgers with Red Onion

1 pound (2 cups) ground
smoked brisket

1 cup unseasoned
breadcrumbs

1 egg, beaten

½ cup minced red onion

½ cup Big-Time Barbecue
Sauce (see recipe, p. 19), or
more to taste

1 tablespoon minced
Italian parsley

Salt and freshly ground
black pepper to taste

4 poppyseed buns

Sweet pickles for garnish

There is no possible way to have rare brisket burgers, so I'm going to make them appear to be rare with the colorful addition of my barbecue sauce. Use an old-fashioned meat grinder for the brisket or the meat-chopping blade of your food processor. Serve the brisket burgers with coleslaw or potato salad. • **Yield: 4 servings**

Prepare the grill for direct cooking at high heat.

In a bowl, combine all the ingredients, except the buns and pickles, and knead with your hands until they are very well mixed. Make 4 fairly thin patties. Grill the patties over high heat for about 2 minutes a side.

Place the patties on the buns and serve with the pickles.

Soft "Machaca" Avocado Tacos

8 corn tortillas

1 onion, finely chopped

1 tablespoon vegetable oil

2 poblano chiles, roasted, peeled, stems and seeds removed, chopped

2 medium tomatoes, chopped

2 teaspoons dried oregano

¼ teaspoon ground cumin

1 pound (2 cups) shredded smoked brisket, warmed in the oven

Diced avocado or guacamole

Chopped cilantro

In the Southwest, *machaca,* or shredded beef, is preferred over ground beef for the best tacos and burritos. It is brisket or beef roast that is boiled with chiles and then shredded. Since you have the extra smoked brisket, you can forget the boiling part. • **Yield: 4 servings**

Wrap the tortillas in a damp towel and aluminum foil and warm them in a 300°F oven for 15 minutes. In a saucepan, sauté the onion in the oil until soft. Add the chopped poblanos, tomatoes, oregano, and cumin, and sauté for 5 minutes. Drain the mixture through a sieve. Place the meat on the warmed tortillas, add the chile and tomato mixture, a little avocado or guacamole, and the chopped cilantro. Fold one side of the taco over the filling and serve.

French Dip Brisket Sandwiches

2 tablespoons butter

1 small onion, chopped

1 tablespoon flour

Two 10¾-ounce cans beef consommé

1½ pounds (3 cups) smoked brisket, sliced very thin

4 *bolillo* rolls or other long rolls, split

Big-Time Creole Barbecue Rub, to taste (see recipe, p. 13)

If you can find them, I recommend using Mexican *bolillo* rolls for these sandwiches, but any long roll will work. Serve the sandwiches with potato salad. • **Yield: 4 servings**

In a skillet, melt the butter and sauté the onion until soft. Add the flour and cook for 1 minute, stirring constantly. Whisk in the consommé gradually and simmer over low heat. Dip the meat into the consommé and place it on the rolls. Sprinkle with the Big-Time Creole Barbecue Rub and serve with small bowls of the consommé mixture on the side for dipping.

Tamale Pie with Brisket

2 tablespoons olive oil

1 medium onion, chopped

2 cloves garlic, minced

1 green bell pepper, chopped

1 pound (2 cups) ground smoked brisket

2 tablespoons red chile powder

Salt and freshly ground black pepper to taste

2 teaspoons minced fresh oregano

½ teaspoon ground cumin

One 28-ounce can crushed tomatoes, drained and chopped

1½ cups tomato sauce

1½ cups chopped black olives

1 cup frozen corn kernels

2 cups water

½ teaspoon salt

1 cup yellow cornmeal

1½ cups shredded cheddar cheese

This is a fun party pie that can be spiced up considerably by just adding more red chile powder. I suggest serving it with pinto beans and Spanish rice. • **Yield: 4–6 servings**

Preheat the oven to 375°F.

Heat the olive oil in a large skillet over medium heat. Add the onion, garlic, and bell pepper and sauté until the onion is soft, about 3 minutes. Add the brisket, red chile powder, salt and pepper, oregano, and cumin and cook for 1 minute. Add the tomatoes, tomato sauce, olives, and corn kernels and bring to a boil. Reduce the heat and simmer, uncovered, until thickened, about 20 minutes.

Transfer the mixture to a greased 9-inch-square baking dish.

In a saucepan, bring 2 cups of water to a boil. Add the ½ teaspoon salt and gradually whisk in the cornmeal. Cook, whisking constantly, until the mixture is thick and smooth, about 1 minute. Spread the cornmeal over the filling.

Bake for 30 minutes, then spread the cheese over the top and continue baking for 10 minutes. Remove from the oven and let stand for 10 minutes before serving.

Brisket Curry

1 tablespoon vegetable oil

1 onion, chopped

1½ pounds (3 cups) ground smoked brisket

2 teaspoons curry powder (imported from India preferred)

2 teaspoons ground cumin

1 teaspoon garlic powder

1 teaspoon ground coriander

1 teaspoon ground allspice

1 teaspoon ground ginger

Two 15-ounce cans tomato sauce

2 cups unflavored yogurt

Cilantro sprigs for garnish

I like to eat curry every once in a while, and the ground smoked brisket works well in this simple one. Serve the curry over hot rice with spicy chutney, finely chopped hard-boiled eggs, chopped pickles, and toasted coconut.

• **Yield: 6–8 servings**

Heat the oil in a large, heavy skillet over medium heat and sauté the onion until soft, about 3 minutes. Add the brisket, curry powder, cumin, garlic powder, coriander, allspice, ginger, and tomato sauce. Cover the mixture and simmer for 1 hour. Remove the mixture from the heat and stir in the yogurt. Garnish with cilantro and serve.

Smoked Pork Dip

½ pound (1 cup) minced smoked pork

1½ cups shredded Swiss cheese

8 ounces softened cream cheese

½ cup mayonnaise

3 green onions, chopped fine

1 tablespoon hot mustard of choice

½ cup finely chopped pecans

Dipping ingredients of your choice

Party hearty with this delicious dip. But what to dip into it? How 'bout your fingers? Just kidding—you can try carrot and celery sticks, small rye bread rounds, or toasted French bread rounds. • **Yield: 6 servings**

Preheat the oven to 375°F.

Combine all the ingredients, except the pecans and dipping ingredients, in a bowl, mix well, and transfer to a casserole or baking dish. Bake until the mixture is golden brown, about 20 minutes. Sprinkle with the pecans and serve on a platter with the dipping ingredients.

Smoked Pork Posole
with Chile Caribe

2 dried red New Mexican chiles, stems and seeds removed

8 ounces frozen posole corn or dry posole corn that has been soaked in water overnight

1 teaspoon garlic powder

1 medium onion, chopped

6 cups water

1 pound (2 cups) smoked pork, shredded or cut in ½-inch cubes

Chile Caribe (recipe follows), flour tortillas, minced cilantro, and chopped onion, for serving

This soup is served in the fall and winter in New Mexico and is usually made with pork loin. But since you have so much smoked pork left, that will work fine. The posole should be served in soup bowls accompanied by warm flour tortillas. Three additional bowls of garnishes should be provided: the chile caribe, freshly minced cilantro, and freshly chopped onion. Each guest can then adjust the pungency of the posole according to their own taste. • **Yield: 4 servings**

Combine the first five ingredients in a pot and boil at medium heat for about 3 hours or until the posole is tender, adding more water if necessary.

Add the pork and continue cooking for 30 minutes. The result should resemble a soup more than a stew. Remove the chile pods before serving. Serve with Chile Caribe and warm flour tortillas, minced cilantro, and chopped onion.

Chile Caribe

6 dried red New Mexican chiles, stems and seeds removed

1 teaspoon garlic powder

Boil the chile pods in 2 quarts of water for 15 minutes. Remove the pods, combine with the garlic powder, and puree in a blender. Transfer to a serving bowl and allow to cool.

Note: For really hot chile caribe, add dried red chile piquins, cayenne chiles, or chiles de arbol to the boiling New Mexican chiles.

Italian Smoked Sausage Hero Sandwich

1 round loaf Italian bread
(2 pounds), unsliced

2 tablespoons olive oil

1 large onion, chopped

2 cloves garlic, minced

1 green bell pepper, seeds
removed, chopped

1 cup tomato sauce

1 cup sliced black olives

3 pounds (6 cups)
crumbled smoked sausage

2 teaspoons Italian
seasoning

1½ cups shredded
mozzarella cheese

Strange but delicious is how I describe this sandwich, which you have to eat with a knife and fork.

• **Yield: 6–8 servings**

Slice the top off the loaf to reveal the soft inner bread. Remove most of the inner bread, leaving a 1-inch-thick shell.

Heat the olive oil in a large skillet over medium heat. Add the onion, garlic, and bell pepper and sauté for 5 minutes, stirring occasionally. Add the tomato sauce, olives, sausage, and Italian seasoning and cook for 2 minutes. Stir in the cheese.

Spoon the mixture into the bread shell, replace the top of the loaf, and wrap the loaf in aluminum foil. Place in the oven and bake for 30 minutes. Unwrap the loaf, remove the top, and separately slice the loaf and the top into wedges. Replace the top wedges and serve.

Sweet-and-Sour Smoked Pork

1 teaspoon sesame oil

1 red onion, chopped

1 pound (2 cups) smoked pork, cut into ½-inch cubes

1½ cups chicken stock

1 green bell pepper, seeds removed, cut into 2 by 1-inch strips

½ cup diagonally sliced celery, cut into ½-inch pieces

1 8-ounce can sliced pineapple, drained and cubed, juice reserved

2 teaspoons brown sugar

2 tablespoons cornstarch

1 tablespoon soy sauce

I know, I know, this is completely old-fashioned and nobody cooks it these days. Except for Dr. BBQ, who is reviving it. Yeah, that's it, reviving it with smoked pork. I even bought a wok, but you can cook it in a skillet if you don't have one. Serve this over hot white rice. • **Yield: 4–6 servings**

In a wok, heat the sesame oil over high heat and sauté the onion until soft, about 3 minutes. Add the pork, stock, bell pepper, and celery and cook for 6 or 7 minutes until the vegetables are cooked but slightly crisp. Add the pineapple and reduce the heat, stirring occasionally, for 1 minute. In a bowl, combine the brown sugar, cornstarch, and soy sauce. Add this to the wok and cook, stirring, until the mixture is thickened.

Creamy Smoked Sausage Fusilli Pasta

1 tablespoon olive oil

1½ pounds (3 cups) smoked sausage, removed from the casing and crumbled

1 teaspoon hot red chile powder

4 cloves garlic, chopped

½ cup white wine

One 28-ounce can crushed tomatoes

½ cup heavy cream

1 cup frozen green peas

¼ cup chopped basil

Salt and freshly ground black pepper to taste

1 pound cooked fusilli pasta, kept warm

Grated Pecorino Romano cheese

Damn, this is good. I find myself cooking this over and over again. At first I used penne pasta, but that's *sooo* ordinary. I looked up "fusilli" in an Italian dictionary and found out it means "springs," which is a perfect description. • **Yield: 6 servings**

In a large skillet, heat the olive oil and add the crumbled sausage, the red chile powder, and the garlic. Cook over medium heat for 3 minutes, stirring occasionally. Add the wine and stir well. Add the tomatoes, increase the heat and bring to a boil, then reduce the heat and simmer for 5 minutes, uncovered. Add the cream and the peas and simmer another 5 minutes, then remove from the heat. Add the basil and salt and pepper, then add the pasta and stir well. Serve topped with the Pecorino Romano cheese.

Smoked Pork Tacos with Spicy Green Chile Sauce

The Sauce

2 tablespoons olive oil

1 cup chopped onion

2 garlic cloves, minced

1¼ cups chopped green chiles

1 large tomato, peeled and chopped

½ teaspoon ground cumin

½ teaspoon ground coriander

1½ cups water

½ teaspoon salt

The Fillings

1 tablespoon olive oil

½ cup chopped onion

2 cloves garlic, minced

1 pound (2 cups) shredded smoked pork

½ teaspoon ground cumin

2 teaspoons chopped chives

½ cup finely minced sweet onion

½ pound good quality goat cheese, crumbled

¾ cup chopped cilantro

12 corn tortilla shells

These tacos are easy to make for a party, and each guest can customize their own taco. Keep the meat and green chile sauce warm in small chafing dishes, and the other ingredients can be lined up next to them on the table. The creamy flavor of the goat cheese contrasts nicely with the pungent green chile sauce. Make the chile sauce first, and while it is cooking assemble the rest of the ingredients. • **Yield: 2 cups sauce; 6 servings (2 tacos each)**

To make the sauce: Heat the oil in a small, heavy saucepan; add the onion and garlic and sauté them over medium heat until the onion is almost transparent, about 2 minutes. Stir in the remaining ingredients, bring the mixture to a boil, and then reduce the heat to a simmer. Simmer for 30 minutes. If after 30 minutes the mixture is not thick enough, increase the heat to a low boil, stirring while the mixture bubbles. Place the sauce in a chafing dish.

To make the fillings: Heat the oil in a large skillet, add the chopped onion and the garlic, and sauté the mixture until the onion is wilted, about 2 minutes. Combine the onion, pork, cumin, and chives in a chafing dish to keep warm.

Place the minced sweet onion, crumbled goat cheese, and cilantro in small bowls and set aside.

Set all of the ingredients out and let your diners dive in to enjoy the feast.

Spicy Smoked Pork–Fried Rice

2 tablespoons vegetable oil

½ cup finely chopped onion

3 fresh serrano or jalapeño chiles, seeds and stems removed, minced

2 cloves garlic, minced

½ pound (1 cup) finely minced smoked pork

4 cups cooked rice

2 eggs, beaten

1 tablespoon fish sauce (*nam pla*), available at Asian markets

2 teaspoons soy sauce

Salt and freshly ground white pepper to taste

¼ cup green onions, finely chopped

⅓ cup thinly sliced cucumber for garnish

3 tablespoons minced cilantro for garnish

This is one of my favorite Thai recipes and it is definitely a main dish. Don't worry about the fish sauce—it smells funny right out of the bottle, but when cooked into the food it tastes great. This is pretty spicy, but you can always cut back on the chiles. This is a very quick dish to make, taking less than 10 minutes—after the pork is cooked, of course. • **Yield: 4 servings**

Heat the oil in a wok or large skillet and fry the onion, chiles, and garlic for about 3 minutes over medium-high heat. Add the pork and fry, stirring, for 1 minute.

Stir in the rice and toss until it is coated with the mixture.

Make a deep well in the center of the rice mixture and add the beaten eggs. Allow them to cook, undisturbed, for about 20 seconds, then start to mix them throughout the rice, cooking for 1 minute.

Add the fish sauce, soy sauce, salt and pepper, and green onions and mix into the rice, cooking for an additional 2 minutes, stirring occasionally.

Place the rice on a heated platter and garnish with the cucumber and the cilantro.

Puttanesca Pork Pizza on the Grill

½ **pound (1 cup) shredded smoked pork**

One 12-inch, pre-baked pizza shell

3 cups chopped fresh tomatoes, such as cherry or plum

2 tablespoons chopped capers

2 tablespoons chopped olives

1 tablespoon chopped fresh basil

2 teaspoons crushed red chile pepper

1 cup grated Pecorino Romano cheese

Garlic salt

Olive oil

A double dose of outside cooking! First the pork is smoked, then it's returned to the grill on a pizza shell for a delicious, spicy treat. Serve it with a garden salad dressed Italian-style and a nice ale. Make sure that your grill is very clean before cooking the pizza. It's easy to cook pizza on a gas grill but more difficult on a charcoal grill because you have to move the coals to adjust the heat if your grill does not move up and down. Because of variations in grill temperatures, it's impossible to give an exact cooking time—you'll have to eyeball it. • **Yield: one 12-inch pizza**

Preheat the grill for direct cooking at medium heat.

Spread the pork over the pizza shell. Place the tomatoes over the pork, then sprinkle the capers, olives, basil, red chile, and cheese over the top. Shake a little garlic salt over the pizza and sprinkle some olive oil over all.

Place the pizza on the grill over medium heat. Close the grill top and cook for five minutes. Open the grill and check the bottom of the pizza to make sure it is not burning. If it is starting to burn, reduce the heat. Rotate the pizza 90 degrees. Repeat this process until the pizza is heated through and the cheese has completely melted.

Smoked Sausage–Stuffed Eggplant

2 medium eggplants

Salt

¼ cup olive oil

1 onion, chopped

2 cloves garlic, chopped

¾ pound (1½ cups) crumbled smoked sausage

2 tablespoons chopped Italian parsley

3 tablespoons chopped fresh mint, or 1 tablespoon dried

2 teaspoons dried thyme

1 teaspoon dried basil

One 8-ounce can tomato sauce

1 ripe tomato, peeled, seeded, and diced

¾ cup cooked rice

Parmesan cheese for garnish

This dish is a great way to eat eggplant because it's simple to make and a meal in itself. Feel free to sprinkle some hot sauce on it. Serve it with dilled carrots.

• **Yield: 4 servings**

Wash the eggplants, cut off the stem ends, and slice in half horizontally. Using a sharp knife, cut around the inside of each eggplant, leaving about a ¼-inch wall. Carefully scoop out the inside with a teaspoon and chop it. Salt both the hollowed-out eggplants and the chopped flesh and allow both to drain in a colander for an hour. Carefully rinse both in cold water before proceeding, taking care not to break the shell or pulverize the flesh.

Preheat the oven to 350°F.

Heat the olive oil in a large skillet and sauté the eggplant, the onion, and the garlic for 3 minutes, taking care not to burn the garlic. Then add the sausage, parsley, mint, thyme, basil, tomato sauce, tomato, and rice and stir. Fill the eggplant halves with the mixture, mounding the tops.

Arrange the halves in a baking dish. They should be close together, so they don't topple over. Bake for 40 minutes, or until the mixture is very hot and the sides of the eggplants are cooked. Sprinkle with grated Parmesan cheese.

Smoked Sausage Rustic Pie

2 pounds potatoes, peeled and cubed

3 tablespoons softened cream cheese

1 egg yolk

½ cup half-and-half

Salt and freshly ground black pepper, to taste

1 tablespoon olive oil

2 cloves garlic, minced

1 onion, chopped

1 carrot, peeled and diced

1 teaspoon minced fresh oregano

1 teaspoon minced fresh thyme

1½ pounds (3 cups) smoked sausage, cut into chunks

2 tablespoons butter

2 tablespoons flour

1 cup beef stock

½ cup frozen peas

2 teaspoons red chile powder

2 teaspoons chopped Italian parsley for garnish

Here's my take on the classic shepherd's pie that Mom used to make before Marie Callender showed up, using any kind of smoked sausage—taken out of the casing, of course. Since the pie has vegetables in it, serve it with bread and a fruit salad. • **Yield: 6 servings**

In a large pot, boil the potatoes until they can be easily pierced by a fork, about 10 to 12 minutes. Drain them and place them in a bowl. In another bowl, combine the cream cheese, the egg yolk, and the half-and-half and mix well. Pour this mixture into the potatoes and mash them until smooth. Add salt and pepper to taste and stir.

Heat the olive oil in a large skillet over medium heat and sauté the garlic, onion, and carrot for 5 minutes, stirring occasionally. Add the oregano, thyme, and sausage and cook for 2 minutes, stirring often. In another skillet over medium heat, add the butter. When melted, add the flour and cook, stirring, for about 2 minutes. Add the beef stock and continue stirring to make a gravy (about 1 minute). Add the gravy to the sausage and vegetables and mix in the peas.

Preheat the broiler. Place the sausage and vegetable mixture in a casserole dish and spread the potatoes over it. Sprinkle the red chile powder over the potatoes. Broil about 8 inches from the heat until the potatoes are well browned. Remove the dish from the oven, garnish with the parsley, and serve.

▼▼▼

Road Apples (Smoked Chicken–Stuffed Tomatoes)

8 medium tomatoes

Salt and freshly ground black pepper, to taste

1 pound (2 cups) chopped smoked chicken

¼ cup prepared pesto

8 slices provolone cheese

This is a recipe I came up with for grill demonstrations. They cook slowly and make the grill look real pretty. They eat pretty well, too. • **Yield: 6–8 servings**

Prepare the tomatoes by cutting the tops off as if you were making a jack-o'-lantern. Then scoop out the seeds and loose flesh from the inside with a spoon. Be careful not to puncture the bottom. Salt and pepper the insides of the tomatoes and set aside.

Preheat the grill for indirect cooking at medium heat.

In a bowl, toss the chicken with enough pesto to coat it liberally. Divide the filling up among the tomatoes and fill them. Place the stuffed tomatoes on a medium indirect grill and cook for about 25 minutes. (Don't cook at a high temperature or the tomatoes will split.) Top each Road Apple with a slice of provolone cheese and continue cooking until the cheese is melted and the temperature of the chicken reaches 160°F.

Spicy Smoked Chicken Frittata

2 tablespoons butter

1 medium onion, chopped

Salt and freshly ground black pepper, to taste

8 eggs

¼ cup half-and-half

½ pound (1 cup) shredded smoked chicken

1 tablespoon minced Italian parsley

¼ cup chopped green chile

1 cup grated cheddar cheese

Fresh fruit for garnish, such as sliced strawberries or melon balls

I've always maintained that frittatas are for people like me who always screw up omelettes. This one is incredibly easy to make and you don't have to flip it. It can be made with any shredded smoked meat. • **Yield: 6 servings**

Preheat the broiler. Place a rack 8 inches from the broiler.

Melt the butter in a medium oven-proof skillet and sauté the onion with salt and pepper to taste until the onion is soft, about 5 minutes. While the onion is cooking, whisk together the eggs and half-and-half in a bowl. To the eggs, add the onion, smoked chicken, parsley, green chile, and cheese.

Pour the frittata mixture into the same hot skillet, and cook, stirring gently for the first minute. Let the mixture cook until the bottom is set, about 4 minutes. Place the skillet in the oven and broil until it is brown and set, 4 to 5 minutes, taking care not to overcook. Remove from the oven and let stand for 5 minutes. Cut into wedges and serve with the fruit.

Smoked Sopa de Lima

2 teaspoons vegetable oil

1 New Mexican green chile, roasted, peeled, seeds and stem removed, chopped (or use 1 small can of chopped green chile)

⅓ cup chopped onion

4 cups chicken broth

½ pound (1 cup) shredded smoked chicken

Salt, to taste

1 tomato, chopped

Juice of 1 lime

4 large lime slices for garnish

16 tortilla chips for garnish

Translated, this is a simple but delicious lime and tortilla soup. Using smoked chicken (usually white meat) adds depth to the flavor. • **Yield: 4 servings**

Heat the oil in a saucepan and sauté the chile and onion until the onion is soft but not browned. Add the chicken broth, chicken, and salt to taste, cover, and simmer 20 minutes. Add the tomato and simmer 5 minutes longer. Stir in the lime juice, taste, and add more if needed. Serve in bowls garnished with one lime slice and with 4 tortilla chips floating on top of the soup.

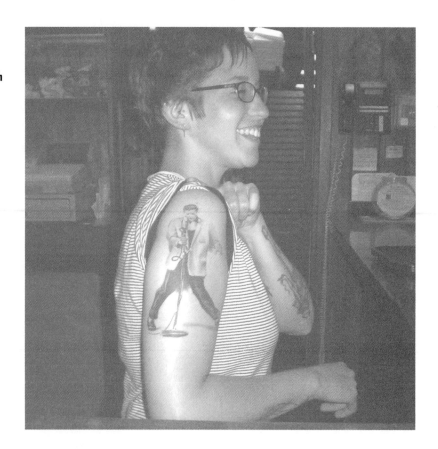

Smoked Chicken Cobb Salad

8 slices bacon, chopped

4 packed cups cut-up romaine lettuce

Juice of 2 lemons

2 avocados, peeled and pits removed

2 ripe tomatoes, peeled, seeded, and chopped

1 red onion, chopped

2 hard-boiled eggs, chopped

¾ pound (1½ cups) chopped smoked chicken

2 cups crumbled blue cheese

I wondered why this salad was named Cobb. It has no corn in it and I doubt that it was named after an old-time baseball player. I looked it up and found that it was named after Bob Cobb, who owned the Brown Derby Restaurant in Los Angeles and invented the recipe in 1945. This is one of those full-meal salads, so serve it with some bread and you're all set. • **Yield: 4 servings**

Brown the bacon in a skillet until crisp. Remove and reserve. In a large bowl, toss the romaine with the lemon juice. Arrange the romaine on a platter. Arrange in rows on top of the romaine: bacon, avocados, tomatoes, onion, eggs, chicken, and blue cheese. Serve it to your guests, making sure each person gets some of every ingredient.

Smoked Turkey Salad with Bacon and Jicama

½ pound bacon, chopped

¼ cup Dijon mustard

1 tablespoon sugar

½ teaspoon freshly ground black pepper

1 pound (2 cups) chopped smoked turkey

½ cup shredded pepper jack cheese

3 hard-boiled eggs, sliced

¼ jicama tuber, peeled and diced

3 medium tomatoes, peeled and chopped

1 small head romaine lettuce, chopped

½ cup chopped green onion

1 large red onion, cut into rings

Here's another Cobb variation made with smoked turkey, a salad so bold that it can be a main dish. The question is: What side dishes do you serve with it? How about a spicy soup and some crusty French bread? Works for me. If you can't find jicama, substitute water chestnuts.

• **Yield: 4 servings**

Sauté the bacon in a pan over medium heat until crisp. Remove the bacon and drain on paper towels, leaving the fat in the pan. Add the mustard, sugar, and pepper to the bacon fat and stir well. Remove the dressing to a small bowl.

In a large bowl, mix the bacon, turkey, cheese, eggs, jicama, tomatoes, lettuce, and green onion. Mix well. Add the dressing mixture and toss well. Divide the salad onto 4 salad plates and top with the onion rings.

Penne Pasta with Smoked Chicken

2 tablespoons olive oil

1 tablespoon butter

3 cloves garlic, chopped

1 small onion, chopped

2 tablespoons flour

½ cup white wine

Juice of 1 lemon

1 cup chicken stock

3 tablespoons capers

1 teaspoon minced fresh oregano

⅓ cup finely chopped Italian parsley

1 pound (2 cups) chopped smoked chicken

1 pound cooked penne pasta, kept warm

Salt and freshly ground black pepper, to taste

Minced green onion tops for garnish

Low-carb, schmo-carb. I've stolen some flavors from veal piccata for this simple pasta meal to use up your extra smoked chicken. Use both white and dark meat for this dish, and serve it with a tomato and avocado salad.

• **Yield: 4 servings**

Heat the olive oil with the butter in a large saucepan. Add the garlic and onion and sauté until soft, about 2 minutes. Add the flour to thicken and cook over medium heat for 2 minutes, stirring constantly. Whisk in the wine and cook for 1 minute, then whisk in the lemon juice and chicken stock. Add the capers, oregano, and parsley and heat for 1 minute. Add the chicken and cook for 2 minutes, stirring occasionally. In a bowl, combine the pasta and the sauce and toss well. Add salt and pepper to taste and serve garnished with the green onion tops.

Herbed Lasagna with Smoked Turkey

2 tablespoons olive oil

1 medium onion, finely chopped

1 pound (3 cups) ground smoked turkey

2 teaspoons minced Italian parsley

2 teaspoons minced fresh oregano

2 teaspoons minced fresh thyme

Salt and freshly ground black pepper, to taste

½ cup butter

½ cup flour

2 cups chicken stock

1¼ cups milk

¾ cup dry white wine

1¼ cups freshly grated Parmesan cheese

12 cooked lasagna noodles (or buy no-cook lasagna noodles at the supermarket)

2 cups cottage cheese

Sprigs of Italian parsley for garnish

Imagine, lasagna without tomatoes. I know it's weird, but I sure like the way this dish turned out—the smokiness of the turkey really stands out. Serve this with buttered beets. • **Yield: 8 servings**

Preheat the oven to 350°F.

In a large skillet over medium heat, add the olive oil and onion and sauté until the onion is soft, about 3 minutes. Add the turkey, parsley, oregano, thyme, and salt and pepper and cook, stirring occasionally, for 2 minutes. Remove from the heat.

In a saucepan, melt the butter over medium heat. Add the flour and, using a whisk, stir while cooking for 2 minutes, taking care not to brown the flour. Add the chicken stock, milk, and wine and bring to a boil, whisking the mixture until it is thick. Reduce the heat and simmer for 3 minutes, whisking often. Add 1 cup of Parmesan cheese and stir. Remove from the heat.

Spread a little of this sauce over the bottom of a 9 by 13-inch baking dish. Place a single layer of 4 overlapping lasagna noodles in the dish and cover with half of the turkey mixture. Spoon on 1 cup of cottage cheese and then one-third of the sauce. Repeat that sequence and top with the remaining noodles and the last of the sauce. Top with the remaining ¼ cup of Parmesan cheese.

Bake for about 50 minutes, or until the top is lightly browned. Remove from the oven and let stand for 10 minutes before serving, garnished with the parsley.

Smoked Turkey Picadillo

3 tablespoons olive oil

5 cloves garlic, minced

3 cups chopped onion

¾ pound (1½ cups) chopped green or red bell pepper

2 pounds (4 cups) chopped smoked turkey

3 cups tomato sauce

¼ cup tomato paste

1 teaspoon ground cumin

1½ cups sliced green olives

6 ounces (½ bottle) beer, not dark (drink the rest)

¼ cup chopped cilantro

¼ teaspoon dried thyme

1 tablespoon red wine vinegar

½ cup raisins

Picadillo is a Cuban favorite that's usually made with pork, but of course I've switched ingredients. It is often served over rice, or just by itself with a fried egg on top. I like it for breakfast or brunch. • **Yield: 8 servings**

Heat the olive oil in a large, heavy skillet, and add the garlic, onion, and bell pepper and sauté on high heat for 2 minutes, or until they are soft. Add the smoked turkey, tomato sauce, tomato paste, cumin, olives, beer, cilantro, thyme, wine vinegar, and raisins. Cover and simmer for 30 minutes while you polish off the remaining beer, stirring frequently.

Green Chile Enchiladas with Smoked Chicken

1 pound (2 cups) of shredded smoked chicken

One 8-ounce package cream cheese, softened

2 cups half-and-half

½ cup chicken stock

¾ cup finely chopped onion

1 cup chopped green chiles

2 fresh serrano chiles, seeds and stems removed, minced

1 jar commercial tomatillo sauce or green enchilada sauce

2 tablespoons minced cilantro

1 egg

Salt and freshly ground black pepper, to taste

3 tablespoons vegetable oil

12 corn tortillas

⅓ cup freshly grated Parmesan cheese

I love these enchiladas and serve them with refried black beans and Spanish rice. This version has a medium heat level, but of course you can spice them up by adding more serrano chiles, cayenne, or even hot sauce. I use the La Victoria brand of tomatillo sauce. • **Yield: 6 servings**

Preheat the oven to 350°F.

In a bowl, combine the chicken with the cream cheese, ½ cup of the half-and-half, ¼ cup of the chicken stock, and the onion. Using a wooden spoon, thoroughly mix until the mixture is smooth. Divide the chicken mixture into 12 portions.

In a blender, combine the green chiles, serrano chiles, tomatillo sauce, cilantro, and the remaining chicken stock. Blend at high speed until the mixture becomes a smooth puree. Add the remaining 1½ cups half-and-half, the egg, and the salt and pepper and blend for 10 seconds more. Pour the mixture into a shallow bowl.

Heat the oil in a small skillet until quite hot. Using tongs, dip each tortilla into the chile sauce and then fry it in the oil for about 10 seconds per side. Drain on paper towels. Place a portion of the chicken mixture on each tortilla, roll it up, and place in a shallow casserole dish. When the 12 rolled-up tortillas are in a single layer in the casserole dish, pour the sauce over them. Top with the Parmesan cheese. Place the dish in the oven and bake for 20 to 25 minutes.

Smoked Turkey Risotto with Apple

1 tablespoon olive oil

4 tablespoons butter

½ cup chopped onion

2 cups Arborio rice

6 cups chicken stock, heated until boiling and kept hot

¾ pound (1½ cups) smoked turkey, cut into short, thin strips

2 cups finely chopped apple

⅓ cup grated Parmesan cheese

¼ cup heavy cream

2 tablespoons chopped Italian parsley

Risotto is usually served as a side dish, but when I add the smoked turkey and chopped apple to it, suddenly it's a main dish. Serve this with tomato salad and a dry white wine. Well, you can serve it that way—I'm having a beer! • **Yield: 6 servings**

In a large saucepan, heat the olive oil and 2 tablespoons of the butter, add the onion, and sauté until it is soft but not browned. Add the rice and sauté for 1 minute, stirring constantly. Add the stock in half-cup increments, stirring constantly. Regulate the heat and your stirring so that the stock is absorbed steadily before adding the next half cup. When the rice has absorbed all the stock (it takes about 20 minutes) stir in the turkey and the apple and cook for 10 minutes on low heat. Remove the saucepan from the heat and stir in the cheese, heavy cream, parsley, and the remaining butter. Serve immediately.

Cayenned Smoked Salmon Dip

1 teaspoon cayenne pepper

1 teaspoon Dijon-style mustard

One 8-ounce package cream cheese

¼ cup white wine

¼ cup grated onion

¼ cup minced Italian parsley

½ pound (1 cup) minced smoked salmon

Whenever I want to stun my friends on the cookoff circuit, I make this dip, which can be served with a variety of carb-laden crackers, or vegetables such as sliced carrots, bell peppers, jicama, or celery. I have never in my life made a toast point, but I hear that they can be dipped. • **Yield: 2 cups**

In a saucepan, combine all the ingredients, except the salmon, and simmer over low heat until thoroughly heated. Remove from the heat, stir in the salmon, and serve.

Smoked Salmon Pâté

¼ cup chopped green chiles

1 pound (2 cups) smoked salmon

3 hard-boiled eggs, chopped

¼ cup chopped green onion

¼ cup chopped Italian parsley

¼ cup chopped toasted almonds

2 tablespoons brandy

1 tablespoon butter

¼ cup mayonnaise

While we're on the subject of smoked salmon dips, I figured that a smoked pâté might get the attention of the gourmands out there who need the flavor of smoke in their Frenchified appetizers. So after researching in some ancient Julia Child cookbooks, I came up with this concoction. I spiced it up a bit just for effect. Do not serve this with saltine crackers—choose some fancy imported ones. • **Yield: 3 cups**

Place all the ingredients in a food processor and puree until smooth. Place the mixture in a mold and refrigerate for a couple of hours before serving.

Smoked Salmon Salad with Dill

1½ pounds (3 cups) chopped smoked salmon, free from any bones

1 red bell pepper, seeds and stem removed, finely chopped

½ cup finely chopped onion

2 tablespoons minced dill

1 tablespoon minced Italian parsley

1 tablespoon capers

2 tablespoons wine vinegar

2 tablespoons olive oil

Salt and freshly ground black pepper, to taste

Here's a quick and easy salad you can whip up while watching a fishing show on TV. Variations include adding a small amount of chopped tomato and/or diced celery. If you want to add some habanero hot sauce to spice it up, be my guest. • **Yield: 4 servings**

Combine all ingredients in a bowl and mix well.

Spinach and Smoked Salmon Soup

2 tablespoons butter

1 medium onion, diced

½ cup chopped celery

1 clove garlic, minced

1 quart chicken stock

1 cup unsweetened coconut milk

½ pound smoked ham, finely chopped

2½ cups washed, coarsely chopped, firmly packed spinach leaves

1 cup sliced okra

1 teaspoon dried thyme

¼ teaspoon freshly ground black pepper

1 habanero chile, seeds and stems removed, minced

1 pound (2 cups) shredded smoked salmon

1 tablespoon melted butter (optional)

Salt, to taste

This soup is based on one from Trinidad that uses a green called callaloo and crabmeat. It is downright delicious, quite spicy, and has a very nice color.

• **Yield 8–10 servings**

Heat the butter in a large saucepan and sauté the onion, celery, and garlic for 2 or 3 minutes. Add the chicken stock, coconut milk, and ham and bring to a boil. Add the spinach, okra, thyme, black pepper, and habanero chile. Reduce the heat to a simmer and cook, covered, for about 50 minutes, stirring occasionally, until the okra is thoroughly cooked.

Whisk the soup until very smooth, or puree it in small batches in a blender. Add the smoked salmon and heat thoroughly. Add the butter, swizzled over the top, if desired, and taste for salt before adding any.

Deviled Smoked Salmon

4 tablespoons butter

2 tablespoons flour

½ cup milk

1 pound (2 cups) shredded smoked salmon

½ teaspoon prepared mustard

2 teaspoons minced Italian parsley

1 teaspoon Worcestershire sauce

1 teaspoon hot sauce of choice

Salt and freshly ground black pepper, to taste

1 egg, slightly beaten

2 tablespoons finely crushed breadcrumbs

Minced chives for garnish

This recipe is a take on deviled crabs. I use a casserole dish because I keep forgetting to buy ramekins. Serve this with hash-browned potatoes and dilled green beans. • **Yield: 4 servings**

Preheat the oven to 350°F.

In a skillet, melt 2 tablespoons of the butter over low heat and add the flour slowly, stirring constantly to make a roux. Mash out any lumps. Add the milk slowly, stirring to make a smooth sauce. Increase the heat to medium and cook, stirring occasionally, for about 8 minutes.

Add the salmon, mustard, parsley, Worcestershire, hot sauce, salt, and pepper and cook for 5 minutes, stirring often. Add the egg, stir, and remove the skillet from the heat.

In a small pan, melt the remaining 2 tablespoons of butter, add the breadcrumbs, and stir to coat them.

Place the salmon mixture in a small casserole dish, top with the breadcrumbs, and bake for 30 minutes. Remove from the oven and let sit for five minutes. Serve topped with the chives.

Paradise Ridge Stuffed Lobster or Lobster Fettuccine

A Recipe from Barbecue All Star Buddy Babb

Paradise Ridge Catering is a family of great cooks and even better folks from Nashville. I first met them at the Amazin' Blazin' BBQ Cookoff in Lebanon, Tennessee, and we have since become very good friends. Buddy gave me some of this dish one day and it was obvious that he had a winner. No surprise that he took first that day and a few other days in the Anything But category. Buddy Babb is a true Southern gentleman and I am proud to have this recipe in my book. There is a little more to the story about the Babb family. In 2000 they were crowned the World Barbecue Champions, so this is one of my Barbecue All Star Recipes.

- **Yield: 6 servings**

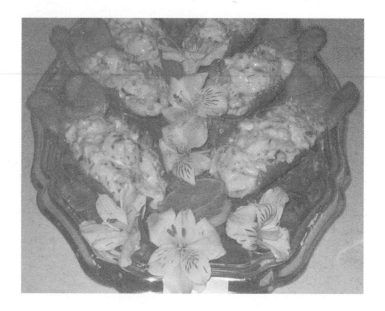

6 wooden skewers, soaked in water for 1 hour

Six 5-ounce rock lobster tails

¼ cup butter

One 8-ounce jar button mushrooms

1 clove garlic, smashed

¼ cup minced Italian parsley and baby spinach, mixed

⅓ cup flour

One 10¾-ounce can chicken broth

1 cup light cream

Salt and freshly ground black pepper, to taste

Light sprinkle cayenne pepper at finish—very light

1 pound fettuccine, cooked per package directions (optional)

Preheat the grill for direct cooking at medium heat.

Place wooden skewers through lobster tails to prevent curling. Grill them for about 4 or 5 minutes on each side, taking care not to let the tails or shells burn. Remove and drop them in ice water to stop the cooking process. The lobster will turn orange on a grill the same as if it was dropped in hot water.

Clip the ribs on the tails with kitchen shears and remove the membrane on the bottom side. Pull out the meat in one piece. Reserve the lobster shells.

In a skillet, melt the butter and sauté the mushrooms, garlic, parsley and spinach until wilted. Stir in the flour. Add the broth and cream and heat over low heat until the sauce thickens, constantly stirring. Dice the lobster meat, add it, and continue stirring. Add salt and pepper.

When the mixture is thick, spoon it back into the lobster shells. Sprinkle *every so slightly* with cayenne. Enjoy while warm, or serve over fettuccine.

Pecan-Encrusted Smoked Salmon Cakes with Lime-Dill Sauce

The Lime-Dill Sauce

¼ cup milk

1 cup mayonnaise

1 tablespoon minced fresh dill

1 tablespoon minced Italian parsley

1 tablespoon grated lime zest

2 teaspoons freshly squeezed lime juice

1 clove garlic, minced

The Smoked Salmon Cakes

1 pound (2 cups) shredded smoked salmon

½ cup breadcrumbs

¼ cup cracker crumbs

1 tablespoon hot mustard of choice

1 teaspoon lime zest

Salt and freshly ground black pepper, to taste

1 large egg, beaten

1 cup finely chopped pecans

¼ cup vegetable oil

Lime wedges for garnish

You can substitute other nuts in this recipe, like pistachios or macadamias. Serve the cakes with coleslaw and boiled new potatoes topped with butter and chopped parsley. Use a chile-infused mustard to heat the cakes up a bit. • **Yield: 4 servings**

Note: This recipe requires advance preparation.

To make the sauce: Combine all the ingredients in a bowl and mix well. Refrigerate until ready to use.

To make the cakes: In a bowl, combine the salmon, breadcrumbs, cracker crumbs, mustard, lime zest, and salt and pepper to taste. Add the egg and mix.

With your hands, make 8 cakes out of the mixture. Place the pecans on a plate and carefully press each side of the cakes into them. Put the encrusted cakes on a plate, cover with plastic wrap, and refrigerate 3 hours.

Heat the oil in a skillet over medium heat. Add the cakes in batches and fry them for about 2½ minutes a side, turning once. Drain the cakes on paper towels and serve with the lime wedges and the Lime-Dill Sauce on the side.

Summer Smoked Salmon Pasta

2 tablespoons olive oil

3 shallots, finely chopped

1 clove garlic, minced

½ teaspoon hot red chile flakes

4 large ripe tomatoes, seeded and chopped

½ cup bottled clam juice

½ cup water

1 pound (2 cups) shredded smoked salmon

1 tablespoon minced cilantro

Salt and freshly ground black pepper, to taste

1 pound cooked bowtie pasta, kept warm

¼ cup minced green onion

I'm always smoking during the summer and I don't mean cigarettes. So I've always got some leftovers—no, make that previously smoked salmon—in the freezer. And when I feel like having a light summer pasta, I cook up some of this and serve it with fresh garden vegetables. There's no cheese topping in this recipe, but I love Parmesan so much that I usually grate some of it over the pasta. • **Yield: 4 servings**

Heat the olive oil in a large skillet over medium heat and sauté the shallots and garlic until soft, about 4 minutes, stirring often. Add the chile flakes and tomatoes and cook for 5 minutes, stirring occasionally. Add the clam juice and water, reduce the heat, and simmer uncovered until the mixture is slightly thickened, about 10 minutes. Stir in the salmon and cilantro and continue to cook for 5 minutes. Add salt and pepper to taste. Place the pasta in a bowl, add the sauce, and top with the minced green onion.

Peppers Stuffed with Smoked Venison

The Peppers and Filling

3 tablespoons olive oil

1 dried red New Mexican chile, crumbled with seeds

1 medium yellow onion, chopped

½ cup chopped mushrooms

1 pound (2 cups) smoked venison, chopped fine

½ teaspoon dried sage

½ teaspoon dried rosemary

½ teaspoon dried mint

2 tablespoons chopped pimiento chile

½ cup beer

2 eggs, lightly whipped

¼ cup dry breadcrumbs

½ teaspoon salt (optional)

4 large whole green (or red) bell peppers

1 cup chicken broth

The Sauce

3 tablespoons olive oil

½ cup chopped scallion

1 clove garlic, minced

4 tomatoes, diced

¼ cup chopped Italian parsley

½ cup dry red wine

Here's an interesting twist on stuffed peppers using smoked venison. Any game—and any smoked meat—will work in this recipe. Serve with oven-baked french fries and green beans. • **Yield: 4 servings**

To make the filling: Heat a Dutch oven until a drop of water quickly sizzles away. Add the olive oil, red chile, onion, and mushrooms; sauté until the onions are limp. Add the venison and cook for 2 minutes.

In a bowl, blend the sage, rosemary, mint, pimiento, beer, eggs, breadcrumbs, and salt, if desired. Add the venison mixture to the bowl and blend to make the filling.

Cut around the pepper stems and remove the seeds; save the stems. Spoon in the filling, taking care not to break the peppers; replace the stems. Reheat the Dutch oven, without cleaning it, and add the chicken broth. Bring it to a simmer. Place the stuffed peppers, stems up, in the broth, cover the Dutch oven, and steam the peppers for 30 minutes. Remove the peppers to a warm plate, keep them upright, and cover with foil to retain the heat.

To make the sauce: Add the olive oil, scallion, garlic, tomatoes, parsley, and wine to the Dutch oven. Bring the sauce to a simmer and cook for 10 minutes with the lid off. Discard the stems from the peppers and serve them covered with the sauce.

The Barbecue Log

Reminders About How to Make Those
High-Falutin' Dishes Work Their Magic

▼▼▼

Side-Steppin'

Side Dishes and Desserts
from Ray's Kitchen

The dishes we serve with barbecue are as important as the barbecue itself. Every barbecue cook knows that the proper accompaniments can make their barbecue meal perfect, and there are some longstanding traditions that should not be ignored in any discussion of barbecue. The list is pretty short and it has a strong Southern influence.

It would be hard to imagine barbecue without beans. Many of us use canned baked beans and put our own spin on them by adding onions, peppers, spices, sweeteners, and smoked meat or bacon. I have included my version and it's pretty simple. My friends in Texas won't hear of using the canned variety. Dried pinto beans are their choice, and they take them very seriously. I've also included white beans, which are very popular in Tennessee and are served with cornbread. It's not a common barbecue side, but I don't think anyone would mind combining the two. There is even a barbecue cookoff in Tennessee where the Friday night contest includes White Beans and Cornbread as a category.

Potato salad in all its incarnations is a staple at backyard barbecues all over the country. Most folks have a serious attachment to the version made by their mom or a favorite aunt. That's what barbecue is all about. The food is very important, but so is the time spent with friends and family. Sharing those great old family recipes is just as good as it gets.

Coleslaw also has many lives in the world of barbecue. It can be based on vinegar, mustard, mayonnaise, or even barbecue sauce. It can be made with or without sugar, onions, carrots, red cabbage, and bell peppers. There is even something called broccoli slaw. Coleslaw can be a side dish or a condiment. In the Southeast you may very well get some slaw right on your pulled pork sandwich. Many people just can't eat pulled pork any other way.

Grilled vegetables have become very popular and they are certainly very good. Many variations of potatoes work well grilled, too.

The common thread among barbecue side dishes is that they are not required to be eaten immediately upon preparation. It's all sort of leisure food. I guess that's why these dishes fit so well with barbecue.

Last, but certainly not least, are desserts. Cobblers, pecan pie, banana pudding, and bread pudding are all as traditional as the barbecue itself. There is a great Southern influence with these desserts and, much like the meats, they are created using humble ingredients.

By the way, you'll notice that many of these dishes are to be prepared in the kitchen. I love my grills and smokers, but you just can't cook *everything* on them. You'll notice that many of the Barbecue All Star recipes appear here. These champions are very generous, but most keep their hardcore barbecue secrets to themselves. They are proud to share the side dish recipes, though, and I have been lucky enough to get some great ones.

▼▼

Barbecue Beans

One 55-ounce can Bush Beans

1 cup brown sugar

½ cup Thick and Sticky Barbecue Sauce (see recipe, p. 21)

1 tablespoon freshly ground black pepper

1 tablespoon Big-Time Barbecue Rub (see recipe, p. 9)

1 tablespoon hot sauce of choice

½ pound (1 cup) cooked pork butt or beef brisket (optional)

These are my typical barbecue beans, made with a can of baked beans as a base. I call these Barbecue Beans because they are so typical of what people serve alongside their grilled and smoked foods. It's easy to do and can be personalized in many ways. My recipe is very simple. I like them without chunks of veggies—but many would disagree. Feel free to customize this one in any way. Some popular items added to this type of bean dish are bell peppers, onions, bacon, hot chiles, molasses, honey, and Liquid Smoke. Barbecue Beans can be cooked in the barbecue or the oven. The cooker gives them another layer of flavor because of the smoke. Just adjust the time to the temperature you're cooking at. • **Yield: 8–10 servings**

Preheat the oven to 350°F. Pour a little of the liquid off the top of the can and discard. Pour the beans and the remaining liquid into a foil pan or a casserole dish. Add all the remaining ingredients and mix well. Put the beans in the oven for about 1 hour, or in the cooker for about 2 hours. If you are making them in the cooker, be sure they are warmed through.

Real Pinto Beans

1 pound dried pinto beans

¼ pound salt pork, cut in 1-inch cubes

One 15-ounce can tomatoes

4 cloves garlic, crushed

1 large onion, chopped

3 tablespoons chili powder

1 teaspoon cumin

3 chipotles in adobo sauce, chopped

1 tablespoon Worcestershire sauce

Salt, to taste

Many cooks wouldn't consider using canned beans. They feel that dried pinto beans are the best and always make the effort to cook them. Cooking dried beans does take a little more time, but they are very good and definitely different. I like them very much. Pinto beans are a common category at barbecue cookoffs in Texas. My friends from Texas tell me that chunks of vegetables and broken beans are not desirable for those contests. They even have a swirling technique that they use to avoid stirring with a spoon, which could break some of the beans. I think some chunks are just fine for serving to my friends and family. These can be cooked in the smoker or grill instead of on the stove. Adjust the time and cook until the beans are tender. • **Yield: 6–8 servings**

Note: This recipe requires advance preparation.

Soak the beans overnight in a big bowl covered with water.

When you're ready to cook, drain the beans and put them in a Dutch oven. Cover with at least an inch of fresh water. Stir in all the other ingredients and bring to a simmer over medium heat. Reduce the heat and continue to simmer for at least 2 hours, until the beans are tender. Add more water as needed. Check for salt and add some at the end, if needed.

Yankee White Beans

½ **pound thick-sliced bacon**

1 medium onion, chopped

1 or 2 chicken thighs, skinned, boned, and chopped

4 cloves garlic, chopped

1 jalapeño, seeds and stem removed, chopped fine

1 teaspoon salt

1 tablespoon freshly ground black pepper

1 pound Great Northern beans

Three 10¾-ounce cans chicken broth

1 can water

Cornbread, for serving

I went to a barbecue cookoff in middle Tennessee where they have a White Beans and Cornbread category on Friday night. Many cookoffs will do this, always using a locally popular dish, and white beans and cornbread are sure popular around there. Being from Chicago, I wasn't really sure how the white beans were supposed to be seasoned, so I just made up my own plan. Chopped chicken, garlic, and a jalapeño sounded good to me. They didn't score very well, but they sure tasted good to me. I now make them regularly. My Bonesmokers Cornbread Casserole (see recipe, p. 257) substitutes very well for traditional cornbread.

• **Yield: about 12 servings**

In a skillet, cook the bacon until some of the fat is rendered. Remove the bacon. Add the onion and chicken to the bacon fat. Chop the bacon. After a few minutes, add the garlic, jalapeño, salt, and pepper.

After the chicken is cooked until it's white and the onion is soft, transfer it and the chopped bacon to a Crock-Pot turned to high. Add the beans, all the chicken broth, and half the water. Stir and cover. Cook for 5 to 6 hours, stirring occasionally and adding more water as needed. When the beans are soft and the liquid is creamy, the beans are done. Check the salt. Serve with cornbread.

Potato salad is another one of those sides that just belong with barbecue. There are a few distinct types that I've presented here, but everybody likes to put their own spin on potato salad. Go right ahead and customize these for your friends and family.

▼▼▼

Miss Judy's Red Potato Salad with Vinaigrette Dressing

2½ pounds red potatoes

Salted water

½ cup olive oil

⅓ cup red wine vinegar

1 tablespoon minced garlic

½ red bell pepper, chopped to a small dice

¼ cup chopped Italian parsley

1 tablespoon sugar

½ teaspoon freshly ground black pepper

½ teaspoon salt

½ teaspoon dried thyme

½ teaspoon paprika

¼ teaspoon dry mustard

2 slices bacon, cooked crisp and crumbled

Judy Stuckey walked up to my barbecue stand one day and said she'd heard I was looking for some help. I told her that I was and she could start the following Wednesday. Turns out that was a good day for me. Judy is a very talented cook and a really hard worker. She's also a nice person who has become my good friend. The barbecue stand is on hold for now and Judy has inherited a pack of Chihuahuas, but we still get together regularly when I'm in Florida. While writing this book I have spent many hours cooking and experimenting, and I was having a hard time getting around to a red potato salad, so I asked Judy to create one for me. She has a background in recipe development, and I knew this would be no problem for her. I think she did great with this one. Thanks, Judy. • **Yield: 6–8 servings**

In a large pot, boil the potatoes in salted water until tender. Drain and cool. When cool cut them into bite-size pieces, leaving the skin intact, and put them in a big bowl.

In a separate bowl, whisk together the oil and vinegar. Add all of the other ingredients, mixing constantly. When they're all blended, pour the dressing over the potatoes and toss gently to coat. Cover the bowl and refrigerate for at least 2 hours.

Creamy Potato Salad

2½ pounds russet potatoes

1½ cups mayonnaise

¼ cup sweet pickle relish

1 large onion, diced small

1 green bell pepper, diced small

1 tablespoon prepared yellow mustard

1 teaspoon salt

1 teaspoon freshly ground black pepper

4 hard-boiled eggs, coarsely chopped

Paprika for garnish

This is just a traditional mayonnaise-based potato salad. • **Yield: 6–8 servings**

Place the potatoes in a large pot and cover with water. Bring the water to a boil, and then turn the heat down so that the water is at a gentle boil. Cook for 15 to 20 minutes. Do not overcook, or you will have mashed potato salad! Drain and let cool. Peel the potatoes and cut into 1-inch cubes. Place them in a big bowl and set aside.

In another big bowl, mix together the mayonnaise, relish, onion, pepper, mustard, salt, and pepper. When well blended, add the eggs and toss gently. Pour the mayonnaise mixture over the potatoes and toss gently. Refrigerate for at least 2 hours. Transfer to a clean bowl and sprinkle with paprika.

Mustardy Potato Salad

4 large russet potatoes

¼ cup white wine vinegar

1 clove garlic, minced

¾ cup chopped green onion

1 cup diced celery

2 hard-boiled eggs, whites only, chopped (feed the yolk to the dog)

¼ cup chopped Italian parsley

⅔ cup peeled, seeded, and diced cucumber

½ cup hot and spicy mustard of choice

¾ cup low-fat mayonnaise

¼ cup plain yogurt

1 tablespoon prepared horseradish

2 tablespoons Dijon mustard

½ teaspoon salt

¼ teaspoon freshly ground black pepper

Here are few recommendations to make this salad as tasty as possible: First, buy good white wine vinegar. Second, make sure you use Italian parsley for its spark, and, if you can't find it, grow it or substitute watercress with its peppery overtones. Third, be prepared to run out because it really is that good. • **Yield: 6 servings**

Place the potatoes in a large pot and cover with water. Bring the water to a boil, and then turn the heat down so that the water is at a gentle boil. Cook for 15 to 20 minutes. Do not overcook, or you will have mashed potato salad! Drain the potatoes and peel quickly—they need to be hot. On a cutting board, slice the potatoes lengthwise, and then slice into ¼-inch-thick slices and put them into a large bowl. Sprinkle the slices with the vinegar.

Add the garlic, green onion, celery, chopped whites of the hard-boiled eggs, parsley, cucumber, and mustard to the potatoes and toss gently.

In a small bowl, whisk together the mayonnaise, yogurt, horseradish, mustard, salt, and black pepper. Pour this mixture over the potato-vegetable mixture and toss gently to coat. Serve slightly chilled.

Coleslaw

I have found coleslaw to be a very controversial subject. Of all the things I serve to people, the coleslaw is the one they all ask about before they'll eat it. It seems that everyone has a family favorite and that's what they want mine to taste like. Then there is the KFC slaw that all others must be measured against. It's impossible to compete with the Colonel or your mom, but here are three good slaw recipes anyway. Try a scoop of any of these on your pulled pork sandwich. Incidentally, "cole" means "cabbage" and "slaw" means "shredded."

▼▼▼

Dr. BBQ's Creamy Coleslaw

1 large head green cabbage, shredded

¼ cup minced onion

1 large carrot, shredded

¾ cup mayonnaise

¼ cup milk

2 tablespoons white wine vinegar

1 tablespoon freshly squeezed lemon juice

¼ cup sugar

½ teaspoon dry mustard

½ cup half-and-half

½ teaspoon salt

½ teaspoon freshly ground black pepper

This is one of my all-time favorites and it is a great accompaniment to smoked meats of any kind.

• **Yield: 10–12 servings**

In a large bowl, toss together the cabbage, onion, and carrot.

In a separate bowl, mix all the other ingredients well. Pour the dressing over the cabbage mixture. Toss well to coat.

Cover and refrigerate and let rest at least one hour. Toss again and serve.

Big Bob Gibson's Spicy Crisp Mustard Slaw

A Recipe from Barbecue All Star Chris Lilly

Big Bob Gibson's is mentioned in a few other places in this book and there is good reason for that. The family has been in the barbecue business for about eighty years and they do it as well as anyone. They have two great restaurants in Decatur, Alabama, and a busy catering and sauce business. Don McLemore is the patriarch of the family and the grandson of Big Bob Gibson. Don and his lovely wife, Carolyn, run the business with their daughter, Amy, and her husband, Chris Lilly. Chris is a great cook and personality in his own right and has appeared and cooked on the Food Network with Paula Dean, Sara Moulton, Bobby Flay, and Martha Stewart and he's also been on the *Today Show*. He always cooks and promotes barbecue with these appearances. Chris is a barbecue man through and through. Big Bob's team cooks on the barbecue circuit when time allows, and they are among the best. They regularly compete at the Memphis in May World Championship Barbecue, and they have won the shoulder division six times and the overall World Championship twice. One day Chris got a call from the James Beard Foundation asking if he would like to be the featured chef one night at the James Beard House. This is truly a high honor for any cook, but unheard of for a barbecue man. There had been barbecue meals served there in the past, but nobody ever brought their trailer with three smokers from Alabama and

1 large head green
cabbage, shredded

1 large white onion,
shredded

1 green bell pepper,
shredded

1 carrot, shredded

1 stalk of celery, shredded

1¼ cups sugar

¾ cup apple cider vinegar

½ cup prepared mustard

½ cup ketchup

½ cup sour cream

¼ cup Alabama White
Barbecue Sauce (see
recipe, p. 24), or substitute
¼ cup mayonnaise

1 tablespoon salt

½ teaspoon cayenne
pepper

parked it on the street in Greenwich Village. Chris is a friend of mine, and when he told me he was going to do this, I immediately volunteered my services as a helper. The answer was yes, and I was invited. The family, along with me and Smokin' John Underwood, were on our way to New York. We cooked a meal of barbecued ribs, pork shoulder, sausage, beans, slaw, and lemon icebox pie. Chris then plated it like the fanciest food you could imagine and the guests loved it. After the meal we were introduced in the main dining room. The woman who introduced us paid us a great compliment. She said, "This was a meal that Mr. Beard would have loved." Of course he would, as he was the author of *James Beard's Treasury of Outdoor Cooking* (1960). Chris has generously shared the slaw recipe from that meal. • **Yield: 10–12 servings**

Combine the cabbage, onion, bell pepper, carrot, celery, and sugar in a large bowl and mix well. In a saucepan, combine the remaining ingredients. Bring to a boil, stirring constantly. Pour it over the cabbage mixture and mix well. Chill and serve.

Dr. BBQ's Tangy Slaw

1 large head green
cabbage, shredded

1 large carrot, shredded

1 medium green bell
pepper, shredded

1 small onion, shredded

¾ cup apple cider vinegar

½ cup sugar

½ cup canola oil

1 teaspoon salt

½ teaspoon celery seeds

Here's a variation on a common theme.
• Yield: 10–12 servings

In a large bowl, toss together the cabbage, carrot, bell pepper, and onion.

In a small saucepan, combine all of the other ingredients. Bring to a simmer, stirring occasionally to dissolve the sugar. Remove from the heat and pour over the cabbage mixture. Toss well to coat.

Cover and refrigerate for at least one hour. Toss again before serving.

▼▼

Marinated Portobellos

6 large portobello mushroom caps

Italian Dressing Marinade (see recipe, p. 28)

6 ounces crumbled blue cheese

Of all the different things I cook for people, these are the most requested and also the thing they go home and cook for themselves more than anything else I show them. It's a very simple recipe and I guess that accounts for some of it, but it's also the exotic nature of the portobellos and the blue cheese. These have converted many a non-mushroom person. • **Yield: 6 servings**

Note: This recipe requires advance preparation.

The morning before you plan to cook, twist the stems off the portobello caps and discard them. Put the caps in a sealable plastic bag and pour the Italian Dressing Marinade over them. Seal the bag and toss to coat. Refrigerate.

Prepare the grill for direct cooking at high heat.

Put the portobellos on the grill with the gill side facing down. Grill for about 5 minutes. Flip and top with the cheese, dividing it equally among the caps. Grill another 5 minutes or until the cheese is melted. The great thing about these is that everything could be eaten as is. If you like the mushrooms al dente, feel free to serve them that way. If you like them grilled hard and crispy, that's fine, too. I like them both ways. Serve whole as an appetizer, or cut into bite-size pieces for grazing.

Grilled Radicchio with Balsamic Dressing

¼ cup balsamic vinegar

½ teaspoon sugar

¼ cup olive oil

¼ teaspoon dried thyme

¼ teaspoon celery seed

¼ teaspoon dried basil

2 bamboo skewers, soaked in water for 1 hour

1 head radicchio, cut vertically into four sections

¼ cup olive oil

Big-Time Herb Rub (see recipe, p. 12)

Radicchio is tasty Italian chicory and is usually served as a salad green. But when you're Dr. BBQ you try to grill everything. Most things work, a few don't. This one worked very well! Radicchio can be found in the produce sections of most supermarkets; it looks like a mini red cabbage. Be sure to soak the skewers in water before grilling.

• Yield: 4 servings

To make the dressing, pour the vinegar into a shaker jar, add the sugar, and shake until the sugar is dissolved. Add ¼ cup of oil, thyme, celery seed, and basil, shake well, and set aside.

Prepare the grill for direct cooking at medium heat. Run 2 soaked bamboo skewers perpendicularly through the radicchio quarters. Brush ¼ cup of olive oil over the quarters and sprinkle with the rub.

Grill for about 4 minutes a side, turning once. Remove to a serving bowl and coat the quarters with the dressing.

Fried Green Tomatoes

A Recipe from Barbecue All Star Marsha Russell

The Breading Mix

- 1 cup flour
- ¾ cup cornmeal
- ¼ cup sugar
- 1 teaspoon salt
- Freshly ground black pepper, to taste

6–8 medium green tomatoes, sliced and placed in a bowl of cold water for a few minutes

Vegetable oil for frying

Bacon grease for frying

This recipe comes via my good friend Marsha Russell from Lynchburg, Tennessee. She is as sweet a Southern belle as you'll ever meet. Marsha spends her weekdays working in the offices at Jack Daniel's and most of her weekends cooking barbecue somewhere. She and John Hale compete as the Late Night Whiskey Smokers, but they also cook for local fundraisers and they play a big part in the Jack Daniel's World Barbecue Championship every October. I once sat at the kitchen island in her house and talked with friends while we watched Marsha make us a wonderful meal of deviled eggs, fried chicken, homemade macaroni and cheese, mashed potatoes, gravy, and fried okra. What a treat. For many of us, this would have been a special theme dinner. For Marsha it was just what she cooks for supper.

- Yield: 6–8 servings

Combine all the ingredients for the breading mix in a bowl. Flour the tomatoes with the mix and let sit for 15 minutes before frying.

I use an iron skillet to fry the tomatoes. Cover the bottom of the skillet with oil, and add 3 to 4 tablespoons of bacon grease to the oil. Fry the tomatoes until they are light golden on one side, then flip and brown the other side. Serve hot.

Grilled Tomato Halves

4 large plum tomatoes

Big-Time Herb Rub, to taste (see recipe, p. 12)

This has got to be the simplest recipe in the book. It's only two ingredients and cooking time is 6 minutes. These tomatoes are a great addition to any plate of grilled food, so I make them often. • **Yield: 8 servings**

Prepare the grill for direct cooking at high heat.

Cut the tomatoes in half lengthwise. With two fingers, scrape out the seeds and loose pulp. Season the cut side with Big-Time Herb Rub. Grill the tomatoes with the cut side down for about 3 minutes. Flip and grill another 3 minutes. That's it.

Grilled Sweet Corn with Barbecue Butter

1 pound unsalted butter

3 tablespoons Spicy Big-Time Barbecue Rub (see recipe, p. 11)

4 ears corn, husks and stalks attached

I've spent a lot of time in Wisconsin, where they have the greatest sweet corn in the world. I like it boiled, steamed, and even grilled like I serve it here. Be sure to buy ears with some of the stalk attached for a great handle. The barbecue butter is a natural. Make a big batch and freeze some in small cups for other uses. Try a pat on top of a grilled pork chop or a steak. • **Yield: 4 servings**

Allow the butter to soften in a bowl at room temperature and mix in the Spicy Big-Time Barbecue Rub. Let sit for at least 1 hour to blend the flavors.

Remove any dried, brownish husks from the corn. Pull the husks back, but don't remove them completely. Remove the silks. Soak the ears in cold water for 30 minutes to prevent the husks from burning.

Prepare the grill for direct cooking at medium heat.

Dry off the corn, brush some of the butter on each of the ears, pull the husks back up over the ears, and secure them with string or a strip of corn husk.

Grill the corn, turning often, for about 15 minutes. It's a good idea to have a spray bottle with water handy in case the husks start to burn. Serve with additional barbecue butter.

Vidalia Onions Stuffed with Sausage

6 Vidalia onions

2 to 3 tablespoons olive oil

Big-Time Barbecue Rub, to taste (see recipe, p. 9)

6 cloves garlic

½ pound spicy Italian sausage

1 aluminum foil pan

The sweet Vidalia onions inspire a cook to do something fun. They are so sweet when cooked that they barely qualify as onions. • **Yield: 6 servings**

Prepare the grill for indirect cooking at 325°F.

With an apple corer or a melon baller, core out the centers of the onions, but don't go all the way through the bottom. The bottom should be kept intact so that the filling doesn't run out. Brush the onions all over with the olive oil and season with Big-Time Barbecue Rub. Drop a clove of garlic in each cavity. Then stuff it full with the Italian sausage.

Put the onions in a foil pan and place it on the grill. Cook for 30 minutes. Cover the pan with aluminum foil. Cook another 30 minutes, or until the sausage is fully cooked and the onions are tender.

Grilled Vidalia Onions with Poblano Cream

2 poblano chiles, roasted and peeled, seeds and stems removed

½ teaspoon salt

1 bunch cilantro, leaves only

1 cup sour cream

Juice of 1 lime

4 Vidalia onions, peeled and halved along the equator

Olive oil

Salt and freshly ground pepper, to taste

Vidalia onions are only available at a certain time of the year. When they're around, I try to use them as often as possible. When they're out of season you can still make this dish, just substitute Texas Sweet onions or the ones from Walla Walla. The Poblano Chile Cream is a great compliment to them. This goes well as an appetizer or side dish, or it can even be served warm as a salad. • **Yield: 8 servings**

Combine the poblano chiles, salt, cilantro, sour cream, and lime juice in a food processor and puree. Chill in the refrigerator.

Prepare the grill for direct cooking at high heat.

Make ¼-inch-deep X-shaped incisions on the flat sides of the onion halves without touching the 2 outside layers.

Grill the onion halves until kind of soft.

Puddle some Poblano Chile Cream on small plates and serve the onion halves in it, flat side up. Drizzle olive oil and sprinkle salt and pepper over the X-shaped incisions.

Whole Smoked Cabbage

1 large head green cabbage

2 to 3 tablespoons olive oil

Big-Time Barbecue Rub, to taste (see recipe, p. 9)

1 stick of frozen butter

Your guests will get a big kick out of this one. When you serve Smoky Corned Beef (p. 67) and cabbage they will think you've lost it, until they taste it. Don't save this only for the corned beef, though. It's simple and delicious and goes with many other things. • **Yield: 6–8 servings**

Prepare the grill for indirect cooking at 325°F, using apple wood for flavor, if desired.

Make a doughnut out of aluminum foil to hold the head of cabbage upright. With a sharp knife, cut the core out of the cabbage. Brush the whole head with olive oil and season with the Big-Time Barbecue Rub. Be sure to season the cavity well.

Place the head on the foil doughnut with the cavity facing up. Put the frozen stick of butter in the cavity. Move the cabbage and doughnut to the grill. Cook for 30 minutes. Wrap the cabbage in foil and continue cooking in the upright position until it is soft and fully cooked. This should take another 30 minutes. This can also be cooked in the slow barbecue cooker. The times will be about twice as long.

Potatoes go with everything, even barbecue.

▼▼▼

Roasted Garlic Stand-Alone Potatoes

3 pounds red potatoes, half peeled (peel some strips off and leave some strips on)

1 head of roasted garlic,* squeezed out of the husks and crushed with a fork

One 3-ounce package cream cheese

1 cup sour cream

½ cup milk

4 tablespoons butter, cut in pieces

1 tablespoon freshly ground black pepper

1 tablespoon salt

*Cut the top off a head of garlic, drizzle with olive oil, and bake in a pan for 30 minutes at 350°F.

I call these stand-alone because they certainly do. No gravy needed. You may, however, be standing alone after eating them if you don't have a breath mint.

• **Yield: 6–8 servings**

In a large pot, boil the potatoes in salted water until soft. Drain and put in a big bowl. Mash the potatoes. Add the other ingredients one at a time, mashing and mixing constantly. The potatoes should still be a little chunky when finished.

Peppered-Up Twice-Baked Potatoes

2 large baking potatoes

Vegetable oil

½ cup grated pepper jack cheese

½ cup sour cream

2 tablespoons melted butter

1 teaspoon salt

1 teaspoon freshly ground black pepper

2 teaspoons dried chives

Paprika

T he pepper jack cheese makes these a little spicy and not your average twice-baked spud.

• Yield: 2–4 servings

Preheat the oven to 375°F.

Wash, prick, and rub the potatoes with oil. Bake until done, about an hour.

Remove the potatoes from the oven and let them cool for at least a half hour. Then cut them in half, scoop out the flesh, and reserve the shells. Put the potato flesh in a bowl with all the other ingredients except the paprika. With a fork crush and mix everything until blended but still chunky. Stuff the mixture back in the shells, mounding the top. Sprinkle with paprika. Put in a 400°F oven for about 15 minutes to brown and reheat.

Baked Sweet Potatoes

4 medium sweet potatoes

Olive oil

Sweeter Big-Time Barbecue Rub, to taste (see recipe, p. 10)

We all seem to forget about sweet potatoes except during the holidays. Try these and you'll be eating them all year long. • **Yield: 4–6 servings**

Preheat the oven to 350°F, or prepare the cooker for indirect cooking at 350°F.

Wash and dry the sweet potatoes. Cut them into quarters lengthwise. Rub the quarters with olive oil. Season all over liberally with Sweeter Big-Time Barbecue Rub. Put the quarters back together and wrap each potato in foil. Cook for about one hour, or until tender.

Bonesmokers Potatoes

One 28-ounce can diced
potatoes

One 10-ounce can diced
tomatoes with green chiles
(get the hot if you like)

1 tablespoon butter

1 tablespoon flour

½ cup milk

1 cup grated cheddar
cheese

2 slices bacon, cooked and
crumbled

½ teaspoon salt

½ teaspoon freshly ground
black pepper

Paprika

These are a true original. I've always been intrigued by mixing tomatoes and potatoes. Then one day I saw these cubed canned potatoes, and thought I needed to do something with them. I put those two together with a little cheese sauce and some bacon and Bonesmokers Potatoes were born. These can be cooked in the barbecue pit with great results, too. • **Yield: 4 servings**

Preheat the oven to 350°F, or prepare the cooker to cook at 250°F.

Drain the potatoes and the tomatoes together in a colander. Melt the butter in a small saucepan. Thoroughly mix in the flour. Add the milk, stirring to blend. Add ½ cup of the cheese, stirring. All the cheese doesn't need to melt into the sauce. Add the bacon and salt and pepper, and stir to blend. Remove from the heat to cool a bit.

Toss the potatoes, tomatoes, and the sauce mixture together in a bowl. Transfer to a greased 2-quart casserole or an 8 x 8-inch pan. Top with the remaining ½ cup cheese and sprinkle with paprika. Bake for 30 minutes at 350°F in the oven, or 1 hour in a 250°F barbecue cooker.

This is where the recipes that don't quite fit anywhere else in the book ended up.
I think you'll see what I mean.

▼▼▼

Bonesmokers Cornbread Casserole

1¼ cups cornmeal

½ teaspoon baking soda

1 teaspoon baking powder

1 teaspoon salt

1 stick butter, melted

1 cup milk

4 eggs, lightly beaten

2 cans creamed corn

I have worn many hats in the barbecue business and one of them has been running a barbecue stand in Florida during the winter. This recipe was created just for that stand. There's something magic about cornbread and barbecue, but traditional cornbread gets dry, so I needed something a little different. This has a texture almost like a cake. The addition of the corn helps out, too. You should be able to cut it into squares. I like it plain, but I have added grated cheese, chopped chiles, or grilled onions and been pleased as well. • **Yield: 6 servings**

Preheat the oven to 350°F.

In a bowl, combine the dry ingredients, then add the butter, milk, and eggs. Mix well. Add the corn and mix well again. Pour into a greased pan and bake for about an hour. Serve warm or at room temperature.

$1000 Maple Bean Pie

4 tablespoons butter

2 tablespoons flour

3 large eggs

1 cup evaporated milk

1 tablespoon real maple syrup

1 teaspoon ground allspice

1 teaspoon ground cinnamon

½ teaspoon salt

1 cup brown sugar

Two 16-ounce cans of Bush Original Baked Beans, drained and mashed

1 large deep-dish pre-made pie crust

My friend Lee Fraser and I competed in the Liberty Bell Cookoff in Philadelphia. They had a beans category. They gave us a can of beans, but the catch was that you were required to make a dish out of the beans instead of just doctoring them up. Lee's friend Dylan suggested a bean pie, and even found a couple of pumpkin and sweet potato pie recipes for us to work with. We all agreed it was a great idea. When we got to the cookoff I set up my Big Green Egg to cook like an oven. I then started mixing and matching the recipes Dylan had found and when it tasted good I poured the mixture into the pie shell and cooked it. It ended up being delicious, so we garnished it with a dollop of whipped cream and a sprig of mint and turned it in. The result was a first-place trophy and a $1000 check. • **Yield: 8 servings**

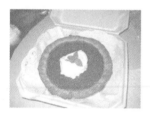

Preheat the oven to 350°F.

In a small saucepan over low heat melt the butter. Stir in the flour and mix until blended. Set aside. In a large bowl lightly beat the eggs. Whisk in the evaporated milk, maple syrup, allspice, cinnamon, and salt. Add the brown sugar and mix until well blended. Add the mashed beans and the flour mixture and mix until well blended. Pour the mix into the pie crust.

Bake the pie on a baking sheet for about 1 hour and 15 minutes, or until a toothpick inserted in the middle comes out clean.

Kinda Dirty Rice

3 tablespoons olive oil

1½ pounds ground chicken

1 teaspoon paprika

1 teaspoon dry mustard

1 large onion, chopped

1 green bell pepper, seeds and stems removed, chopped

3 stalks celery, chopped

2 tablespoons minced garlic

2 bunches green onions, green tops and white parts separated and finely chopped

3 tablespoons Big-Time Creole Barbecue Rub (see recipe, p. 13)

1 can cream of celery soup

1 can French onion soup

2 cups long-grain rice, uncooked

1½ cups water

Dirty rice is a Louisiana specialty, and the name refers to the addition of meat that makes the rice look dirty. This one isn't very traditional, but it's easy and very good served with barbecue. • **Yield: 8–10 servings**

Preheat the oven to 350°F.

In a skillet over medium heat, add the oil, then brown the chicken, stirring as needed. Add the paprika, mustard, onion, bell pepper, celery, garlic, green onion whites, and barbecue rub. Continue cooking for approximately 5 minutes, stirring occasionally. Add the celery soup and onion soup, stir well, cover, and continue cooking until the mixture begins to bubble.

Add the rice, stir well, and remove from the burner. Add the water. If the rice is not completely covered by the liquid, add more water. Transfer to a baking dish, cover, and place in the oven. Bake for 45 minutes, checking occasionally. If the mixture appears dry or the rice is not completely cooked, add water, cover, and return to the oven until the rice is tender and moist.

Serve garnished with the green onion tops.

Dr. BBQ's Macaroni and Cheese

8 ounces elbow macaroni

4 tablespoons butter

4 tablespoons flour

3 cups whole milk

1 teaspoon salt

¾ teaspoon cayenne
pepper

2 eggs, beaten

4 cups shredded mild
cheddar cheese

Paprika

I like my macaroni and cheese plain and traditional. If you want to add something else to it, go ahead. Some suggestions would be chopped onion, green bell pepper, diced tomato, small shrimp, any spicy chile, or some of those fried onions in the can. You can substitute or mix and match the cheese, too. • **Yield: 6–8 servings**

Preheat the oven to 350°F.

Cook the macaroni in boiling water to al dente stage, then drain.

While the macaroni is cooking, make the sauce. In a medium saucepan, melt the butter over medium heat. Add the flour and mix well until all the lumps are gone. Add the milk, salt, and cayenne and cook until the sauce simmers and begins to thicken. This should take about 10 minutes. Temper the eggs (mix a few spoonfuls of sauce into the eggs, then add the eggs to the sauce in the saucepan) and mix them into the sauce. Remove from the heat. Add 3 cups of cheese and stir until it's melted and blended in.

In a large bowl, fold the macaroni together with the sauce. Transfer to a greased baking pan or casserole dish. Top with the remaining cup of cheese and a sprinkle of paprika for color. Bake for 20 to 30 minutes, depending on the dish you've chosen. It should be brown and bubbly when done.

Grilled Fresh Pineapple on the Half Shell

1 large pineapple

½ cup brown sugar

2 ounces rum

Grilled pineapple works very well. It has just the right texture to get tender and crispy while holding its shape and staying together. This dish can easily be served as a dessert, but I prefer to serve it right on the buffet with dinner, kind of like a sweet fruit salad. • **Yield: 6–8 servings**

At least an hour before you plan to cook, stand the pineapple on a cutting board. The goal is to split the pineapple in half while keeping the top leaves all on one side. That side will serve as the bowl later. Now take a long, sharp knife and start right under the leaves. Cut in on an angle, but quickly turn the blade down toward the board. Continue the cut straight down through the whole pineapple. You should end up with two halves, one with all the leaves and one without. Now you must cut the flesh out of the two halves, preferably in big wedges. First cut out the core. Try the non-leaf half first; you'll be discarding that shell anyway. Cut along the outside skin deep into the flesh from top to bottom. Now cut from the center back toward the first cut. With a little practice you can get most of the pineapple out in two big wedges. Repeat the cuts on the leaf half, being careful not to cut through that shell. I will often buy a second pineapple so I will have enough flesh for a refill at the table. You can take the second pineapple and cut it in a traditional fashion into wedges, discarding all the skin.

Place the wedges in a sealable plastic bag. Mix the brown sugar and the rum together and pour over the pineapple. Seal the bag and toss to coat evenly.

Prepare the grill for direct cooking at high heat. Place the wedges directly on the grate. Grill until brown and crispy, turning occasionally. This should take 8–10 minutes. Remove the wedges to a cutting board. Cut them into bite-size pieces and place them in the reserved half shell.

Mrs. Basso's Light Rolls

A Recipe from Barbecue All Star Ray Basso

This story is much more about the Internet than about these rolls. In 1998 I bought a computer. I didn't really need one and I didn't know what I was going to do with it, but I saw what was going on around me and I knew that I needed to get on the bandwagon or I was going to be left behind. It has turned out to be a wise move. Needless to say, I now use my computer for business all the time, but the Internet is the real story here. As I said, I had no plan for this computer, so I signed onto the Internet and searched on barbecue. I arrived at The KC BBQ Connection. I now know that this was the second-ever Internet page related to barbecue. The first-ever barbecue Web page was created by Mark Haggitt from Nashville, Tennessee. Mark is still around cooking and judging on the barbecue circuit, but that first Web page is history. The KC BBQ Connection is a whole different story. It is still up and running at *www.kcbbqconnection.com* and has spawned the busiest barbecue sites on the Net. Specifically, *www.bbqsearch.com* and the biggest thing to ever happen to competition barbecue, The BBQ Forum. The address is *www.bbqforum.com.* The BBQ Forum is an Internet bulletin board that all competition barbecue cooks go to for information and interaction. It has enabled many of us from around the country to meet each other and exchange cooking information as well as information about the world of competition barbecue. We have a lot of fun, too. All these sites and everything associated with them have been created by Ray Basso.

Ray is a soft-spoken guy with huge vision. When he looks at the Internet he sees things that most of us don't see. I can tell you first-hand that Ray Basso and his Internet projects have been critical in advancing my career over the past few years. I've also made some lifelong friends because of Ray. He is one of them. This recipe means a lot to Ray and I'm proud to include it here. I will use his words to introduce it.

Nobody knows where this recipe came from. All anyone knows is my mother, Maxine Basso, had this recipe for many years and it delighted a lot of people. She guarded it closely and would give it to nobody. Well, over the years, she forgot what went into the recipe and lost the "hard copy" of it. So it was lost forever, or so it appeared. It disappeared for over thirty years. After she passed away the recipe was discovered in an old cookbook. At first I decided that I would only sell it because it was so good and worth money. However, I have decided to give it to anyone who wants it. Since some of the finest people in the world visit this Web page, I think it's only fair that you should have it. —Ray Basso

¼ cup butter, melted

1 cup milk

¼ cup sugar

½ tablespoon salt

1 package yeast

1 egg

3 cups flour

• **Yield: about 12 rolls**

Mix the butter and ½ cup of the milk. Add the sugar and salt, then heat this mixture slightly (95°–105°F). Stir in the yeast. Let this mixture sit for a few minutes until the yeast starts to activate. You can tell this is happening when the yeast starts to bubble up—it takes about 10 minutes. Then put the rest of the milk in a separate container and beat the egg into this milk.

Mrs. Basso's Light Rolls (continued)

Pour the milk and yeast mixture into a large bowl. Sift in the flour. After about half of the flour has been worked in, add the milk and egg mixture. Gradually add the rest of the flour, mixing it in with a spoon.

Cover it loosely with plastic wrap, place in a warm, draft-free place, and let it rise to about double in size. This should take about 30 minutes. Flour your hands, because the dough will be sticky, and shape 12 round balls about the size of a golf ball. Place them on a greased cookie sheet. Cover with plastic wrap and place in a warm, draft-free place to rise to about double in size. This should take another 30 minutes.

Preheat the oven to 350°F. Bake for about 13 minutes or until golden brown.

Bonesmokers Bahama Mamas

2 quarts light rum

1 quart dark or Myers's rum

2 quarts coconut rum

1 gallon freshly squeezed orange juice

1 gallon pineapple juice

1 quart freshly squeezed lemon juice

16 ounces grenadine

Ice

Man cannot live on food alone. Occasionally he must drink, too. I came up with this drink to quench the thirst of some friends at a cookoff. The nice thing about staying up half the night and sleeping in a lawn chair is that nobody has to drive. David Roper, the well-known barbecue eater and Jack Daniel's tour guide, once sampled these and said, "The only thing these need is drinking." This recipe will serve a large party. • **Yield: 4 gallons**

Mix everything together in a 5-gallon water cooler.

Dessert has curiously become a popular category at barbecue cookoffs. It's really popular with the judges. Not surprisingly, dessert is also a popular category with guests who are at your house for dinner. Here are some fabulous versions of the traditional favorites.

▼▼▼

Banana Pudding

1 large box of instant vanilla pudding mix

One 8-ounce package cream cheese, at room temperature

1 large can sweetened condensed milk

1 extra-large tub of nondairy whipped topping

2 boxes of vanilla wafers

6 bananas, sliced thin

1 small tub of nondairy whipped topping for topping

Shaved chocolate for garnish (optional)

This is a great version of a very popular Southern dessert. Try making it in a trifle bowl.

• **Yield: 8–10 servings**

Prepare the pudding as directed on the box, then set aside.

Soften the cream cheese in another bowl, add sweetened condensed milk, and blend well. Add the pudding to the cream cheese mixture and blend well. Gently fold in the large tub of nondairy whipped topping.

In an extra-large bowl, layer the bottom of the bowl with vanilla wafers, then sliced bananas, then the pudding mixture. Repeat the layers a couple of times and finish with sliced bananas on top. Spread the small tub of nondairy whipped topping over the top. Garnish with the shaved chocolate or a few vanilla wafers. Chill for 2 hours.

Bread Pudding with Dr. Jack Sauce

4 eggs, lightly beaten

1 cup brown sugar

1 quart heavy cream

½ stick butter, melted

1 teaspoon vanilla

½ teaspoon cinnamon

2 bananas, mashed

½ cup pecan chips

6 ounces bittersweet chocolate, chopped

16 slices day-old white bread without crust, cubed

This is the dessert I came up with for my first trip to the Jack Daniel's World Championship Invitational Barbecue. Dessert is always a category there, and the cooks really go all out. I think they see it as an opportunity to show off that they can do more than just cook giant hunks of meat. The judges love this category. I didn't win anything with this, but it sure did get eaten up. The sauce is full of uncooked liquor, so be careful not to serve it to any kids or friends who are on the wagon. • **Yield: 12 servings**

Preheat the oven to 350°F.

Butter a 9 x 13-inch baking pan. In a large bowl, whisk together the eggs, brown sugar, cream, butter, vanilla, and cinnamon. Mix in the bananas, pecans, and chocolate. Fold in the bread until fully wet.

Pour into the prepared pan. Bake about 1½ hours, until set.

Dr. Jack Sauce

2 ounces Jack Daniel's whiskey

3 ounces Dr. McGillicuddy's Vanilla Schnapps

½ cup sweetened condensed milk

Combine and serve over the pudding. Do not cook.

Classic Vanilla Flan

3 tablespoons brown sugar, mixed with 1 tablespoon of water

One 12-ounce can sweetened condensed milk

Enough milk to fill the empty can of sweetened condensed milk

3 eggs

1 teaspoon vanilla extract

The great thing about flan is how such basic ingredients can make such a delicious dessert. It's not really a common barbecue dessert, but it's a close cousin to custard pie, which is, so let's just consider this a fancy version of a custard pie. • **Yield: 6 servings**

Preheat the oven to 350°F.

In a small, heavy saucepan, melt the sugar mixed with the water and caramelize it by heating it until it is thick and brown. Coat the bottom and sides of a glass 1½-quart baking dish with the sugar mixture.

Pour the sweetened condensed milk into a blender. Fill the empty can with milk and add that to the blender along with the eggs and vanilla. Blend at high speed for one minute. Slowly pour this mixture into the coated baking dish.

Place the dish in a water bath. (The water for the water bath should be very hot, and should come up to about two-thirds the height of the baking dish.) Bake, uncovered, for 50 to 60 minutes. The middle of the flan, like custard, should still be a little "jiggly." Do not overbake. Remove the flan from the oven and allow it to reach room temperature before it is refrigerated.

The flan can be served slightly warm or chilled.

Peach Cobbler

A Recipe from Barbecue All Stars Bill and Barbara Milroy

1 cup flour

1⅓ cups sugar

1½ teaspoons baking powder

¼ teaspoon salt

½ cup milk

1 stick butter

One 15-ounce can sliced peaches, drained

I began cooking in barbecue contests in 1982. You have to look real hard to find anyone who goes back further than that and is still active today. Bill and Barbara Milroy are on that short list. They started in the 1970s! That is prehistoric times in the world of barbecue cookoffs. These folks have done it all and still do. Using the name Texas Rib Rangers, they have cooked in hundreds of barbecue contests and have won a roomful of awards, including the prestigious "Best Sauce on the Planet" at the American Royal. They are also very busy in the barbecue business. They travel the country vending barbecue at all the big events, they have a flourishing sauce and seasoning business, and they sell barbecue in the infield at Texas Motor Speedway. They also do a lot of catering when they are home in Denton, Texas, and Barbara always talks about how much folks like her cobblers. So when I was writing this book I asked her if she'd be so kind as to share that recipe. Bill and Barbara are two of the nicest folks you'll meet anywhere, and I'm glad to be their friend.

- **Yield: 6–8 servings**

Preheat the oven to 350°F.

Mix the flour, 1 cup of the sugar, the baking powder, salt, and milk in a large bowl until well blended. Melt the butter in a 9 x 13-inch baking pan. Pour the batter into the pan, spreading it evenly. In a small saucepan, warm the peaches and the remaining ⅓ cup sugar just until the sugar is melted. Pour the peach mixture over the top of the batter.

Bake for 45 minutes. Allow to cool for 10 minutes before serving.

Trish Trigg's Pecan Pie

A Recipe from Barbecue All Stars Trish and Johnny Trigg

3 eggs, lightly beaten

1 cup sugar

1 cup Karo light corn syrup

2 tablespoons butter, melted

1 teaspoon vanilla

1¼ cups whole pecans

1 9-inch pre-made pie shell, unbaked

This is one very famous pecan pie recipe, and I'm really proud to include it here. Trish Trigg and her husband, Johnny, are regulars on the barbecue cookoff circuit. Their team name is Smokin' Triggers, and they are among the best ever to compete. They have won just about everything there is to win, and as I'm writing this they are the current World Barbecue Champions. Johnny cooks the barbecue and Trish does the presentations. Trish also cooks the desserts, and over the years this pecan pie recipe has probably won more awards around the country than any other dessert. When you try it you'll understand why. Thank you, Trish. • **Yield: 8 servings**

Preheat the oven to 350°F.

In a large bowl, stir together the first 5 ingredients until well blended. Stir in the pecans. Pour the mixture into the pie crust.

Bake for 50 to 55 minutes, until set. Let cool on a wire rack.

Key Lime Meringue Pie

Two 12-ounce cans sweetened condensed milk

1 cup freshly squeezed key lime juice or bottled key lime juice

8 egg yolks

1 prepared graham cracker pie crust

8 egg whites

½ teaspoon cream of tartar

⅓ cup confectioner's sugar

Lime slices for garnish

Key lime pie isn't a common dessert at barbecue joints, but it would be if the limes were more available. Key limes are small and are only grown in southern Florida. Typical limes are not the same. The key limes have a tart flavor that just isn't like anything else. I love key lime pie, but don't expect it to be sweet. If it's properly made the tartness wins out. If you can't find the small, round key limes, try the bottled stuff from Nellie & Joe's. The meringue on this one makes good use of the spare egg whites.

• **Yield: 6 servings**

Preheat the oven to 350°F.

To make the filling: In a bowl, whisk together the condensed milk, lime juice, and egg yolks until completely smooth. Set aside.

To make the meringue topping: Using a hand mixer, whip the egg whites to soft peaks. Add the cream of tartar and whip to stiff peaks. Add the sugar and whip until well mixed.

Pour the filling into the prepared crust and spread the meringue over the top. Place in the oven and bake for 20 to 25 minutes, until a toothpick comes out clean. Remove from the oven and allow it to sit for at least 1 hour. Slice into 6 sections. Place a slice of lime on top of each section as a garnish.

Baked Apples in the Cooker

6 large red apples

1 aluminum foil pan

1 stick butter

6 cinnamon sticks

½ cup brown sugar

These are just like Grandma used to make. The barbecue cooker is perfect for them. If you are using a lot of smoke for something else, just cover them with foil.

• **Yield: 6 servings**

Prepare the cooker to cook at 350°F, or preheat the oven to 350°F.

Core the apples with a melon baller, trying to leave the bottom intact so the filling won't run out. Put the apples in an aluminum foil pan. Cut the stick of butter into 6 pieces and put one in each apple. Put a cinnamon stick in each apple and top each one with part of the brown sugar. Use a little more brown sugar if you like.

Put the pan in the cooker or grill and cook until the apples are soft. The time will depend on how hot you are cooking. At 350°F it should be about 30 minutes.

The Barbecue Log

My Best Match-Ups Between Sides and Mains

▼▼

Barbecue and Grilling Glossary

Alder wood. Imparts a light flavor that works well with fish and poultry. It is native to the northwestern United States, and is the traditional wood for smoking salmon.

Apple wood. Has a sweet, mild flavor and is used mostly with pork and game, but can be used for ham as well.

Baby back ribs. Tender pork ribs cut from the loin or back section.

Barbacoa. The Spanish word for barbecue, this generally refers to the head of a cow that is wrapped in cloth and cooked slowly in a pit.

Barbecue. As a verb in the most general sense, to cook outdoors. More specifically, to smoke meats by indirect heat and then to finish them with sauces. As a noun, it means the entire unit used to grill.

Barbecue sauce. A condiment used to finish the barbecue after the meat is smoked.

Bark. The crust of smoked meat formed by the rub.

Baste. To apply a mop, sop, or marinade during the grilling or smoking process.

Beef back ribs. Large ribs cut from the loin of the cow.

Beef short ribs. Thick ribs cut from the bottom end of the cow's rib cage.

Brining. Soaking meat in a salt and spice mixture prior to smoking.

Briquettes. A processed charcoal that looks and burns consistently.

Brisket. The chest muscle of a cow and one of the favorite cuts of Texas-style barbecue.

Burnt ends. The blackened, crisp, fatty portion of the tapered end of a smoked brisket. A favorite in Kansas City barbecue.

Butt. The butt end of a whole pork shoulder. Also known as a **shoulder blade roast.**

Cherry wood. This wood is used for ham, but some cooks think that its smoke is too acrid.

Country-style spareribs. Meaty sections from the rib end of the pork loin.

Curing. Treating meat or fish with a salt and spice mixture prior to smoking.

Drip pan. An aluminum pan placed below the grill surface to catch fat, juices, and excessive basting sauces.

Grate. The metalwork holding the fuel in a smoker or barbecue.

Grill. The lattice of metal that the meat is placed upon for grilling or smoking. In a more general sense, the entire unit is called a grill or barbecue. As a verb, to cook over the direct heat of flames or coals.

Grill brush. A brush with metal bristles used to clean the grill.

Hickory wood. This is probably the most famous smoking hardwood, the wood of choice in the Southern barbecue belt. It imparts a strong, hearty flavor to meats, and is used mostly to smoke pork shoulders and ribs.

Instant-read thermometer. A probe temperature device that tells the internal temperature of grilled and smoked meats in seconds. Do not use this as an oven thermometer.

Jerk. A style of smoke-grilling popular in Jamaica that uses an allspice and chili pepper–based marinade.

Lump. Charcoal or charred wood in its natural state.

Maple wood. This has a mild and mellow smoke that imparts a sweet flavor that is traditional for smoking ham but is also good with poultry, pork, and seafood.

Marinade. A seasoned sauce that meat is soaked in prior to cooking in order to tenderize it.

Mesquite wood. This is better for grilling than smoking because the smoke tends to be resinous and bitter. Despite all the hype about mesquite of late, few serious barbecuers use it exclusively except for the grill or for in-ground pit barbecues, because of their limited amounts of smoke. Mesquite is the strongest-flavored wood used in outdoor cooking, and it is popular with restaurant grills that cook meat for a very short time.

Oak wood. The favorite wood of Europe, strong but not overpowering. It is a very good wood for beef or lamb and is probably the most versatile of the hardwoods. Do not use acorns for smoking.

Pecan wood. This is similar to hickory, but milder. It's also a Southern favorite, and is becoming the smoking wood of choice in the Southwest because of the extensive pecan groves in Texas, New Mexico, and Arizona.

Picnic. A lunch in the park or the lower arm portion of a hog's shoulder.

Pig pickin'. Slicing or pulling hunks of meat by hand from a pork shoulder.

Pit. A hole in the ground for cooking meats over coals; or a manufactured unit for smoking meats.

Rub. A dry spice mixture rubbed over meat prior to cooking.

Skewer. A metal or bamboo stick used to grill kabobs, seafood, and vegetables.

Skirt steak. Beef diaphragm muscle that is used for fajitas.

Slab of ribs. The entire side or top of the rib cage. Should be 13 bones.

Smoke ring. The pink ring just below the surface of smoked meat that proves it is true barbecue.

Smoker. A metal unit for smoking meats by the indirect heat method.

Sop. A basting sauce applied to the meat during the cooking process. Also called **mop**.

Spareribs. The lower portion of a hog's ribs. This term refers only to pork ribs.

Cookoff List

Here's a list of barbecue events around the country. Contact information is provided for each event. For the most recent information, take a look at *www.barbecuenews.com*. That's the best Web site for up-to-date barbecue cookoff information.

National Events

FEBRUARY

Houston Livestock & Rodeo Show, World Championship Bar-B-Que
Houston, TX
www.hlsr.com

National Barbecue Association's Annual Conference and Exposition
Marriot Westchase Hotel, Houston, TX
Contact: National Barbecue Association at 512-454-8626 or *www.nbbqa.org*

MAY

World Championship Barbeque Cooking Contest
Memphis, TN
Contact: Memphis in May, 88 Union Ave., Suite 301, Memphis, TN 38103, 901-525-4611 (MIM)

SEPTEMBER

Whose Sauce Is the Boss?
Montego Bay, Jamaica
Contact: Rocky Danner at 931-433-2651 or *rocbbq@vallnet.com* (not sanctioned)

OCTOBER

American Royal Barbeque
Kansas City, MO
Contact: Tracy Satterfield at 816-221-9800 ext. 113 or *tracys@americanroyal.com* (KCBS)

Jack Daniel's World Championship Invitational Barbecue
(always 4th Saturday in October)
Lynchburg, TN
Contact: Tana Schupe at 931-759-4221

Sanctioned Events

This includes events sanctioned by the Kansas City Barbecue Society (KCBS), Memphis in May (MIM), and the International Barbeque Cookers Association (IBCA). This also includes events sanctioned by smaller regional groups that have a monopoly on an area: The Florida Barbeque Association (FBA), The Lone Star Barbeque Society (LSBS), and Central Texas Barbeque Association (CTBA).

New England

Connecticut

AUGUST

**Podunk Bluegrass Music Festival
Connecticut State Championship**
East Hartford, CT
Contact: C. Roger Moss at 860-282-8241 or
rmoss@ci.easthartford.ct.us or
www.podunkbluegrass.net or
www.podunkbluegrass.com (KCBS)

Massachusetts

JUNE

Cape Cod Rib and Brisket Festival
Peters Pond Campground, Sandwich, MA
Contact: John Martell at 781-834-7721 or
gjem3@aol.com (KCBS)

New Hampshire

JUNE

New Hampshire State BBQ Championship
Anheuser-Busch Brewery, Merrimack, NH
Contact: Jim McGrath at 978-369-2835 or
jimmcgra@bellatlantic.net

Vermont

JULY

**Harpoon New England Barbecue
Championship**
Windsor, VT
Contact: Angela Archer or Charlie Storey at
802-674-5491 ext. 656 or
aarcher@harpoonbrewery.com or
cstorey@harpoonbrewery.com (KCBS)

Southeast

Alabama

MARCH

**The Mitchell Company BBQ Championship
and Hog Wild Festival**
Mobile, AL
Contact: Lee Corrigan/Lee Butler at 251-479-4900
or *lcorrigan@ucpmobile.org* (KCBS)

MAY

Rocket City BBQ Cook-Off
Huntsville, AL
Contact: *www.rocketcitybbq.com*

JULY

Taste of Freedom BBQ Cookoff
Albertville, AL
Contact: Kathy Poe at 256-878-5188 or
Joan Killian at 256-878-9352 (KCBS)

SEPTEMBER

**10th Annual Riverfest Alabama State
Championship**
Decatur, AL
Contact: 256-350-2028 or *sqee@decaturcvb.org*
(KCBS)

DECEMBER

Alabama State Championship BBQ Cook-Off
Demopolis, AL
Contest contact: Paul Willingham, 1201 Al's Lane,
Demopolis, AL 36732, 334-289-2856. Judges contact:
Traci Hurst, 703 The Cove, Demopolis, AL 36732,
334-289-8229 (MIM)

Arkansas

APRIL

Festival of Two Rivers BBQ
Arkadelphia, AR
Contact: Angela Nesbett at 870-246-2793 (IBCA)

5th Fire Up Your Grill in Bentonville
Bentonville, AR
Contact: Jeff Latham at 479-271-7171 (KCBS)

MAY

Bordertown Bash BBQ Cookoff
Fort Smith, AR
Contact: Greg South at 479-648-0534 (KCBS)

Florida

JANUARY

Lakeland Pig Festival at Tiger Town
Lakeland, FL
Contact: Tina Winnett at 863-533-0528 or
twinnwtt@cfifl.com (KCBL)

FEBRUARY

Top of the Lake BBQ Affair,
Okeechobee Main Street Inc. BBQ Contest
Okeechobee, FL
Contact: Craig Guinn at 863-763-3437 (FBA)

APRIL

Hog Wild–Pig Crazy
Lake City, FL
Contact: Heyward Christie at 386-758-5448 (FBA)

JUNE

Blueberries, Barbeque and Bluegrass Festival
Callahan, FL
Contact: Tom Pippin at 904-491-6285 or
tpip@msn.com (FBA)

SEPTEMBER

Q-Fest
Grant, FL
Contact: Robin Tibbitts, P.O. Box 655, Grant, FL
32949, 321-952-4938

OCTOBER

Mulberry Fine Swine at the Pit
Mulberry, FL
Contact: American Legion City of Mulberry and
The Mulberry Chamber of Commerce, Patricia
Jackson at the City of Mulbery, P.O. Box 707,
Mulberry, FL 33860, 863-425-1125 or
city.mulberry@vesgmail.net

NOVEMBER

Plant City Pig Jam
Plant City, FL
Contact: Jodi Smith at 813-752-5863 or
smith.jodi@myfloridahouse.com (KCBS)

DECEMBER

Arcadia All-Florida Championship Rodeo &
BBQ Contest
Contact: Susan or Todd Rachles at 863-990-1867 or
863-990-1868 or *dsrachles@earthlink.net* (FBA)

Georgia

MARCH

Perry Shrine Swine Cookoff
Perry Shrine Club, Macon, GA
Contact: Alan Shaw at 478-987-0313 or
alan.shaw@att.net or Stump McDonald at
478-987-0993 (FBA)

AUGUST

9th Annual Dillard Bluegrass & Barbeque
Festival
Dillard, GA
Contact: Jane Tomlin at 706-746-9936 or
jane@rabun.net (KCBS)

Big Pig Jig
Vienna, GA
Contact: Rhonda Lamb Heath, P.O. Box 308,
Vienna, GA 31092, 229-268-8275, or
lambheath@firstnetline.com. Judges contact:
Dana Gambrell, P.O. Box 308, Vienna, GA 31092,
229-268-8275 (MIM)

OCTOBER

Sand Town Festival
Cusseta, GA
Contact: Sandy George at 706-989-3796 or
706-989-3749 or *coltvp@mindspring.com* (KCBS)

NOVEMBER

Pig Fest
(always 2nd weekend in November)
Richland, GA
Contact: Diane and Charles Lee at 229-887-3377;
Peggy Jo Scott, 5775 W. Centerpoint Rd., Richland,
GA 31825, 229-887-3460 or *dascott@sowega.net*.
Judges contact: Helen Blanton, P.O. Box 126,
Richland, GA 31825, 229-887-2132 or
hbla274093@aol.com (MIM)

Kentucky

AUGUST

**Lions Club Oldham County, Kentucky,
BBQ & Bluegrass Fest**
Crestwood, KY
Contact: Tom Temple at 502-241-4912 (KCBS)

Lousiana

NOVEMBER

**Lions Gulf Coast Barbeque
Cook-Off & Festival**
Slidell, LA
Contact: John Stevenson at 985-641-6430 or
info@lionsbbq.org or *jsteven1@bellsouth.net* (KCBS)

Mississippi

JUNE

**Byhalia Clydesdale Christmas Store
Barbeque Festival**
Byhalia, MS
Contact: Ronnie Luther at 662-895-2828 (KCBS)

SEPTEMBER

**The Benton County Fair & State
Championship**
Ashland, MS
Contact: 662-224-8933 or *cathym@ext.msstate.com*
(KCBS)

Heavenly Hogs Championship BBQ
Madison, MS
Contact: Keith Obert, P.O. Box 2081, Madison, MS
39130, 601-856-9690 or *obertlaw@bellsouth.net*.
Judges contact: Frank Collins, P.O. Box 2081,
Madison, MS 39130, 601-982-5580 (MIM)

Hog Wild in Corinth
Corinth, MS
Contact: Tammy Bonds, 629 Constitution Drive,
Luka, MS 38852, 662-243-2468 or
tammybonds@dixie-net.com (MIM)

OCTOBER

Cleveland Octoberfest
Cleveland, MS
Contact: Elise Jenkins, P.O. Box 490, Cleveland,
MS 38732, 662-846-4210 or *jenkins2@tecinfo.com*.
Judges contact: Donna Gaines, 662-843-2712 or
geomtech@telepak.net (MIM)

Roast-n-Boast, Inc.
Columbus, MS
Contact: David Darby, 801 Hwy 45 N., Columbus,
MS 39701, 662-328-5026 or *scat@tilc.com*. Judges
contact: Melissa Clark, 47 Savannah St.,
Columbus, MS 39702, 662-328-4410 (MIM)

North Carolina

APRIL

Kings Mountain Firehouse Cook-Off
Kings Mountain, NC
Contact: Frank Burns at 704-734-0555 or
frankb@cityofkm.com (KCBS)

JUNE

Blue Ridge BBQ Festival
Tryon, NC
Contact: Bob Bolen at 828-859-7427 or
bbqfestival@alltel.net (KCBS)

Lincolnton Hog Happenin
Lincolnton, NC
Contact: Brad Guth or Holly Kiser at 704-736-8915
or *downtown@ci.lincolnton.nc.us* (KCBS)

SEPTEMBER

Bikes, Boogie & BarBQue
Galstonia, NC
Contact: Aja Rennie at 704-867-2855 or
orders@carolinaharley.com (KCBS)

NOVEMBER

Hog Happenin–Tar Heel BBQ Championship
Shelby, NC
Contact: Jerry Gardner at 704-482-4202 or
www.hoghappnin.com (KCBS)

South Carolina

SEPTEMBER

Main Street Laurens Squealin' on the Square
Laurens, SC
Contact: Jenny Boulware at 864-984-2119 or
mail@mainstreetlaurens.org (KCBS)

Uniquely Union BBQ Festival
Union, SC
Contact: Carroll Sailors-Lane at 864-429-8420 or
csailors@uniquelyunion.org (KCBS)

Tennessee

APRIL

High on the Hog
Winchester, TN
Contact: Fred and Linda Gould at 931-469-0080 or
winchesterhoth@aol.com (KCBS)

JUNE

Wild Turkey Bourbon BBQ Championship
Lawrenceburg, TN
Contact: Carl Counce at 931-762-3399 or
ccounce@bellsouth.net or
www.lawrenceburg.com/Kiwanis (KCBS)

AUGUST

Amazin' Blazin' BBQ Cookoff
Lebanon, TN
Contact: Wanda McKee or Kristina McKee at
615-444-5730 or *tnamazinblazin@aol.com* (KCBS)

Smokin on the Square Coffee Pot Challenge
Manchester, TN
Contact: Fantasy 101.5 FM, P.O. Box 1015,
Manchester, TN 37349, 931-728-3458 (FBA)

SEPTEMBER

Conroe Lions PRCA Rodeo and Cookoff
Conroe, TN
Contact: James Boys at 936-672-9700 or Lindy
Bingham at 936-856-5991 (IBCA)

Cookeville Cookoff
Cookeville, TN
Contact: Tony Stone at 931-526-1063 or
tony@stonebrotherswelding.com (KCBS)

OCTOBER

Arlington Barbecue Burnout
Arlington, TN
Contact: Josh Anderson, 11754 Douglass St., Arlington, TN 38002, 901-867-8905 or *arltown@bellsouth.net*. Judges contact: Robin Bumpus, 11271 Pleasant Ridge Rd., Arlington, TN 38002, 901-867-9601 or *bikermemaw@aol.com* (MIM)

Cookin' on the Cumberland
Clarksville, TN
Contact: Wayne Abrams at 931-552-3512 or *waynes@clarksville.net* (KCBS)

Hatchie Hollow Hog Fest
Bolivar, TN
Contact: Susanne Rhea, 707 Cliff Street, Bolivar, TN 38008, 731-658-9913 or *susannerhea@clarksville.net* (KCBS)

World's Oldest Bar-B-Que Cooking Contest
Covington, TN
Contact: CH Sullivan or *csullivan@downhomebank.com*. Judges contact: Amanda Ralph, 855 Deen Rd., Brighton, TN 3801, 901-475-1077 or *fmcmortgage@aol.com* (MIM)

Midwest

Illinois

JUNE

King City Barbeque Showdown
Mt. Vernon, IL
Contact: Troy Heitmeyer at 618-242-4020. Entry fee also covers Kids-Q (KCBS)

SEPTEMBER

Wabash Ribberfest
Mount Carmel, IL
Contact: Chuck Johnson at 618-262-8378 or *cqujohnson@earthlink.com*. Judges contact: Tom Ford at 618-262-3673 or *tford@mtcarmelonline.com* (MIM)

Iowa

JUNE

State Center Rose Festival BBQ
State Center, IA
Contact: Paul Lengeling at 641-385-2263 or *reflats@aol.com* (KCBS)

JULY

Main Street Waterloo BBQ'Loo and Blues Too!
Waterloo, IA
Contact: 319-291-2038 or *mswaterlootpb@acesiowa.net* (KCBS)

AUGUST

Lynch Livestock Pig Stampede/Iowa State BBQ Championship
Waucoma, IA
Contact: Chris Bouska at 563-776-3311 or *chris@lynchbbq.com* (KCBS)

Kansas

APRIL

Hank Lumpkin Memorial Red, Hot & Wild
Topeka, KS
Contact: George Liesmann or Randy Goldsmith at 785-228-7220 or 785-228-7265 or *geliesmann@aol.com*, *george.liesmann@radionetworks.com,* or *mark.elliot@radionetworks.com* (KCBS)

Smoke in the Spring BBQ Championship
Contact: Don Cawby at 785-528-3735 or
drcawby@osagecity.com (KCBS)

JUNE

Kansas Masters BBQ Cookoff
Wichita, KS
Contact: CJ Maley at 316-612-6891 or
cjjmaley@aol.com (KCBS)

Tonganoxie Days
Tonganoxie, KS
Contact: Jim Gambrill at 913-369-2869 or
913-369-9013 (KCBS)

JULY

Anthony Downs Barbeque Contest
Anthony, KS
Contact: Allen Thomas at 620-842-3796 (KCBS)

Central Kansas BBQ Cookoff
Great Bend, KS
Contact: Kent Romaine at 620-793-7829 (KCBS)

AUGUST

Christian Barbeque Contest & Festival
Bonner Springs, KS
Contact: Mary Smith Blakey at 913-3345-1811 or
fsfaith37@aol.com (KCBS)

Paola Roots Festival BarBQ Championship
Paola, KS
Contact: Steve Mcmullin at 913-294-0015 or
mcmullin@classicnet.net (KCBS)

SEPTEMBER

Beaumont Blazin' BBQ
Beaumont, KS
Contact: Jerry Albert at 785-841-3100 or
jalbert@hotelsic.com (KCBS)

Sterling Silver Premium Meats &
Air Capital Cook-Off
Wichita, KS
Contact: Jill Nestleroad at 316-267-2817 or
jill@wichitafestivals.com (KCBS)

When Pigs Fly BBQ & Fly-In
McPherson, KS
Contact: Cheryl Lyn Higgins at 620-241-3303 or
chamber@mcphersonsks.org (KCBS)

Michigan

JULY

Taste of Grand Rapids & Barbecue Contest
Grand Rapids, MI
Contact: Rich Berry or John Bates at 616-459-1919
ext. 111 or *rberry@clearchannel.com* (KCBS)

Minnesota

MAY

Minnesota in May BBQ Contest
Cambridge, MN
Contact: Mark Born at 651-388-6393 or
markborn@pressenter.com (MIM)

Missouri

MARCH

North Kansas City BBQ Championship
North Kansas City, MO
Contact: Jay McClintick at 816-455-0210 (KCBS)

APRIL

Marshall Rotary Club BBQ
Marshall, MO
Contact: Charles Cooper at 660-886-5871 or
coop@cdsinet.net (KCBS)

Pigs in the Garden
Charleston, MO
Contact: Lisa Hillhouse at 573-683-6509 or
chamber@charlestonmo.org (KCBS)

Sugar Creek Bar-B-Que Cookoff
& Craft Show
Sugar Creek, MO
Contact: Sue Mikula at 816-252-4413 or
smikula@sugar.creek.mo.us (KCBS)

JUNE

Black River Festival BBQ Contest
Poplar Bluff, MO
Contact: Jerry Hillis at 573-785-9666 or 573-686-7262
(KCBS). Judges contact: *cope@tcmax.net*

Platte City Barbecue Fest
Platte City, MO
Contact: Karen Wagoner at 816-858-5270 or
karewwagoner@earthlink.net (KCBS)

Sedalia Lions Club MO Blues & BBQ Fest
Sedalia, MO
Contact: Chris Koetting at 660-221-2080 or
ckoetting@smelectric.com (KCBS)

JULY

Johnson County Fair BBQ Contest
Warrensburg, MO
Contact: Connie Skelton at 660-747-3354 or
www.johnsonsoncountyfairassociation.com
(KCBS)

AUGUST

Laurie Hillbilly BBQ
Laurie, MO
Contact: Susann Huff at 573-374-8776 or
laurievents@aol.com (KCBS)

St. Louis BBQ Fest
St. Louis, MO
Contact: *marvism@earthlink.net* or
terry@supersmokers.com (MIM)

SEPTEMBER

Mighty Missouri Pig Fest Featuring
the Scism Sizzle
Park Hills, MO
Contact: Willa Dean Meyer, #1 Airline Dr.,
Farmington, MO 63640, 573-756-6118 or
wmeyer@marmc.org. Judges contact: Richard
Womack, 1148 Spring Brook Park Dr.,
Farmington, MO 63640, 573-756-6475 or
dickw@jcn.net (MIM)

Nebraska

JULY

John C. Fremont Days Festival/BBQ Cookoff
Fremont, NE
Contact: Mollie Brown at 402-721-7565 or
unsinkablemollie@yahoo.com (KCBS)

SEPTEMBER

Last Fling Til Spring BBQ Contest
West Point, NE
Contact: Richard Sterling at 800-422-3664,
fax 402-372-5423 or *rsterling@kwpnfm.com* (KCBS)

Ohio

OCTOBER

Ohio Smoked Meat & BBQ Festival
Nelsonville, OH
Contact: 740-753-3531 or Steve Grinsted at
740-753-9100 (KCBS)

Wisconsin

AUGUST

VAHA BBQ Faceoff
Viroqua, WI
Contact Jeff May at 608-637-8661 or
mayflies@frontiernet.net (KCBS)

West Coast

California

MAY

Modesto Street Scene Barbeque
Modesto, CA
Contact: Sheilia Doberenz at 209-577-5757 ext. 111
(KCBS)

AUGUST

West Coast Barbeque Championship
Fairfield, CA
Contact: Jeff Jones at 925-639-7436 or
jeff@jeffbbq.com (KCBS)

Mid-Atlantic

Delaware

SEPTEMBER

Smokin' on the Fairgrounds
Harrington, DE
Contact: Bob Nay, toll-free, 1-877-742-7827 or
ktl@ezy.net (KCBS)

Maryland

APRIL

Pork in the Park
Salisbury, MD
Contact: Sandy Fulton at 410-548-4914 or
slfulton@comcast.net (KCBS) or
www.porkinthepark.org

JUNE

Smokin on the Chesapeake
Gambrills, MD
Contact: Bob Nay, toll-free, 1-877-742-7827 or
ktl@ezy.net (KCBS)

AUGUST

Maryland BBQ Bash
Bel Air, MD
Contact: Craig Ward and Jim Welch at 410-638-1023
or *bbq@fredward.com* (KCBS)

New Jersey

SEPTEMBER

King of the Grill
Ocean City, NJ
Contact: Willis Lynch at 609-399-4291 or
bchwillie@aol.com (KCBS)

Virginia

MAY

Pigs in the Park
Danville, VA
Contact: Rosalee Maxwell or Bill McMann at
434-793-4636 or *specialevents@visitdanville.com*
(KCBS)

SEPTEMBER

James River BBQ Festival
Contact: John Wynne at 434-386-6301 or
jlw@cfbonline.com (KCBS)

Washington, D.C.

JUNE

Safeway's National Capital Barbecue Battle
Washington, D.C.
Contact: Allen Tubis, 4335 Northview Dr., Bowie,
MD 20716, 301-860-0630 or *barbecue1@aol.com.*
Judges contact: Doug and Kathy Halo, 3809
Washington Woods Dr., Alexandria, VA 22309,
703-799-0523 or *kshalo1@aol.com* (MIM)

Rocky Mountains

Colorado

JUNE

Annual Boats, Blues & BBQ
Pueblo, CO
Contact: HARP Authority at 719-595-0242 or
info@puebloharp.com (KCBS)

JULY

Rocky Mountain BBQ
Denver, CO
Contact: Steven Marrs at 303-288-0011 (KCBS)

AUGUST

BBQ at the Summit
Dillon, CO
Contact: Brenda at 888-499-4499 or
www.bbqatthesummit.com (KCBS)

Pikes Peak Bar-B-Que Festival
Colorado Springs, CO
Contact: Bob Tretheway at 719-597-1821 (KCBS)

Southwest

New Mexico

MARCH

**New Mexico 2005 Pork & Brew State
Championship**
Rio Ranchero, NM
Contact: Art Perez, 505 896 8731 or
aperez@ci.rio-rancho.nm.us (KCBS)

Oklahoma

APRIL

**Stillwater Elks State Championship BBQ
Blazethon**
Stillwater, OK
Contact: Pat Pittman at 405-372-3726 or
patpitman@wilsonchevroletjeep.com (KCBS)

MAY

Bixby BBQ 'n' Blues Festival
Bixby, OK
Contact: Jim VerHoef at 918-231-2476 or
jim@olp.net (KCBS)

JULY

Sapulpa Elks State Championship
Sapulpa, OK
Contact: Brian Cooper at 918-224-0457 or
918-299-1722 or *bman1957@excite.com* (KCBS)

AUGUST

Art of Barbeque
Tulsa, OK
Contact: Mary Rankin at 918-584-3333 ext. 11 or
mrankin@transfund.com (KCBS)

Cherokee Strip BBQ & Chili Cookoff
Ponca City, OK
Contact: Susie Roberts at 580-762-5651 or
susier@pbtok.com (KCBS)

Texas

JANUARY

Hold'em & Hit'em & Anything But
Houston, TX
Contact: Lee Johnson at 832-642-3205 (IBCA)

LSBS BBQ Cookoff & 2004 COTY Awards
Fairfield, TX
Contact: Jimmy Lee at 903-389-3719 or Pat or
Glenn Nichols at 817-261-9507 (LSBS)

San Antonio Livestock BBQ
San Antonio, TX
Contact: Miltie McDonald at 210-832-0902 (IBCA)

FEBRUARY

Bastrop LBA VFD
Bastrop, TX
Contact: Ann Butterfield at 512-321-2315 (CTBA)

Chilly BBQ & Chili
Austin, TX
Contact: Dee Dee Barton at 512-365-7821 (IBCA)

CUPID Bar-B-Q Cook-Off
Bastrop, TX
Contact: Ann Butterfield at 512-321-2315 (CTBA)

Humble Rodeo BBQ
Humble, TX
Contact: Stacy Williams at 281-831-5780 (IBCA)

Irving Elks Lodge
Irving, TX
Contact: David Boedeker at 972-579-0005 (IBCA)

Victoria JC Livestock Show BBQ
Victoria, TX
Contact: Candace Hollis at 361-582-4392 (IBCA)

MARCH

API BBQ Cookoff
Caldwell, TX
Contact: Glenn or Pat Nichols at
nich1@airmail.net (LSBS)

Copperas Cove Downtown Association BBQ
Copperas Cove, TX
Contact: Glenn or Pat Nichols at
nich1@airmail.net (LSBS)

Cypress Creek EMS Beef N Bird
Houston, TX
Contact: Josh Fetner at 281-397-7844 (IBCA)

LaGarto Store
Benefiting HALO Flight, LaGarto, TX
Contact: Mary Schumacher at 361-547-2929 or
Dick Payne at 361-224-7904 (IBCA)

Que & Show
Hubbard, TX
Contact: Tommy Roberts at 254-576-1546 (CTBA)

Richest BBQ Cookoff
Palestine, TX
Contact: Glenn or Pat Nichols at
nich1@airmail.net (LSBS)

**Rocky Hill Bike Ranch Spring Wing Ding
Cook-Off**
Smithville, TX
Contact: Sherry Lovekamp at 512-237-3847 (CTBA)

Rotating Lodge Cook-Off
This event is always held in central Texas at a SPJST Lodge.
Contact: Brian Banick at 1-800-72S-PJST or Jessie Pospisill at 512-365-1110 (CTBA)

Technology Spring Festival
North Harris College, Houston, TX
Contact: Jerry Pierce at 713-851-4614 or Ginny Patten at 281-618-5730 (IBCA)

Walnut Springs Lions Club
Walnut Springs, TX
Contact: Kelly Olsen at *Kelly@htcomp.net* or 254-797-3721 (LSBS)

West VFD BBQ
West, TX
Contact: Cody Dragoo at 254-826-3570 (IBCA)

APRIL

Buc Days
Corpus Christi, TX
Contact: Steve DeWalt at 361-882-3242 (IBCA)

Cameron Dueberry Festival
Contact: Chamber of Commerce at 254-697-4979 (LSBS)

Hardin City Relay for Life BBQ
Sour Lake, TX
Contact: Ron Latil at 409-287-3171 (IBCA)

Hoot-n-Howler BBQ Cookoff
Atlanta, TX
Contact: Atlanta Chamber of Commerce at 903-796-3296 (LSBS)

Houston AGC BBQ Cook-Off
Houston, TX
Contact: Carl Lee at 281-447-8100 (IBCA)

KC 3203 2nd BBQ/Chili
Odessa, TX
Contact: Ed Kelley at 432-520-7117 (IBCA)

Liberty Hill VFW Post 8200
Liberty Hill, TX
Contact: Cliff Whitt at 512-260-0986 (CTBA)

Limestone County Youth Fair and BBQ
Groesbeck, TX
Contact: Donny May at 254-729-8255 (CTBA)

Live Oak County Cabrito Cookoff
Sweeny Switch, TX
Contact: Linda Barnes at 361-449-2733 (IBCA)

Marble Falls Highland Lakes Chili & BBQ Cookoff
Marble Falls, TX
Contact: Larry Kinnison at 830-693-5502 (CTBA)

Mauriceville Crawfish Festival BBQ
Mauriceville, TX
Contact: James Rash at 409-745-3577 (IBCA)

Melody Oaks Ranch BBQ Cook-Off
Contact: Gayle Jones at 325-356-5231 (CTBA)

Mills County Goat BBQ Cookoff
Goldthwaite, TX
Contact: Chamber of Commerce at *gcc@centex.net* or Glenn and Pat Nichols at *nich1@airmail.com* (LSBS)

Oenaville, Texas Cook-Off
Oenaville, TX
Contact: Debbie Ellis at 254-984-2422 (CTBA)

Spring Turkey Hunt BBQ Cookoff
Deleon, TX
Contact: *chamber@deleontexas.com* or Barbara Helbert at 254-893-3702 (CTBA)

Terrell Heritage Days
Terrell, TX
Contact: Sarah at 972-524-5703 (IBCA)

VFW Post 6525 Cook-Off
Rockdale, TX
Contact: James Adcock at 254-984-2422 (CTBA)

War Memorial BBQ Cookoff
Brown Wood, TX
Contact: Glenn or Pat Nichols at
nich1@airmail.net (LSBS)

MAY

Annual Rib Burn Off
Heartland Mall, Early, TX
Contact: Charlotte Parrack at
marketing@pbrg.com or Glenn or Pat Nicholson at
nich1@airmail.com (LSBS)

Blanco Days Cookoff
Blanco, TX
Contact: Glenn or Pat Nicholson at
nich1@airmail.com (LSBS)

Bruceville-Eddy Mayfest
Bruceville-Eddy, TX
Contact: Bob Miracle at 254-859-5874 (CTBA)

Buckholts Cotton Festival
Buckholts, TX
Contact: Jay Beckhusen at 254-593-4175 (CTBA)

Electra Goat BBQ Cookoff
Electra, TX
Contact: Chamber of Commerce at 940-496-3577 or
Glenn or Pat Nicholson at *nich1@airmail.com*
(LSBS)

Elks Lodge BBQ & CASI Chili Cook-Off
Amarillo, TX
Contact: Johnny Wiseman at 806-676-0614 (LSBS)

Harvest House BBQ Cookoff
Burleson, TX
Contact: Glenn or Pat Nicholson at
nich1@airmail.com (LSBS)

Highland Lakes BBQ
Burnet, TX
Contact: Donna Fritsch at 512-756-8080 (IBCA)

Knights of Columbus BBQ Cookoff
Somerville, TX
Contact Glenn or Pat Nicholson at
nich1@airmail.com (LSBS)

Marble Falls Rootin' Tootin' BBQ
Marble Falls, TX
Contact: Lindsey Brickerton at 830-693-6759
(CTBA)

Masonic Lodge Cookoff
Groesbeck, TX
Contact: Glenn or Pat Nicholson at
nich1@airmail.com (LSBS)

Special Olympics BBQ Cookoff
Colleyville, TX
Contact: Glenn or Pat Nicholson at
nich1@airmail.com (CTBA)

World Bison Championship Cookoff
Santa Ana, TX
Contact: Montie Guthrie at 325-348-3826 (IBCA)

JUNE

Alvord Pioneer Days
Alvord, TX
Contact: Mike Hardy at 940-427-9172 or
atkinsonfam67@ntws.net (LSBS)

Bosque County Go Texas BBQ Cookoff
Meridian, TX
Contact: Glenn or Pat Nicholson at
nich1@airmail.com (LSBS)

FFA Ag Boosters BBQ Cookoff
Penelope, TX
Contact: Danny or Tammy Christian at
254-533-5678 or *dchristian@hilcozap.net* or Glenn
or Pat Nicholson at *nich1@airmail.com* (LSBS)

FFA Boosters BBQ Cookoff
Caldwell, TX
Contact: Glenn or Pat Nicholson at
nich1@airmail.com (LSBS)

Homers Backyard Ball & BBQ Cookoff
Amarillo, TX
Contact: Lemon Wall at 806-564-2468 (LSBS)

Itasca C/C BBQ
Itasca, TX
Contact: Bob Wilson at 254-687-2331 (IBCA)

Smokin' on the Winfield Rails
Winfield, TX
Contact: Jan Worsham at 903-524-2247 or Glenn or
Pat Nicholson at *nich1@airmail.com* (LSBS)

Summer Taste Challenge
Dubli, TX
Contact: Glenn or Pat Nicholson at
nich1@airmail.com (LSBS)

Texas Paralyzed Veterans BBQ
Houston, TX
Contact: Randy Elston at 713-729-0258 (IBCA)

Wild Horse Prairie Days & BBQ Cookoff
Haskell, TX
Contact: Mike Harrell at *tti@dtnspeed.net* or
940-864-8042 or Glenn or Pat Nicholson at
nich1@airmail.com (LSBS)

JULY

Band Boosters BBQ Cookoff
Contact: Paul or Joann at 254-386-3365 or
254-784-3522 or *gomez@htcomp.net* (LSBS)

East Texas Youth Sports Association Cookoff
Whitehouse, TX
Contact: Roger Gipson at 903-521-3856 (LSBS)

Home Town BBQ Cookoff
Hughes Springs, TX
Contact: Judi at 903-639-2351 (LSBS)

Knights of Columbus Cookoff
Levelland, TX
Contact: Joseph Honesto at 806-891-5830 or
bosohonesto@aol.com (IBCA)

No Adult Supervision BBQ Cookoff
Contact: Kelly Draper at 806-781-8520 or
kelly@odsy.net (LSBS)

Peppermint Lounge HWY 36 Cookoff
Temple, TX
Contact: Roy Lee Butler at 254-933-1409 (CTBA)

Spring Ho BBQ Cookoff
Lampasas, TX
Contact: Jill Jones at
lampasaschamber@thegateway.net (LSBS)

Star Hall SPJST Lodge #47
Seaton, TX
Contact: Edwin Pechal at 254-985-2282 (CTBA)

Trinity Fourth of July BBQ
Trinity, TX
Contact: Kelly or Tim at 936-594-2141 (IBCA)

Wichita Falls VFD BBQ Cookoff
Wichita Falls, TX
Contact: Carolyn King at 940-767-4823 or
Sunflowervfd@aol.com (LSBS)

AUGUST

Chisolm Trail BBQ Cookoff
Morgans Point, TX
Contact: Joe Medrano at 254-0780-1334 (CTBA)

Hoof en Hair BBQ
Fort Richardson State Park, Jacksboro, TX
Contact: 940-567-3506 (LSBS)

Hot Summer Nights BBQ Cookoff
Gainsville, TX
Contact: 940-665-2831 or 888-585-4468 (LSBS)

Hotter Than Hell BBQ Cookoff
Hearne, TX
Contact: C. Demottier at 979-272-8358 (LSBS)

Knights of Columbus #12292
Brownfield, TX
Contact: Jimmy Garzat at 806-637-2226 or
806-637-7881 (IBCA)

Mount Vernon Sheriff's Posse Cookoff
Mount Vernon, TX
Contact: Mike Betts at 903-568-2462 or
bettswelding@bluebonnet.net (LSBS)

SEPTEMBER

Barnie McBee Memorial BBQ Cookoff
Comanche, TX
Contact: Darlene Causey at
chamber.dc@itexas.net (LSBS)

Bronze Bass BBQ Cookoff
Canyon Lake, TX
Contact: Reva Weatherly at *revabbw@gtvtc.com*
(LSBS)

**Little River Catfish Association Pinto Bean
and BBQ Cook-Off**
Academy, TX
Contact: Lyndale Rea at 254-982-4056 (CTBA)

Newton County Go Texan
Newton, TX
Contact: Rick Richman at *tx_rick_99@yahoo.com*
(LSBS)

Shin Oaks Springs BBQ Cookoff
Gorman, TX
Contact: Janet at 254-734-2202 or *dna@cctc.net*
(LSBS)

OCTOBER

Best Little BBQ in Texas
McKinney, TX
Contact Terri Kurlan, 202 S. Waddill St.,
McKinney, TX 75069, 972-547-9789 or
kurlan@sbcglobal.net. Judges contact: Linda
McNeff, 2100 Cliffside St., Plano, TX 75023,
972-562-0607 or *buyingprincess@aol.com* (MIM)

Breast Cancer Research BBQ
Midland, TX
Contact: Patsy Childress at 915-520-4433 (WTBA)

Captain Daingerfield Days
Daingerfield, TX
Contact: Hewitt Wheeles at *Hhwheless@aol.com*
(LSBS)

Come Hell or High Water BBQ Cookoff
Stamford, TX
Contact: Staci Robertson at 325-773-8780,
325-773-2705, or *stacirob@yahoo.com* (LSBS)

LaGarto Store Benefiting Masons
LaGarto, TX
Contact: Mary Schumacher at 361-547-2929 or
Dick Payne at 361-224-7904 (IBCA)

Ogletree Gap BBQ Cookoff
Copperas Cove, TX
Contact: Mary Pat Seal at Seal,
aa@copperascove.com or 254-547-7571 (LSBS)

Pumpkin Festival Cookoff
Paris, TX
Contact: Linda Suarez at *lss@paristex.com* or
call 1-800-PARISTX (LSBS)

Tynan Recreation Club BBQ
Tynan, TX
Contact: Wanda Wilson at 361-354-2326 (IBCA)

NOVEMBER

Harp's Fun Days
Bryan, TX
Contact: Wes Harper at 979-778-7921 (IBCA)

Lions Club BBQ Cookoff
(1st weekend in November)
Fairfield, TX
Contact: Jimmy Lee at 903-389-3719 or
fax 903-389-4034 (LSBS)

**Rowlett Festival and Exchange Club
BBQ Cookoff**
Rowlett, TX
Contact: Kyle French at *kefrench@ev1.net* (LSBS)

DECEMBER

Christmas on the Square
Angleton, TX
Contact: Chamber of Commerce, 979-849-6433
(IBCA/T)

Nonsanctioned Events

This includes local events that are not affiliated with
larger organizations. These events do not abide by a
governing body's rules, nor are the winners eligible
to compete in invitational cookoffs or state cookoffs
run by the governing bodies.

Southeast

Arkansas

APRIL

**14th Annual Hogskin Holidays Festival &
Pork Cook-Off**
Hampton, AR
Contact: Floyd Nutt at 870-798-4818 or 870-798-2100
(NS)

Florida

JANUARY

Central Florida BBQ Fest
Sebring, FL
Contact: Richard McClain or Dave Travers,
P.O. Box 1981, Sebring, FL 33871, 863-385-3247 or
hcfa@strato.net (FBA)

MARCH

**Eastpoint VFD 3rd Annual Charity Rib
Cookoff**
Eastpoint, FL
Contact: James Shiver at 850-670-4127 or
George Pruett at 850-670-9000

Georgia

MARCH

Hasan Shrine Spring Festival BBQ Cook-Off
Albany, GA
Contact: Hasan Shrine at 229-432-1011 or
wpantone@aol.com

**The Hawkinsville Civitan Club's 11th Annual
Shoot the Bull**
Hawkinsville, GA
Contact: Hazel Miller at 478-892-2839 (NS)

APRIL

Greater Columbus Pig Jig Cookoff
Columbus, GA
Contact: 706-323-7979 or *franhcf@hotmail.com*

MAY

May Day Festivities
Doerun, GA
Contact: Sharon Baird at 229-782-5918

SEPTEMBER

A Walk in the Pork
Loganville, GA
Contact: Charlie Eavenson at 770-554-02020 or 770-
815-6028 or *cseavenson@bellsouth.net* (NS)

NOVEMBER

Best of the Best Invitational Cook-Off
Douglas, GA
Contact: Kell Phelps at 1-800-385-0002 or
www.BestoftheBestbbq.com (N/S)

Smokin' on the Square IV
Douglas, GA
Contact: City of Douglas at 912-383-0277 or
www.BestoftheBestbbq.com (N/S)

Mississippi

APRIL

Southaven Springfest
Southaven, MS
Contact: *mrbarbq@hotmail.com*

OCTOBER

Hogs Championship BBQ Contest
Madison, MS
Contact: 601-856-9690

North Carolina

MAY

Charlotte Ribfest
Charlotte, NC
Contact: 828-628-9626 or 304-984-2412 or
wcpro@bellsouth.net

OCTOBER

Lexington Barbecue Festival
Lexington, NC
Contact: 336-956-1880 or *www.barbecuefestival.com*
(N/S)

South Carolina

MARCH

**Prestigious Palmetto Pig Pick'n
Championship**
Exchange Park, Ladson, SC
Contact: Tommy Brush at 843-766-5576 or
tbrush@brushlawfirm.com or Jim Trolley at
843-729-0906 or *jrtrolle@msn.com*

APRIL

Smoke at the Lodge
Summerville, SC
Contact: Kenny Craven at 843-270-6963 or
www.smokeatthelodge.com (N/S)

MAY

Carolina Children's Home BBQ Cookoff Festival
Columbia, SC
Contact: Elizabeth Southern-Caulk at 803-790-6541 ext. 216 or *southern@carolinachildrenshome.com* (N/S)

Foothills BBQ Festival
Spartanburg, SC
Contact: James Eubanks at 864-576-4768 or *barbecueman@charter.net*

JULY

South Carolina Festival of Discovery BBQ Cookoff
Contact: Paula Brooks at 864-942-8448 or *uptown@co.greenwood.sc.us.*

Tennessee

MAY

Sertoma 48 BarBQ
Contact: Thomas Howe at 785-842-2772 or *Thomas@tehowe.com*

West Virginia

JULY

Charleston Ribfest
Charleston, WV
Contact: Bill Picozzi at 304-984-2412 or *fonzie@isp.com* or *www.bbqribfest.netfirms.com*

Midwest

Kansas

MARCH

Kookers Kare Event
Kansas City, KS
Contact: Craig Kidwell at 816-230-7522 or *BBQBOY@worldnet.att.net*

Missouri

APRIL

Rock n Ribs BBQ Festival
Springfield, MO
Contact: Phoebe at 866-894-3398 or *teams@rocknribs.com* or *www.rocknribs.com*

West Coast

Washington

SEPTEMBER

1st Annual Gig Harbor "Blues, Bones & Brew Festival"
Gig Harbor, WA
Contact: Dick Suess at 253-857-3383 or *pifl98@aol.com* (NS)

Mid-Atlantic

Virginia

JUNE

Shenandoah Valley BBQ Cookoff
Harrisonburg, VA
Contact: Greg Marrow at *marrow@rica.net* or *www.shenvalleybbq.com* (N/S)

Virginia Barbeque Fest
Fredericksburg, VA
Contact: Richard Ivey at 804-448-9877 or
www.virginiaabbq.com

Southwest

Texas

APRIL

Texas Rio Grande Valley Onion Fest
Weslaco, TX
Contact: Arnie Segovia at 956-495-8947 or
quetex@rgv.rr.com or Fred Macaleb at 956-975-1996
or Martha Nowell at 956-778-3977

West Texas Open BBQ Cook-Off & Kingsford Shootout
Post, TX
Contact: Danny Cooper at 806-495-0693

MAY

Alvin Rotary Club Bar-B-Que Cookoff
Alvin, TX
Contact: Buddy Lindsey at 281-585-4013 or
Jerry Barnett at 281-331-6549

OCTOBER

Trader's Village Barbecue
Grand Prairie, TX
Contact: Allan Hughes at 972-647-2331

Kerr County Fair Champion Cook-Off
Kerrville, TX
Contact: Chad Parker at 830-257-6833 or
kcfa@ktc.com

Index